BAD

BUSINESS

CORPORATE
CRIME
IN CANADA

Laureen Snider

QUEEN'S UNIVERSITY

Nelson Canada

© Nelson Canada,
A Division of Thomson Canada Limited, 1993

Published in 1993 by
Nelson Canada,
A Division of Thomson Canada Limited
1120 Birchmount Road
Scarborough, Ontario M1K 5G4

Canadian Cataloguing in Publication Data

Snider, Laureen, 1944–
  Bad business : corporate crime in Canada

Includes bibliographical references and index.
ISBN 0–17–604144–3

1. Commercial crimes – Canada. 2. Corporations –
Canada – Corrupt practices. I. Title.

HV6771.C2S62 1992   364.1'68'0971   C92–094596–1

Acquisitions Editor   Dave Ward
Supervising Editor   Nicole Gnutzman
Developmental Editor   Cynthia Boylan
Art Director   Bruce Bond
Cover Design   Bruce Bond
Cover Illustration   Michael Herman
Text Design   Matthews Communications Design

Printed and bound in Canada
1 2 3 4   WC   96 95 94 93

To

Bill, Cameron, and Carolina

Contents

Foreword

For many people, terms such as "violence," "theft," or "criminal" conjure up a rather restricted set of stereotypical images. We are apt to think of violence as a drunken quarrel that results in a homicide, of theft as a garden-variety convenience store robbery, and of criminal as a disreputable member of an urban underclass.

Such images dominate public opinion about the "crime problem" and they pervade the crime news and crime drama that we routinely encounter in the mass media. It is also true that throughout much of its history, criminological theory and research have, with few exceptions, been similarly focused on "crime in the street."

However, in recent years, an increasingly large number of criminological researchers have begun to emphasize the study of criminal activity engaged in by the more respectable members of Canadian society. While the first studies of "corporate criminals" were actually done several decades ago, it has been only during the last few decades that criminological theories and research methodologies have matured sufficiently to allow the complexity of the issue to be adequately addressed.

Bad Business: Corporate Crime in Canada provides a comprehensive and systematic examination of the problem of corporate crime with particular reference to Canada. In this volume, Professor Snider critically reviews what is known about the dimensions, causes, and consequences of corporate offending. The picture that emerges challenges conventional views about the sources and effects of criminal harm in this society.

Much of the strength of Professor Snider's analysis derives from the fact that it is informed by the insights of a wide range of disciplinary approaches including sociology, law, economics, and history. Her approach illustrates that the investigation of a problem as multifaceted as corporate crime is poorly served by the (sometimes) artificial barriers that separate one scholarly approach from another. This is particularly true with respect to one key issue to which Snider devotes considerable attention—the social and legal control of corporate crime.

Bad Business: Corporate Crime in Canada fills a large void in Canadian criminology literature. Not only does it provide a state-of-the-art review of corporate crime theory and research in Canada, but it also helps to establish an agenda for future study of an area central to the interests of modern criminology students.

Leslie W. Kennedy, University of Alberta
Vince Sacco, Queen's University

Preface

Corporate crime is a multifaceted and increasingly multidisciplinary subject. It touches on areas as diverse as ethics and forensic science, and ranges over disciplines from sociology and political studies to economics, business, and environmental science. No one book can hope to encompass all of these aspects. The aim of this book is to give the reader an idea of the scope of the area and present a wide-ranging theoretical framework to bring it together and make it comprehensible. Above all, I hope to make clearer the complexity of the issues, and the ways they relate to our philosophical, psychological, and economic systems, and indeed to our wasteful but luxurious standards of living. To understand the roots of corporate crime is to come closer to effective models of controlling it—and if this overview makes anything clear, it is that we are a long way from achieving this goal. The complexity of corporate crime will make it difficult to move toward effective measures of control without building up levels of formal social control to such a degree that traditional concepts of privacy and civil rights disappear. And if history is any guide, one may be assured that the primary populations victimized by moves such as this will not be the primary perpetuators of corporate crime.

This book is based on research carried out over the past decade, as part of a personal and intellectual quest (shared by many) to piece together the many components of corporate crime and understand why it has proved so difficult to control. Parts of Chapters 4, 6, and 7 originally appeared in articles in *Law and Policy* 9, no.1 (January 1987); *Crime and Delinquency* 36, no.3 (July 1990); *The International Journal of the Sociology of Law* 19 (1991); and in "Commercial Crime," in V. Sacco, ed., *Deviance: Conformity and Control in Canadian Society* (Prentice-Hall, 1992). Chapter 5 is being published simultaneously in Michael Blankenship's *Understanding Corporate Criminality* (Garland Press, 1992).

As with every book of this nature, my debts to friends and colleagues are legion. Frank Pearce, Vince Sacco, and Elizabeth Comack have provided much appreciated personal support and intellectual counsel. I have benefited also from numerous discussions with colleagues over the years at conferences, in person, and through letters. Natalie Forknall in the Faculty of Arts and Science at Queen's University regularly saved my life by rescuing endangered disks from the computer monster and finding those that "the experts" were sure had been erased. The book owes much to her efficiency and good humour, and to the cheerful dedication of Diane Reid as well. Indeed, there is no one in the

Dean's Office of the Faculty of Arts and Science who did not help bring this book to completion—by filling in when I was absent on research days, cheerfully taking extra phone messages, or persuading my computer to communicate with the library. I am grateful to everyone there.

I would also like to thank the two editors of this series, Les Kennedy and the aforementioned Vince Sacco. Dave Ward of Nelson Canada provided encouragement as well as delivering unfailingly polite but persistent nudges when the manuscript was late and the author apparently reluctant ever to complete it. Three reviewers, Walter DeKeseredy (Carleton University); Robert Gordon (Simon Fraser University); and Carl Keane (University of Western Ontario) improved the final product with perceptive and intelligent critiques. And finally, Ross MacMillan cheerfully, capably, and quickly sorted out ten years of bibliographic references scrawled on everything from hotel napkins to magazine articles, found those that were missing, and matched sources in the bibliography with those in the book itself. Without his help the manuscript would have been both later to surface and considerably less professional. However, it goes without saying (although authors always say it) that all remaining errors and imperfections are mine alone.

Introduction

THE EXTENT AND COSTS OF CORPORATE CRIME

This book is about corporate crime, acts committed by businesses large and small in the interests of making profits or avoiding losses. Although corporate crime receives much less publicity than the assaults, thefts, and rapes most people think of when they hear the word "crime," it actually does more harm, costs more money, and ruins more lives than any of these. Corporate crime is a major killer, causing more deaths in a month than all the mass murderers combined do in a decade. Canadians are killed on the job by unsafe (and illegal) working conditions; injured by dangerous products offered for sale before their safety is demonstrated; incapacitated by industrial wastes released into the air or dumped into lakes and rivers; and robbed by illegal conspiracies that raise prices and eliminate consumer choice. Every six hours, a worker in this country dies on the job. Canadians are twenty-eight times more likely to be injured at work than by assault (Reasons, 1986). Occupational deaths are the third leading cause of death (and heart disease and cancer, in number one and two spots, are frequently related to corporate criminality as well). People are ten times more likely to be killed by conditions at their workplace than to be victims of homicide (Reasons et al., 1981).

Nor are Canadians unique. Every year in the United States 30,000 people are killed and an estimated 20 million receive serious injuries from buying unsafe consumer products, according to the National Product Safety Commission. Industrial accidents, a substantial percentage of them due to employers' illegally violating safety codes to maximize company profits, claim another 14,000 deaths per year. An additional 100,000 deaths annually, it is estimated, result from occupationally induced diseases. Comparing this total with the average 20,000 homicides committed annually in the United States (itself the highest rate in the developed world), one can see the magnitude of the problem (Coleman, 1989:7–8).

In Britain, too, 600 people are killed annually by accidents in the workplace, and an additional 12,000 injured. As in Canada and the United States, the majority of these accidents are thought to originate with the negligence of employers, through illegal acts of omission or commission. Indeed, workplace accident rates in Britain have been rising throughout the 1980s under the impact of policies designed to reduce the costs of regulation and get government "off the backs" of the business community. One result of such policies has been a "dramatic increase in major injuries," and an accident rate standing at ninety accidents for every 100,000 workers (Pearce, 1990a:19). There is evidence, as well, that the "real" accident rate is much higher. A recent victimization survey study (the Second Islington Crime Survey) questioned 889 residents of a working-class community in London about their personal experiences with crime during the previous year. Departing from the usual survey conventions (most of which focus exclusively on traditional offences of violence and theft), these researchers included certain corporate violations. Thus, in addition to the usual questions about assault, theft, and burglary, respondents were asked whether they had experienced various unsafe conditions in their place of work, or had been victimized in the marketplace as consumers through faulty merchandise or illegal credit charges. The rate of victimization thereby uncovered for corporate offences in the workplace indicates that the real accident rate may be *thirty times* higher than official government figures make it out to be (Pearce, 1990a).

The following examples provide some indication of the range and extent of corporate criminality. In particular, they illustrate the wide variety of behaviours commonly subsumed under the terms corporate and white-collar crime.

ITEM

Nearly 200 people died when the ironically, if appropriately, named *Herald of Free Enterprise* went down in the English Channel in 1987. The accident occurred when the ferry left the dock before the bow doors were properly secured. Subsequent investigation showed there was no means of communication between the bow and the bridge, which meant that the captain had no way of ensuring that the doors in the bow were safely closed. Visual communication was impossible without leaving the bridge (which would be dereliction of duty) and walking to the back of the ship. Yet roll-off, roll-on ferries are designed to maximize ease of loading and unloading. Such a design means they capsize easily and quickly if any appreciable amount of water is taken on board. In subsequent investigations it was revealed that the ship's masters, aware of the design flaw, had repeatedly asked the company to install a system of warning lights on the bridge to allow them to make sure the bow doors were securely closed, but the request was rejected in "authoritarian and contemptuous terms." Such safety measures increase costs, therefore cutting margins of profit for the owners (Clarke, 1990:203–4).

ITEM

In the early 1980s, the multinational giant Union Carbide Company, faced with a declining market for carbamate pesticides, cut operating costs at its plant at Bhopal, India, by employing fewer staff, reducing the training time offered new employees, and cutting back on plant maintenance. The subsequent disaster, an accidental release of poisonous gas in 1984, killed more than 3000 people outright and caused debilitating and chronic injuries in thousands of others. The company never accepted responsibility for the accident; indeed, it tried to shift blame onto the Indian government on the grounds that its regulatory machinery was inadequate. There is not a shred of evidence that Union Carbide ever sought more effective regulation. Indeed, one of the reasons multinationals such as Union Carbide set up plants in the Third World is to reap the advantages of lower levels of regulation, which translate into lower production costs. Thus, the return on capital received by the U.S. chemical industry is considerably higher in less regulated countries. The industry spends less than half as much on pollution and safety control in its overseas operations as in the United States, where a more efficient regulatory system forces it to invest approximately 12 percent of total revenues (1976 figures) to meet environmental and safety standards. After years of courtroom wrangling and political intrigue, Union Carbide has, to date, agreed to an out of court settlement requiring it to pay $470 million in damages to victims. Two hundred million dollars of this is covered by insurance. The appeals and counter-appeals continue, with no relief in sight for the victims and their relatives, or the community (Pearce, 1990b:422–24).

ITEM

In the United States, the Bolar Pharmaceutical Company admitted to selling adulterated and mislabelled drugs, and lying to investigators from the federal Food and Drug Administration (FDA) about the quality and origin of the medicines it sold. The company pleaded guilty to twenty counts and was fined a total of $10 million plus $238,000 in other costs ($500,000 per count), the largest fine ever imposed in a case of this kind. However, the company amassed $140 million from sales on one drug alone during the five months it was offered to the public; the drug received FDA approval in August 1987, and was pulled off the market in January 1990. (*The New York Times*, Sunday, March 24, 1991: 26; and *The Orlando Sentinel*, Thursday, February 28: A17).

ITEM

Mer/29 (triparanol), a drug developed by Richardson-Merrell to reduce cholesterol levels, was introduced to the American market in 1960. It soon became popular, with sales to more than 300,000 patients. However, the federal regulatory body, the Food and Drug Administration, began receiving complaints that recipients of the drug were developing skin damage, cataracts, and changes in their reproductive organs. Subsequent investigation revealed that the company had discovered these potentially lethal side-effects much earlier, through animal tests in its own labs, but purposively suppressed the information and evidence (Clarke, 1990:205).

ITEM

From 1960 to 1972, Reed Paper, a processing plant in Dryden, Ontario, dumped an estimated 9000 kilograms of mercury into the surrounding river and lake system. Despite evidence showing more than twice the allowable concentration of mercury in area fish, as well as symptoms of mercury poisoning in the people of the Grassy Narrows Ojibwa band downstream, the company ignored an order from the Ontario government to cease dumping for five years, from 1970 to 1975. The Ojibwa, whose main source of food has traditionally been fish, were found to suffer from brain damage, for mercury poisoning destroys parts of the brain, resulting in a form of cerebral palsy characterized by shaking hands, a halting walk, slurred speech, and eventually blindness and deafness. The social consequences of this destruction of their traditional way of life, combined with the effects of the poisoning, have led to record-high levels of murder, suicide, and assault on and off the reserve (Reasons, 1986; Science Council, 1977; Sass and Butler, 1982).

ITEM

An employee of a food processing company in Moncton, New Brunswick, a 30-year-old father of two, was killed when he fell into a giant meat grinder. Testimony showed that the safety switches, intended to guard against accidents by stopping the machinery the instant foreign matter was introduced, were corroded shut. No criminal charges were preferred; one charge was laid against the employer under the provincial Occupational Health and Safety Act, an act that only allows a low maximum fine of $50,000. In this case, the company was fined one-tenth of the maximum, $5000, for negligence (Kingston *Whig-Standard*, December 7, 1989).

Corporate crime, then, is a major killer, responsible for thousands of deaths and injuries each year. But it also causes staggering losses in financial terms, as an examination of some comparative figures reveals. While the average robber in the United States nets $338, the average federally convicted white-collar criminal takes $300,000 (Shapiro, 1984). Moreover, the latter offender, unlike the former, frequently escapes punishment entirely. In a reverse Robin Hood process, antitrust offences and tax evasion transfer billions of dollars from the poor to the rich. Barnett (1979:184) says that high financial returns due to illegal monopoly power may account for one-quarter of the total value of corporate stock held by the wealthiest stockholders in the United States. All the street crime in a given year in United States costs an estimated $4 billion, less than 5 percent of the average yield of corporate criminals. In Britain, Clarke reports that the amount of dollar loss at risk in fraud cases investigated by the Metropolitan

Police (fraud division) was £1,349,000 in 1985. That same year, the combined losses from all burglaries, robberies, and thefts totalled less than 40 percent of this amount—and these figures refer to losses for one small subsection of corporate crime overall (Clarke, 1990:147). As Reiman has summarized:

> The general public loses more money *by far* ... from price-fixing and monopolistic practices and from consumer deception and embezzlement, than from all the property crimes in the FBI's Index combined. Yet these far more costly acts are either not criminal, or if technically criminal, not prosecuted, or if prosecuted, not punished, or if punished, only mildly. In any event, although the individuals responsible for these acts take more money out of the individual citizen's pocket than our Typical Criminal, they rarely show up in arrest statistics, and almost never in prison populations. (Reiman, 1984:51; emphasis in original)

ITEM

The giant Inco Limited of Toronto pleaded guilty to violating the Ontario Water Resources Act after a tailings pond discharged pollutants into watercourses in Sudbury. Despite the fact that the maximum fine under the act is $100,000, and the fact that Inco profits in 1990 totalled $514,801,000, the fourth largest in Canada that year, the company was fined $50,000 (*The Globe and Mail*, Monday, December 17, 1990: B3; *The Financial Post*, Summer 1991:88).

ITEM

In the United States, the owners and operators of nearly half of all underground coal mines have systematically tampered with the dust samples sent to federal safety inspectors. The samples are monitored to determine and control the risks of black lung disease to miners. More than 5000 incidents of sampling fraud have been discovered thus far, a systematic scheme that directly risks workers' lives in order to enhance company profits. Only one company has been sanctioned to date: the Peabody Coal Company pleaded guilty to three counts of tampering and was fined $500,000. Similar civil penalties will be sought in the other cases, according to a government official from the Mine Safety and Health Administration (*The Washington Post*, Thursday, April 4, 1991:1 and A15). Approximately 4.5 percent of all coal miners have contracted black lung disease thus far; 4000 deaths a year are attributed to it (Cullen et al., 1987:69).

ITEM

On May 18, 1988, over 4200 dead fish floated down the Tiger River in Spartanburg County, South Carolina. The giant Canadian multinational Laidlaw Incorporated admitted that two waste-water instrumentation systems on its incinerator upstream had malfunctioned that day, dumping more than 2750 gallons of excess caustic solution into the river over a twelve-hour period. The company admitted no criminal or civil liability—the vice-president of Laidlaw Environmental Services Incorporated argued that the fish kill "just happened to coincide" with the malfunction. However, "to settle the matter," the company negotiated a consent order with the state's Department of Health and Environmental Control. The order required it to donate $5000 to restock the river with fish, and pay a $20,000 fine (*The Globe and Mail*, Monday, December 17, 1990:B1–2).

ITEM
On March 3, 1991, junk bond king Mike Milken began serving a ten-year prison sentence at a minimum security facility in Pleasantville, California, for violating federal securities laws. Milken and his company, Drexel Burnham, pleaded guilty to insider trading and six felony counts, and were assessed $650 million in fines. (After paying this, Milken still possesses a personal fortune estimated to be in excess of $500 million.) He faced criminal charges for ninety-eight racketeering and securities fraud offences, including insider trading, failure to disclose information, and assorted others. As head of the junk bond division of Drexel Burnham, Milken was responsible for developing an innovative scheme to fund corporate takeovers by issuing junk bonds—raising money from companies previously considered too risky to issue shares. This new source of capital, combined with the "feeding frenzy" of greed that characterized corporate America in the 1980s, led to a series of raids and takeovers that preyed upon many legitimate, hitherto productive companies. With few exceptions—the small number of companies that emerged from the leveraged buyout craze leaner and more efficient than they were—the takeover mania of the 1980s was counterproductive even in financial terms. It created no new wealth, and enriched only short-term investors, investment bankers (raiders such as Drexel Burnham), and the hundreds of lawyers pressed into service to resist or facilitate takeovers. The costs to the social fabric were widespread and serious. In some sectors of the economy, such as savings and loan companies, such practices became linked with a series of illegal acts that constitute a new type of crime dubbed "collective embezzlement." Collective embezzlement, which resembles the takeovers of legitimate business by organized criminals, is defined as crime by the corporation *against* corporate interests; that is, managers put in place by these takeovers systematically loot the assets of the company they are in charge of, engage in irresponsible buying sprees, use trust dollars to finance personal holidays and other perks, and pay themselves excessive salaries. In the end, the company goes bankrupt and the corporate managers walk away millionaires, and then buy up new companies in a never-ending cycle (Calavita and Pontell, 1990; Bruck, 1988).

The 1980s were a time when government regulation of business, particularly in the United States, was seen as a fetter on free enterprise, an onerous burden to be removed as quickly as possible. This philosophy resulted in slashing the budgets and reducing the powers of all federal regulatory agencies. In the savings and loan industry, the Reagan administration moved to "liberate" the industry by phasing out restrictions on interest rates such companies could offer. But it simultaneously increased federal bail-out provisions, by raising the federal government insurance on money deposited from $40,000 to $100,000 per deposit, thereby creating a risk-free environment for those who managed and owned savings and loan companies. This, plus competition for business, greed, and the new availability of money through junk bonds, had disastrous results. Risky and fraudulent investments in the overheated investment climate of the 1980s have led (thus far) to the bankruptcy of 312 savings and loan companies in all parts of the United States. Two to three hundred more banks and loan companies are known to be in trouble. Because the deposits put at risk (and now lost) were insured by the American government, the cost of the bail-out, which will ultimately be borne by the American taxpayer, is immense.

Meanwhile, most of the corporate embezzlers escaped untouched. (Milken and Ivan Boesky, another financier convicted of inside trading, were two visible symbols who did not.) The collapse of the savings and loan industry in the United States has rightly been called "the costliest series of white-collar crimes in history" (Calavita and Pontell, 1991:94). The General Accounting Agency, the top "watchdog" for the U.S. Congress, puts the minimum cost of this series of corporate crimes at $352 billion; the maximum at $1.4 trillion; and the "realistic" estimate at more than $500 billion. Such numbers are so huge they lose all meaning. To put them in perspective, $300 billion was the total defence budget of the United States in 1989. The gross national product of Saudi Arabia, one of the richest countries in the world, is $100 billion. The collapse of the savings and loan industry is expected to cost every household in the United States a minimum of $5000. It means there will be less money to improve the environment, finance medical care for the 40 million Americans who have no medical insurance, rebuild roads, house the homeless, or do similar essential tasks. The cost to foreign governments and their institutions, since many of these investments were international, is an added but still largely unknown factor (*The New York Times*, June 10, 1990; *The Observer*, April 8, 1990; Calavita and Pontell, 1990).

As the savings and loan debacle illustrates, the potential of corporate fraud to impoverish the lives of millions of people in dozens of countries distinguishes it in the clearest way from "ordinary," blue-collar thefts and robberies. While no one would

deny that the latter are serious offences that cause much harm—
because they often involve personal confrontations that generate
fear, and they usually victimize those who are most powerless
and vulnerable—corporate crimes kill, rob, and maim immeasur-
ably greater numbers of people.

DEFINING AND CONCEPTUALIZING CORPORATE CRIME

The preceding discussion has assumed that we all know what
corporate crime actually *is*. However, this is not the case. The
term itself is derived from the broader concept of "white-collar
crime," whose meaning has preoccupied scholars for decades. The
white-collar label itself is generally credited to Edwin Sutherland, a respected American criminologist who spoke about the
criminal acts of the privileged classes in his presidential address
to the American Society of Criminology in 1939, sparking a
debate that has raged ever since. Sutherland's original definition
was very broad. To him, white-collar crimes were "all offences
committed by a person of respectability and high social status in
the course of his occupation (Sutherland, 1940:1). His larger purpose, a polemical and political one, was to remind the academic
community of that era of something it had largely forgotten:
namely, that lower-class males had no monopoly on the commission of amoral or criminal acts. Respectable, middle-class people
with no discernible pathology were responsible for much antisocial, harmful, and criminal behaviour. Sutherland's definition,
then, allowed scholars to focus upon the many and varied
offences associated with the business and professional classes,
from income tax fraud to political corruption to malpractice. It
represented an attempt to wrest the discipline of criminology
from its obsession with the crime-prone tendencies of the poor,
young, and ethnic, but also made a genuine contribution on the
intellectual level.

Although Sutherland may have coined the term "white-collar
crime," he was certainly not the first social analyst to point out
the criminal proclivities of the powerful and privileged. Early
social theorists such as Karl Marx and Friedrich Engels, nineteenth century British socialists, the "muckraking" movement in
turn of the century America, and even an early criminologist, Wilhelm Bonger, all talked about the cross-class character of antisocial behaviour. However, because the capitalist class virtually
owned the political state until well into the 20th century, the
characteristic acquisitive activities of this class were not sanc-

tioned by criminal law, and thus were not formally "crimes." In general, capitalists and entrepreneurs were not only allowed, but encouraged by the state to amass as much money and power as possible in whatever method seemed most efficient. Because of this power to shape law to reflect its interests, criminal laws characteristically focused on acts that the poor and powerless were most likely to commit; robbery, vagrancy, and homelessness, for example, were all crimes.

The tendency to believe that one's own acquisitive acts (and those in one's peer group or class) are moral, socially beneficial, and even necessary is not limited to the upper classes. Delinquents, con artists, those specializing in petty theft or welfare fraud all have distinctive sets of rationalizations for their acts, rationales that justify these behaviours to those who eventually commit them. However, while all classes believe in the innocuous nature of their activities, they do not all have the power to enshrine their point of view in legal statutes, or to avoid the imputations of criminality that the victims of their behaviour seek to impose. Only the upper classes—specifically capital—have consistently been able to exercise this degree of power.

It is therefore not surprising that dominant classes at the turn of the century argued, publicly and vociferously, that certain behaviours were "morally neutral." These actions included paying wages too low to allow employees to maintain their health or dignity; forcing workers to labour in conditions that caused thousands of injuries and deaths; and buying legislatures through secret rebate deals (as the Standard Oil Company, the precursor of Exxon, did in Pennsylvania) (Weinberg and Weinberg, 1961). Such behaviours, it was argued, were essential, part of the cost of doing business, the price of progress. For business to remain competitive, sacrifices had to be made, and if it happened that the employee made the sacrifices while the employer reaped the benefits, that was merely the inexorable result of the laws of capitalism. Moreover, it was argued, the capitalist and not the worker was risking his or her money by setting up a business, and the capitalist provided the chance of employment in the first place (Bliss, 1974). Therefore, incentives, in the form of high profit potential and maximum administrative control, were necessary to ensure that the "engine of progress," the capitalist with money to invest, would continue to do so. These "facts" were self-evident to those who benefited by this set of arrangements; thus, decades of struggle, resistance, and debate were necessary to challenge and surmount them. The eventual extension of the right to vote, awarded first to middle-class males, then lower-class males, and finally to women, was crucial in forcing governments to act against capital. Thus, it would have been difficult for Sutherland to talk about white-collar crime fifty or 100 years earlier than he did, not because antisocial behaviours did not exist, but because laws that defined such acts as deviant had not been passed.

By Sutherland's time, however, a few laws regulating business behaviour were in existence in the United States. Most of these were not criminal statutes; thus, technically speaking, most of the white-collar and corporate crimes he spoke against were really not "crimes." This became the first target of Sutherland's many critics. To this day the majority of laws that govern business—those that prohibit the sale of unsafe or dangerous products, fixing prices, making false advertising claims about products, dumping poisonous residues into the water or air, firing workers for organizing to get more pay—are not proscribed by criminal law. Although most of these acts are now regulated, the statutes involved are largely civil and administrative in character. In Canada, for example, crimes are those acts proscribed by the (federal) Criminal Code, an omnibus statute that includes traditional crimes such as break and enter, burglary, robbery, sexual and regular assault, and homicide (to name just a few), and only these. Behaviours specified in the Criminal Code have a particular stigma attached to them, special standards of proof and evidence required for conviction, and the official presumption that defendants are innocent until proven guilty. In other words, they are infested with procedures and presumptions that do not characterize most other types of law. Thus, the first criticism of the concept of white-collar crime revolved upon the fact that most of the acts Sutherland singled out were not technically criminal, and could therefore not be labelled and studied as crimes.

As Coleman (1989:2–3) points out, Sutherland made himself unnecessarily vulnerable by the examples he chose to illustrate white-collar crime. In his paper he concentrated the discussion upon a subset of violations of U.S. federal regulations such as price fixing and false advertising. These were relatively new laws in Sutherland's time (with the exception of antimonopoly statutes that became the Sherman Act passed in 1890), and there was still much debate about whether they were "really" offences at all (particularly in the business community). Had Sutherland concentrated instead on crimes of violence, for example, the manufacture of unsafe drugs, or corporate cover-ups of dangerous materials (such as asbestos) in the workplace causing death and disease to workers, the connection between corporate crime and "real" crime would have been immediately obvious despite the absence of a criminal designation in law. As it was, critics argued that Sutherland's definition, because it included acts not officially defined as crimes, was too broad and subjective. Any way of accumulating profits that someone, somewhere defined as socially or morally wrong could theoretically be considered a white-collar crime, they said. Therefore, if the concept was to be useful, they argued, white-collar crime had to be limited to those acts that violated existing criminal codes (Tappan, 1947). Furthermore, only white-collar criminals who had actually been charged with a criminal offence and found guilty could be included in such discussions. This narrow definition of white-collar crime, had it carried the day, would have reduced the field to the study of the least serious offences and the least powerful offenders.

However, Sutherland successfully challenged such critiques with a series of counter-arguments. First, he pointed out that decisions about which laws are excluded from criminal codes, and which included, are determined by the power of the groups involved, not by the intrinsic harmfulness of the behaviour in question. Second, although most of the laws that define white-collar crimes are not found in criminal codes, most of the penalties these laws prescribe are; that is, the punishments for white-collar offences, the fines and imprisonment judges have at their disposal, are essentially criminal sanctions, identical to those used for criminal offences. Sutherland interpreted this to mean that the lawmakers who proscribed white-collar offences did indeed define them as serious transgressions. For this reason his definition of white-collar crimes included only those statutes that contained criminal-like sanctions. Because he saw power as a crucial variable, Sutherland strongly resisted Tappan's contention that only convicted offenders could be studied as white-collar criminals. For him, the crux of the definition of white-collar crime lay in the fact that these acts were *punishable*; the power of the classes to whom the laws applied meant then, as now, that enforcement processes would necessarily be weak.

This is not the end of the definitional debate, however. On the other side of the political spectrum it is argued that Sutherland's original definition, far from being too broad, was not broad enough. According to these analysts, all harmful acts committed by people with power should be defined as crimes. The key variable should be the damage a particular willful act causes, not the presence or absence of laws against it, because laws reflect the relative power of a particular group, not the morality of its actions. By this standard, all acts that offend against basic human rights, such as the right to food, shelter, and bodily integrity, can be defined as crimes. Many acts of commission and omission by business—for example, behaviours that deny workers sufficient pay to meet their needs (however needs are defined in that particular society), or force employees to work in dirty and dangerous conditions—are by this definition as criminal as acts that deprive people of their possessions (burglary), or of their right to bodily integrity (assault) (Sheleff, 1982; Pepinsky, 1974; Michalowski, 1985; Michalowski and Kramer, 1987; Simon and Eitzen, 1990).

The rationale here is that a "true" definition of crime must encompass all harmful or exploitative acts, and a preliminary list of these would include terrorism, genocide, environmental pollution, sexism, looting of Third World art treasures by First World collectors, unfair labour practices, and the depletion of natural resources (Sheleff, 1982). The fact that certain groups, especially powerful and privileged males, are able to use their influence to escape legal sanctioning is no excuse for social scientists to refuse to recognize, conceptually and through research, the damage such acts cause. To accept the self-serving perceptions of the privileged, and see crime only where laws (criminal or not) have been passed or, even worse, enforced, is to concur in the fiction that law passage and punishment are uncontaminated by class or power. Using the legal status quo to define immoral or harmful acts is tantamount to colluding with the privileged to define crime in a way that concentrates exclusively on the antisocial acts of those classes that lack the ability to resist such definitions.

Thus, Pepinsky (1974) sees white-collar crime as a form of exploitation, while Michalowski (1985) introduces the concept of crimes of capital. Simon and Eitzen, going further, would replace the terms white-collar or corporate crime with "elite deviance." Elite deviance covers three types of acts: economic domination, government and governmental control, and denial of basic human rights (1990:34). The first category, acts of economic domination, includes many behaviours Sutherland defined as white-collar crimes, such as price fixing, monopolistic practices, and violations of minimum wage statutes. But it also includes "unethical deeds" such as sexual harassment, laying off older workers to avoid the obligation to provide them with pensions, or firing workers after their probationary period expires to avoid the legal responsibility to assume a share of their benefits, and encompasses acts that betray the interests of local communities, such as corporate relocations to areas with cheaper labour or laxer laws. Many such behaviours are both legal and common; dumping unsafe products in poor Third World countries with no regulatory laws or government officials to protect the population, for example, is a flourishing $1.2 billion business. Such acts, Simon and Eitzen point out, have real consequences: more than 400 deaths and 5000 injuries resulted when an organic mercury fungicide, banned in the United States, was sold to Iraq and used to coat byproducts of wheat and barley (Simon and Eitzen, 1990:35). Similarly they see the manufacture and promotion of tobacco as elite deviance.

Tobacco addiction affects both First and Third World populations, results in nearly 1000 deaths a day in the United States, and costs some $50 billion a year in time off work, medical bills, and related expenses. This far exceeds the revenue realized from tobacco sales through profits and taxes (Simon and Eitzen, 1990:286). Most of these acts would certainly escape conventional definitions of white-collar or corporate crime. Their common thread is the contention that all behaviours that cause demonstrable harm—physical, financial, or moral—must be conceptualized as deviant or criminal.

Persuasive as such arguments are, they too have problems. The concept of harm, although it seems an "objective" standard, is largely in the eye of the beholder. Moreover, it must be balanced against the concept of "acceptable risk," and the value placed on "individual liberty." Some people will maintain, for example, that they are personally harmed every time a teenager in the next county puffs on a marijuana cigarette, whenever a woman has an abortion, or whenever the name of the Christian God is taken in vain. How does one sort out "valid" from "invalid" claims? Including every act that some person or group sees as harmful means including virtually all human behaviours. This makes it impossible to conceptualize white-collar crime as a meaningful category, and broadens the criminological field so much that the distinctive characteristics of white-collar crime are thereby obscured.

None of these debates has been successfully resolved. However, most theorists have yielded to pragmatic concerns and agreed that the concept of white-collar crimes must be limited, for most purposes, to acts that have been legally, though not necessarily criminally, proscribed. However, the dawn of the computer age, and the resultant widening of access to technology and mass communications, has demanded continual conceptual rethinking. The opportunity structure for some types of white-collar crime has been democratized beyond the ken of earlier scholars. Computerization has meant that certain sophisticated fraud schemes, for example, can now be undertaken by anyone with a modem and access to (or the ability to figure out) passports or entrance codes. Therefore, attaining a position of trust in an organization is no longer an essential precondition to commit such frauds. Similarly, modern communications have made it possible to transfer massive amounts of capital outside a particular nation-state in the blink of an eye, blurring conceptional and legal as well as jurisdictional boundaries. It is also now widely recognized that white-collar crime can occur outside the context of occupational roles, income tax fraud being the most obvious example. Despite this, most definitions retain the link between white-collar crime and a particular occupational position and/or status. Definitions, then, have become pragmatic devices rather than holy grails, whose parameters shift according to the questions the researcher is addressing. What this approach sacrifices by not strictly adhering to traditional concepts of scientific method is more than recompensed by the fact that it allows finely textured studies of real life behaviour to be undertaken.

Most present-day definitions of white-collar crime, then, include some combination of the following characteristics: (1) they are offences committed as part of a lawful occupation; (2) a violation of trust is involved; (3) there is no direct physical force, although physical harm may well result; (4) the goals are money, property, power, or prestige; (5) there is a specific intent to profit by the act; and (6) there is an attempt to conceal the crime or use power to prevent the application of sanctions. In simplified form, white-collar crime can be seen as "a violation of the law committed by a person or group of persons in the course of an otherwise respected and legitimate occupation or financial activity" (Coleman, 1985:5). This definition highlights the classic distinctions between traditional and white-collar Criminal Code offences: only the latter are characterized by the use of positions of power for illegal gain, with resulting harm to a variety of victims (Reiss and Biderman, 1980).

A further, and absolutely critical, distinction must be made within the ranks of white-collar crime, dividing occupational (or employee) crime from corporate (or organizational) crime. Occupational crimes are white-collar offences committed by an individual or group of individuals exclusively for personal gain (Coleman, 1985:8). The victim is an organization, public or private, business or government, often though not necessarily the offender's employer. Examples include embezzlement of corporate funds, expense account fraud, commercial bribery, tax evasion, and most computer crime. Corporate crimes, on the other hand, are white-collar crimes committed by legitimate formal organizations, through the individuals inside them, with the aim of furthering the interests of the corporation as well as those of the individuals involved. They are committed by companies or individuals on the company's behalf, and they are punishable by law. They may not always be "punished," however, since corporate crimes are more often excused than sanctioned. In addition, the body of law involved is not necessarily criminal; many civil or administrative rules also qualify. Examples of corporate crime include conspiracies among oil companies to restrict the supply and raise the price of gasoline, dumping hazardous wastes into landfills or nearby lakes and oceans, paying kickbacks to retailers to attain prime display space on supermarket shelves, or paying workers less than the minimum wage. The corporate criminal benefits from such acts because he or she usually has both direct and indirect reasons to seek increases in corporate profits. For example, the actions may improve his or her promotion chances (or avoid demotion), increase prestige, or heighten financial remuneration from personally owned company stocks.

In this book the following definition of corporate crime is used: "illegal acts of omission or commission by an individual or group of individuals in a legitimate formal organization in accordance with the operative goals of the organization, which have a serious physical or economic impact on employees, consumers, or the general public" (Box, 1983:20). By adding "other corporations" to the list of victims, one covers corporate crimes that victimize business competitors. Similarly, violations against civil, criminal, or administrative law can all be included if the conditions specified above apply (Box, 1983:19–23).

The key differences between occupational and corporate crime, then, can be summed up by asking who benefits and who is victimized. Corporate crime benefits both the individual and the organization/employer, while occupational crime victimizes the organization, benefiting only the employee. It is therefore in the interests of the powerful corporate sector to oppose the passage and enforcement of laws against corporate crime. On the other hand, business has good reason to support laws and enforcement actions against occupational criminality, and even seek to strengthen them. This difference is crucial in understanding the laws and sanctions that purport to control corporate crime. Although the primary focus in this book will be on corporate crime, instances of occupational crime will be used for comparative purposes from time to time.

TYPOLOGIES OF CORPORATE CRIME

There are as many ways of classifying corporate crime as there are definitions. One typology focuses on the types of harm inflicted, thereby dividing corporate crime according to whether it causes mainly financial, physical, or moral harm. Financial crimes include various commercial and corporate frauds, false advertising, and price fixing. Physical offences encompass, for example, many acts of pollution, the manufacture and sale of dangerous products, and unsafe dumping and disposal practices. Victims range from employees to neighbours to consumers, as well as the community at large. Offences causing moral damage are harder to specify; indeed, many corporate crimes inflict moral damage in addition to financial or physical harm. However, it is argued that because white-collar crime always involves a violation of trust (Shapiro, 1990), some misuse of a position that the incumbent was supposed to respect, the offence inflicts a heavy moral cost on the community. Because the values and responsibilities attached to this position have been betrayed, the level of cynicism and distrust in the society—especially destructive public traits in democratic systems—goes up. Such a classification is seductive; however, when most corporate crimes simultaneously involve all three types of harm, these distinctions are not particularly useful for our purposes.

The taxonomy adopted by the United States Attorney General's Department is very different in scope and emphasis. The primary purpose of this classification is to highlight issues of importance to enforcement bodies, although there is a secondary focus on generating official definitions of harmful acts. This classificatory scheme designates seven distinct types of offences: (1) acts that threaten the integrity of government institutions and processes; (2) defrauding government (by reducing the effectiveness of its programs, thereby creating higher costs); (3) victimizing business enterprises; (4) victimizing consumers; (5) victimizing investors and/or the marketplace; (6) victimizing employers; and (7) threatening the health and safety of the public (Varrette et al., 1985). Since one can only assume the authors' list reflects a rough but official order of priority, it is interesting to note that threats to public health and safety are last, and that harms caused to employees by employers do not even make the list!

More useful are the typologies enunciated by Shapiro (1984) and Edelhertz (1970). Shapiro singles out fraud (use of deception and misrepresentation); self-dealing (using an organizational position to appropriate resources); corruption (insiders using their positions to direct resources to favoured outsiders); and regulatory offences (violating administrative regulations on the conduct of business, the use of public facilities, or the obligations of citizenship). Edelhertz focuses upon the distinction between individual and organizational crimes. The former are offences committed by individuals either on their own (cheating on taxes, welfare or unemployment benefits, for example), or as employees (stealing from the organization). Organizational or corporate crimes are divided into those where the illegal act furthers the business operation (which includes most of the behaviours defined here as corporate crime), as opposed to those where crime is the central activity of the business (here he cites fraudulent home improvement or bankruptcy frauds, where taking money illegally is the primary and sometimes the only purpose for setting up the organization) (Edelhertz, 1970:4–6). Yet another typology for organizational crimes subdivides them into those involving fraud or deception (for example, false advertising or tax evasion); those aimed at controlling the marketplace (predatory pricing, price fixing); violent offences (unsafe products and production); bribery and corruption (commercial and political offences); and violations of civil liberties (Coleman, 1989:13–79).

To debate the merits of these diverse classification schemes is beyond the scope of this book. Moreover, the details are only important insofar as they help sort out a vast array of very different offences. However, these attempts do illustrate the diverse nature of white-collar crimes, and the multitudinous range of offences subsumed under a small number of terms. It is important to realize that corporate crimes vary widely in scope, in the number of primary and secondary victims, in motivation, and in harmfulness. Classifying such acts together and labelling them all "corporate crime," then, is more an act of faith than one of science. These are heuristic divisions that should be utilized when they are useful for analytic purposes, and discarded (or replaced) when they are not.

WHY WE STUDY CORPORATE CRIME

Why should corporate crime be studied? On one level, the answer is glaringly obvious. An activity must be understood if one hopes to regulate or control it, and corporate crime is more harmful, in terms of lives destroyed and financial damage inflicted, than traditional crime. Despite this, the amount of legal attention and enforcement resources devoted to its control has been minimal, and efforts at intensifying control have been characterized more frequently by failure than success. We need to understand why this happens if we wish to prevent the despoliation of the environment, the destruction of financial markets through fraud, the strain on social services caused by wholesale tax avoidance, insider trading and price fixing, or the unnecessary deaths and injuries meted out through dangerous products and unsafe working conditions.

This understanding necessitates, as we shall see, an examination of the role of the state, the primary control mechanism for corporate crime. Moreover, because corporate crime is linked to capitalist economies, which are premised upon allowing the business sector a high degree of autonomy and freedom from regulation, one must ask whether corporate crime can be adequately controlled without sacrificing the high standards of living that prevail in Western capitalist countries. Can we have effective regulation while allowing the fluidity of capital and maximization of profit that a healthy business sector requires (or claims to require)? Does the need to rein in corporate cupidity conflict with the ability of a particular nation to compete with those jurisdictions that are able to offer lower business costs (and therefore potentially higher profits) because they lack regulatory structures? What, indeed, can people in a developed or undeveloped nation expect in the way of good corporate citizenship from the business sector?

Second, we should study corporate crime because it illustrates so dramatically the class bias in law creation and enforcement. The extent of the double standard employed, at all levels and by all major players including "the public," is breathtaking. When comparing nonviolent traditional crimes such as theft or break and enter (typically committed by lower-class/blue-collar people) with similar corporate offences such as false advertising or restraint of trade (typically committed by corporate officers or businesses), one finds that the wording of the respective statutes, the enforcement priority and resources, and the severity of sanctions are all much heavier for the former as opposed to the latter group (Snider and West, 1980; Reiman, 1984; Johnson, 1986). As pointed out in later chapters, the bulk of corporate criminals and companies either escape punishment completely or receive minimal sanctions, while traditional offenders may still get incarcerated for stealing bicycles or cheating the welfare office out of $50. And, while the black killer of three will be front-page news for days, and will eventually receive a long prison term (or face execution in many countries and an increasing number of American states where capital punishment is still allowed), the mining executive who causes 200 deaths by flouting safety regulations may not even be publicly identified. He or she will almost certainly escape imprisonment, although a token fine may, or may not, be assessed. (Typically such fines are paid by the corporation, and are entirely or partially tax deductible.) The study of corporate crime richly rewards those who seek to understand and confront these systemic biases.

Understanding corporate crime is also important from a scholarly perspective; as an intellectual puzzle; as a corrective and challenge to sociology of law and criminology; and as a contribution to a growing literature on the limits of reform. Is it true, as traditional criminological works have insisted, that criminality is characteristic of the young and alienated, people with short attention spans and an inability to defer gratification (Gottfredson and Hirschi, 1990)? What role do social factors such as poverty or exposure to violent media play in the commission of illegal acts? Are upwardly mobile business executives from impoverished backgrounds more likely to commit corporate crimes than their privileged, private school peers? The study of corporate crime also allows us to investigate questions such as the degree to which legal punishments (such as fines and imprisonment) serve as deterrents. If, as many argue, corporate criminals cannot be deterred by punitive sanctions, then surely traditional offenders cannot be either. Why, then, are levels of punishment increasing against traditional offenders while the activities of corporate criminals are being decriminalized (see Chapter 6)? What reason can there be to take increasingly punitive measures against the poor and powerless—incarceration rates, for example, skyrocketed throughout the 1980s and are still going up (Chesney-Lind, 1991; MacLean, 1986a; Ratner, 1986; Colvin, 1986)—while adopting more cooperative and conciliatory responses to the harmful activities of the rich and privileged? These, then, are the kinds of questions the study of corporate crime leads one to investigate.

OUTLINE OF CHAPTERS

The book is organized in the following manner:

- Chapter 1 looks at the prevalence of corporate crime, and examines techniques and methodologies that have been developed to measure it.

- In Chapter 2, the spotlight turns to explanation: What social theories have been developed to explain the phenomenon of corporate crime? How do such explanations fit into more general theories of deviance and conformity, within and outside complex organizations?

- This theme is developed in specific terms in Chapter 3, which examines the causes of corporate crime. Major individual, organizational, and macro-level theories of causality, and their strengths and weaknesses, are explored here.

- Chapter 4 examines historical forces. It describes and analyzes the long, fierce, definitional and legal struggle that was necessary to force governments to acknowledge the harmful antisocial acts of business. The rise of capitalism, the explosion of productive forces set loose by the Industrial Revolution, and the social changes thereby unleashed set the stage for a new era in social history. The predominant attitude of those who owned and controlled business and government was a facilitative and extraordinarily uncritical one. Thus, it took some time before any laws governing the behaviours of employers were passed.

- In Chapter 5, enforcement is examined; specifically, the development, purpose, and function of the main enforcement vehicle for corporate crimes, the regulatory agency, is discussed.

- Chapter 6 looks at the sanctioning record of governments and agencies: What kinds of punishments, against what kinds of corporate offences, have actually been assessed? It quickly becomes apparent that the enforcement record is an extremely weak one.

- Chapter 7 tries to make sense of this record, and of regulatory ineffectiveness more generally. The goal here is to understand regulatory failures so that potentially more effective reforms can be put forth. Several ameliorating strategies with greater chances of success are described.

- Finally, the Conclusion summarizes the major arguments of each chapter and then briefly addresses the policy question: "Where do we go from here?"

Prevalence, Incidence, and Measurement

INTRODUCTION

The first recorded white-collar crime took place in 360 B.C. in Syracuse, Sicily. A shipowner persuaded a buyer to advance him cash for a load of corn purportedly in the ship's hold. In reality, the ship was empty. The owner's apparent intention was to scuttle the ship, pretend the corn was lost at sea, and pocket the buyer's advance payment. When the passengers discovered the owner's plans, he panicked, jumped overboard, and drowned (Clarke, 1990:13). Individualistic white-collar crimes by the merchant classes and other privileged groups can be found throughout recorded history. Real corporate crime, however, had to await the invention of the corporate form, a special mode of organization that presents unique opportunities for owners of capital. The first modern corporation, the Dutch East India Company, was founded in 1602, although it did not take its present corporate form until sometime after 1700. The first corporation in Canada, one which had a profound influence on Canadian history, was the Hudson's Bay Company founded in 1670. By 1850, less than 200 years later, the corporate form had become the dominant mode of organization, and all significant business enterprises were organized in this way. Historically speaking, then, corporations represent a relatively new and very significant phenomenon.

This chapter examines the history of the corporate form and its subsequent growth, setting the stage for its present-day domination over virtually every institutional sphere in the modern world. However, we shall concentrate on its growing centrality in the economic sector, as well as the increase in corporate concentration that has gone hand in hand with this growth. Following this, the focus will shift to the measurement of corporate crime:

looking at studies that seek to discover the prevalence of corporate and white-collar crime (how common it is), and its incidence (how many offences of each type are committed in a given time period). The various methods scholars have used to measure prevalence and incidence, the estimated rates that follow from this, and the strengths and weaknesses of the different methodologies employed will be examined.

HISTORY AND GROWTH OF THE CORPORATION

The most important characteristic of the corporation is the provision of limited liability to investors. There are three basic models for business firms: single proprietorship, partnership, and corporation (Odagiri, 1981). The first two models are ancient, and differ only in the number of owners involved. Both require owners to assume full liability for any debts the business incurs. The corporation model, on the other hand, allows each owner or stockholder to be liable only for the amount he or she has invested. This is a significant difference, because it allows vast sums of money to be pooled, and it provides increased incentive for those with money to put it into business (rather than land, for example, or material goods).

The right to incorporate was originally a privilege granted by government to encourage the formation of new businesses and attract capital. Limited liability was first codified in English law under the Joint Stock Act of 1844, but it was only through a series of legal "accidents," culminating in the *Salomon v. Salomon* case in 1910, that this principle became enshrined in English law (and thereafter in most Commonwealth countries) (McQueen, 1990). There are still many European countries where limited liability does not apply, and corporate laws that force active members of small corporate enterprises to remain liable for an unlimited amount of debt under certain conditions are still found (McQueen, 1990:2).

In the early years, when limited liability was still seen as a privilege, the corporation had to provide certain services for the community, and give assurances that it would act in the public interest, to secure permission to incorporate (Finn, 1969; Seavoy, 1978; McNully, 1978). By the middle of the 18th century, however, governments began to realize the revenue-enhancing possibilities of corporate charters, and the idea of selling them to the highest bidder was born. As capitalist ideology gained strength, governments came to see the development and growth of the corporation as an unalloyed source of good, for corporations represented "progress" and brought prestige to a community, in addition to revenue and employment opportunities. Moreover, since the decision-makers in government often had interests in business themselves (and were frequently directly involved as owners and investors, especially in North America where there was no land-based aristocracy), they took the interests of the capitalist class very seriously. The result was that the concepts of public interest and service were quickly supplanted by the belief that the only legitimate goal of corporations was profit maximization, and their only real responsibility was to owners/shareholders. Thus, through a combination of litigation and government laxity, the needs of capital were permitted to dominate the political process, and incorporation became a routine service. In the United States, for example, by 1875 virtually every state was granting incorporation automatically in exchange for nothing more than a corporate promise to comply with state law (Cochran, 1977).

One consequence of this has been a continuous increase in the size and power of corporations. This process has accelerated in the last half of the 20th century, as capitalism has moved into the monopoly stage predicted by Karl Marx 130 years ago. Monopoly capitalism refers to the tendency of corporations to get bigger and bigger, concentrating power and wealth in an ever smaller number of hands. The number of dominant corporations declined from 170 in 1951, to 113 in 1972 (Clement, 1975, 1977; Porter, 1965). By 1983, through a combination of takeovers and mergers, twenty-five conglomerates encompassing a total of 585 corporations controlled 34 percent of all industrial assets, 32.6 percent of all corporate profit (outside the finance sector), and 23.5 percent of all sales (Veltmeyer, 1987; Marchak, 1988; Francis, 1986). This has also meant an increase in foreign ownership, as the number of corporations under Canadian ownership and control continues to decline.

In practically every sector, a few giant firms have secured the lion's share of the market, while scores of small companies fight for the scraps (Marchak, 1975). The largest 100 companies (less than 1 percent of all corporations in Canada) control more than 50 percent of all industrial sector property and profits, and more than one-third of all sales. A mere thirty-two family dynasties (for example, the Westons, Thomsons, Molsons, and Eatons) control assets whose combined revenues of $123 billion in 1985 were greater than the $80 billion income of the entire federal government (Francis, 1986). Concentration varies by sector, with petroleum, banking, and manufacturing among the leaders. The "big five" banks control 90 percent of banking assets in the country. In manufacturing, 2 percent of the corporations control 79.4 percent of the assets, 72.3 percent of the sales, and 68.9 percent of profits; while in petroleum, four multinational corporations (Imperial Oil, Texaco, Gulf, and Shell) control 58 percent of all retail outlets and 64 percent of Canadian refineries. (Petro-Canada is excluded because it is still publicly owned at the time of writing.) Accompanying this increase in concentration has been a change in the nature of the Canadian workforce, with the percentage of white-collar and service jobs doubling from 1901 to 1971, from 25 percent to 57 percent of the labour force (Tepperman, 1975:33). This trend has intensified in the 1980s and 1990s, as the computer revolution and free trade have taken away jobs in the primary (raw products) and secondary (manufacturing/industrial) sectors, leaving largely low-paying part-time jobs in service industries in its wake.

In the United States, the largest 500 industrial corporations now control 75 percent of all manufacturing assets; fifty out of 67,000 companies in transportation and utilities control two-thirds of the airline, railway, communications, electricity, and gas industries; four firms control most of the revenues and audiences in the movie business; two insurance companies alone have 25 percent of the industry, while fifty of the remaining 1890 companies account for the next 50 percent (Simon and Eitzen, 1990:12). A similar picture emerges in manufacturing and banking: less than 1 percent of U.S. manufacturers hold 88 percent of all industrial assets and take 90 percent of all profits, while under 1 percent of American banks have 70 percent of all deposits (Pearce, 1991:4–5).

As in Canada, a mammoth increase in the size of corporations has occurred. In 1983, annual sales of the 500 largest industrial corporations exceeded $1.7 trillion, and the revenues of Exxon alone (over $97 billion) were greater than the gross national products of every country in the world except the United States and the Soviet Union (as it then was). It is estimated that forty-six of the top 100 economies of the world are not countries at all, but multinational corporations. For example, in 1988–89, Mitsui, General Motors, and C. Itoh all had sales revenues larger than the gross domestic product of countries such as Denmark, Finland, or Norway (Pearce, 1991). Moreover, corporate economies, growing at rates double and triple those of nation-states (Veltmeyer, 1987; Cavanaugh and Clairmonte, 1983), now supply 80 percent of all jobs in the American economy and similar percentages elsewhere (Coleman, 1985:12–14). Most world trade is not between different countries, but within transnational corporations (Pearce, 1991:5). Transnational corporations are still rare in numerical terms—companies with assets of $250 million or more represent only 0.1 percent of all corporations filing returns with the Internal Revenue Service in the United States (Dugger, 1988). However, this minuscule percentage controls nearly three-quarters of all corporate assets, and receives over half of all corporate receipts and more than two-thirds of all corporate income. A few giant firms, then, dominate the U.S. and world economic systems "to an extent undreamed of in earlier years" (Dugger, 1988:80).

Although wealth and income have never been equally distributed in any capitalist democracy, they became even more concentrated in the 1980s under conservative leaders such as Ronald Reagan and Margaret Thatcher. Since the time of the American Civil War, the richest 1 percent have owned one-quarter of that nation's wealth (the combined market value of *everything*); and the top half of this 1 percent have owned a full fifth of this total (Zeitlin, 1978:14–19). However, in the last decade, thanks to tax cuts, loopholes, tax incentives, subsidies, and various price supports for the rich, the holdings of this one-half of 1 percent at the top jumped dramatically and now stand at 38 percent (Kolko, 1988:344). Moreover, one-twentieth of 1 percent of American adults own 20 percent of all corporate stock, 40 percent of all bonds and notes, and nearly 70 percent of state and local bonds. The richest 1 percent own one-seventh of all real estate and all cash (Simon and Eitzen, 1990:12). A similar shift has been reported in Britain under Margaret Thatcher, where the pre-tax income share of the top 10 percent of income earners has gone from 26.1 percent in 1978–79 to 29.5 percent in 1984–85, and the post-tax share from 23.4 percent to 26.5 percent (Leys, 1989:172).

All of this means that the productive capacity of the world is controlled by a very small group of people and corporations. None of them is democratically elected to its position, and it is increasingly difficult for even the largest and richest nation-states to monitor or control such vast concentrations of wealth. Such conglomerates can raise and allocate capital internally, thereby evading even the meagre level of social control exerted by nation-states when companies rely on external capital markets. As one economist points out, this growth leads not to increased efficiency, but to an unhealthy domination of corporate institutions over all noncorporate institutions—the family, community, and unions to name a few (Dugger, 1988:9). As corporate empires expand, the increasing complexity of form and operation made possible by computer technology means that gaining access to information on their activities, finding out what they are doing, and where and how they are doing it, is almost impossible. As Marchak puts it: "They (corporations) make decisions that affect not only their shareholders ... and not only their employees ...

but the entire population, and the economic environment and the political possibilities of the entire nation (indeed of many nations). Yet they make these public decisions in private and with reference to private goals and private profit" (Marchak, 1988:71–72).

This increase in the size, power, and scope of the corporate sector has direct consequences for discovering, assessing, and measuring the amount of corporate crime. The 1980s were a period of conglomerate-building and takeovers, with corporations gobbling up profitable companies wherever they could be found, to stave off bankruptcy or unfriendly takeovers themselves. This means greater opportunities for corporate criminality, because territorially based nation-states are now charged with controlling international empires. Capital can be transferred overnight from a country with many regulatory laws to one with none. High-polluting industries can be shifted to the Third World where governments are too weak and desperate for foreign investment to establish effective controls; Third World countries are also useful for trying out potentially dangerous drugs, or dumping drugs banned in the First World (Braithwaite, 1980). Profits can be hidden and taxes evaded by having one branch of a multinational sell goods at excessive prices to a subsidiary in a low-tax country. Moreover, because the resources of the corporations typically dwarf those of the regulating country, the chances of being held responsible for such offences are small in First World countries and virtually nonexistent elsewhere (barring major disasters such as Bhopal where the international media act as countervailing pressure groups). For corporate management, then, temptations and opportunities increase as companies get larger.

This does not mean smaller companies are crime-free; only that different factors come into play for both company and regulator. Because small companies are typically less mobile, more restricted to one geographic location, and much less powerful, regulatory bodies typically find it easier to hold them accountable for corporate offences. However, because their survival is usually more precarious than that of large companies (with takeover threats and declining profit margins as continuing problems), such businesses can find themselves with backs against the wall, fighting to retain a precarious market share. At least one author claims there is evidence that such a situation increases the company's likelihood of lawbreaking. Antitrust offences are particularly tempting because small companies, unable to realize economies of scale, know that collaborating with the competition to fix prices may guarantee the high profit levels they need for survival (Simpson, 1986).

MEASURING INCIDENCE AND ESTIMATING PREVALENCE

All this means, then, that motives and opportunities to commit white-collar crime are plentiful throughout the business world. However, measuring the amount of crime that actually occurs is quite a different matter. Corporate and occupational criminality present distinctive measurement problems. Traditional criminal offences such as thefts, burglaries, and assaults are usually reported to policing agencies by victims, witnesses, neighbours, or businesses. A small number of offences are uncovered through routine police patrols. Once an incident is classified as criminal, it is then recorded on official forms and submitted to a government agency (Statistics Canada in this country), which is responsible for collating and reporting all such instances on an annual basis. This system forms the base of statistics on the number of crimes committed. In the academic community it is supplemented by victimization surveys, which ask a cross-section of the population whether it has been victimized by particular criminal acts over a given time period. This method provides a cross-check on the accuracy of official (police-generated) statistics, and taps into a different public constituency. Comparing the two results provides a more accurate picture of how much crime is actually occurring.

Although such statistics are inevitably flawed, they provide at least benchmark data over time. However, this level of comprehensiveness is absent for white-collar crime. Generally speaking, basic data are lacking at every stage of the process, on incidence, identification of offenders, and enforcement actions. Nothing is known about the "dark figure" of white-collar crime—the number of offences that "actually" occur. Little more is known about attrition rates; that is, the number and percentage of cases dropped at each stage of the enforcement process (and thereby lost from official records), from incidence to investigation, prosecution, and sanctioning. Virtually every study that has examined the issue has found that attrition rates for corporate and occupational crimes are very high (Jamieson, 1985; Carson, 1980a, 1980b; Edelhertz, 1970; Casey, 1985). As Shapiro said in her study of data on securities and exchange violations: "The official record overrepresents the decisions not to prosecute common criminals and underrepresents those not to prosecute white-collar ones" (Shapiro, 1985). We know that many (probably most) white-collar crimes are never uncovered; those few that are will most likely be handled without recourse to official sanctioning agencies. Thus, no written record of offence or sanction (in the unlikely event there is a sanction) will exist. The sources most likely to know the number and type of offences occurring, namely business and regulatory agencies, both have good reasons to conceal such information from outsiders.

Because it is so difficult to obtain reliable statistics on white-collar crime, many investigators have been forced to concentrate on the few offences that are officially recorded and sanctioned. This means looking at offenders who have been charged with criminal offences and processed in criminal courts, because such records are public information. Unfortunately these data present a misleading view of incidence, prevalence, and punishment. The vast majority of white-collar offences are either ignored, processed informally, or handled through the civil or administrative procedures of regulatory agencies. By looking at the atypical few who end up criminally indicted, one has eliminated at least 95 percent of the overall sample of wrongdoers, and virtually 100 percent of those offences committed by powerful corporate forces (since power, by definition, tends to allow the redefinition of offences in ways that avoid criminalization) (Katz, 1979). Despite this, researchers are often forced to rely on such data if they wish to say anything at all. To quote Shapiro once more:

> Given the sublety and complexity of white-collar offenses, the possibility of masking illicit activities in everyday routines or hiding them in the privacy of corporate suites or complicated inter-organizational networks, the opportunities to manipulate the time over which events unfold, the frequently consensual nature of the illicit behaviors, and the often diffused quality of victimization, one might expect the dark figure of undetected violations [for white-collar offences] to greatly overshadow that of most common serious crimes. (Shapiro, 1985:181)

While this book is basically about corporate crime, our most reliable data are, unfortunately, about occupational crime.[1] This is not surprising, because offences such as embezzlement, tax evasion, theft by employees, computer crime, or commercial bribery have an obvious and powerful victim—the employer or government from which valuables are taken. Such offences, therefore, are likely to be noticed, acted upon, and with some exceptions, reported. Official records and statistics are thereby generated. For corporate crimes, however, victims are many and diffuse—the general public, consumers, the corporation's employees, or the government; the crime is complex; and the corporation is a chief beneficiary of the offence. Data on corporate crimes, therefore, are most likely to be concealed because those in a position to know and report them have every reason to keep such knowledge secret. Corporate offences are only going to be uncovered by accident, or when regulatory agencies do proactive investigations. Investigations are expensive, and most agencies have undergone at least a decade of morale- and personnel-sapping budget cuts. Moreover, the complexities of corporate form make cover-ups and deception easy. Thus, luck plays a large role in uncovering corporate crime. For example, a careless remark to a regulatory official played a key role in the recent discovery of a multimillion dollar bid-rigging scandal. When asked in casual conversation why his company had not submitted a bid for a major contract, the employee apparently replied that it was not their "turn" to get a contract. Subsequent investigation revealed a major undetected conspiracy that had been going on for years (Canada, 1989). Similarly, the chief executive officer of the Grays Building Society in England, who embezzled £2 million over a forty-year period, was caught only when the auditors were changed following the retirement of the firm's accountant (Clarke, 1990:21).

Even data on crimes where the victim is a corporation, however, must be treated with care. Employers are frequently reluctant to press criminal charges because they fear loss of face from the resulting publicity, or they decide that the time and expense involved in criminal investigation and the resultant court appearances are not worth it. When investigating theft, data on inventory—the amount of wholesale goods purchased—would seem to provide accurate loss records, but these, too, have their problems. Specifically, it is impossible to know how much inventory shrinkage (the disappearance of company property) is due to employee crime, and how much to inefficient filing or purchasing systems, or errors in counting. It is known that shrinkage, measured after known shoplifting offences are subtracted, accounts for up to 75 percent of merchandise losses from retail stores and manufacturers. This would seem to indicate that a lot of theft by employees (and/or undetected outside shoplifters) is occurring. Indeed, theft from all sources (shoplifters, suppliers, other outsiders, and employees) is estimated to add between 2 and 4 percent to the cost of retail goods (Jaspan 1960, 1974; Cameron, 1970; Hollinger and Clarke, 1983).

Dominant patterns of sanctioning for occupational crimes are important insofar as similar tendencies can be expected to shape sanctions for corporate crimes. We know that the likelihood of an offender being charged for an offence varies directly with his or her economic and organizational status (Cameron, 1964, 1970; Bequai, 1978); that is, nonemployees (especially young people) are more likely to be charged than employees, and employees at the bottom of the organizational ladder are more likely to be charged than those higher up. Robin (1967), for example, found that charges were laid against 60 percent of cleaning staff, 32.4 percent of executives, and 26.3 percent of those in sales. A study of shoplifters in an American city found that 24 percent of all charges were laid against black people, despite the fact that they comprised only 6.5 percent of those arrested, *and* that fewer than thirteen of every 100 suspects faced charges (Cameron, 1970).

This is not because lower-level or people of colour steal more valuable objects. Indeed, while the chances of being charged decrease as one ascends the occupational ladder, the amount actually stolen increases; it varies directly with rank and status (Benson, 1985). Thus, employees cause heavier losses than ordinary shoplifters, and executives do more damage (by far) than clerks or workers. The average amount stolen by outsiders in one recent American study was $5279, while that stolen by insiders (employees) was $17,106 (Wheeler and Rothman, 1982); another study reports that the average robbery nets $338, while the average federally convicted white-collar criminal takes $300,000 (Shapiro, 1984; also Coleman, 1985; Bequai, 1978; Simon and Eitzen, 1986; Hollinger and Clarke, 1983). Finally, the average computer criminal (77 percent of whom are corporate employees) nets some $400,000 per job, although losses reported in one survey varied from $1 to $10 million (Coleman, 1985:81; Hollinger and Clarke, 1983). Such findings have profound implications for studying corporate crime because they mean that studies that use statistics derived from court records will overestimate the criminality of those groups most vulnerable to sanctions (lower-class or ethnic people), and underestimate both the number of crimes and the amount of damage done by more powerful segments of the population (middle- and upper-class whites).

Still other data on prevalence come from owners of security services (Jaspan, 1960, 1974), from studies of private police (Shearing and Stenning, 1983), and from government studies, many of them American. It was estimated in the late 1960s that tax fraud cost the U.S. treasury $40 billion a year; embezzlement cost organizations $200 million; and larceny from retail businesses cost $1.3 billion (Smigel and Ross, 1970; Jaspan, 1974). By 1976, the U.S. Chamber of Commerce had upped these estimates and was reporting that $44 billion per year was lost to white-collar crime. This figure is probably understated; a 1977 study of frauds against government programs found losses of $25 billion in a mere seven agencies (Meier and Short, 1982:24). The U.S. Internal Revenue Service (IRS) estimated the total revenue loss in 1981 due to tax evasion (which may or may not be occupational crime) at \$97 billion; \$66.1 billion of this due to nonreporting of income by individuals and \$4.9 billion to nonfiling (Brooks and Doob, 1990:123). In 1987, the U.S. Chamber of Commerce estimated that one of every ten insurance claims was fraudulent, at a total cost of \$15 billion per year, and that 12 percent of all fires on insured property were purposively set (Clarke, 1990:72–78). Other reports find that from 50 to 76 percent of retail workers admit stealing (usually occasionally rather than systematically) from their employer (Schmidt, 1975; Tatham, 1974).

For Canadian data, we have to rely on official records such as those collected from police forces by Statistics Canada. For what they are worth (and it is not much), data for 1980 show that there were 76,556 cases of shoplifting reported to the police, 75,335 frauds involving cheques and credit cards, and 26,920 other types of fraud (Canada, 1982:81–82). Such offences comprised 11.4 percent of all known offences. By 1989, numbers had risen to 103,559 shoplifting offences, 90,962 frauds involving cheques and credit cards, and 39,783 other frauds (Statistics Canada, 1990:2–3). However, these figures are subject to all the problems discussed above; moreover, they do not distinguish between employee versus outsider offences. We can therefore be sure that most of the crimes committed by upper-level, powerful people are not revealed in these statistics.

Moving closer to corporate criminality, let us examine data on tax evasion, a crime that is, by definition, more characteristic of the affluent than the poor, it being impossible to evade taxes one does not owe. Tax evasion, moreover, is potentially much more profitable, and easier, for the incorporated (organization or individual) than the unincorporated, given the plethora of tax shelters incorporation allows. Therefore, although all tax evaders are not corporations, many corporations are tax evaders. Entire branches of companies, indeed, are devoted to minimizing and avoiding tax. While tax avoidance is legal, tax evasion is not. The distinction between the two frequently becomes obvious only after successful court action has been taken by tax authorities (Revenue Canada in this instance) (McBarnett, 1992). Unfortunately, the statistics available provide little solid information about the amount of tax owed by high-status individuals or corporations. Here we face once again the basic problem of determining the incidence of criminal acts committed by powerful bodies: they are uniquely advantaged in hiding their offences from researchers, regulators, and police; and they are better able to resist enforcement efforts when offences are discovered. These advantages are sometimes strengthened by government policy. The federal government of Canada, for example, has long had a policy of not prosecuting tax evaders if they can pay up when caught (Tepperman, 1977); therefore, only impecunious or recalcitrant tax evaders show up in the statistics.

All the same, certain inferences can be made. It was estimated in 1978 that the "real" amount of income tax lost to the Canadian government through evasion or fraud was between $5 and $10 billion a year (Varrette et al., 1985). There is enough work to keep the 400 RCMP officers who staff their Special Investigation Unit busy looking into 900 to 1000 annual cases of tax evasion. Although cases take up to four years to prepare and prosecute, convictions are obtained in virtually all of them. (This may only tell us, however, that the RCMP have such a conservative policy on prosecutions that they drop all cases they could conceivably lose early in the process.) In addition, Revenue Canada's 2400 auditors annually conduct 90,000 audits, although they only prosecute an average of ten per year. This is not because no additional taxes are owed; indeed, it has been calculated that each and every hour of an auditor's time yields, for companies with over $200 million of sales annually, an average of $6000 in tax owing. Not all of this is collected, however. In 1976, $550 million of an estimated $2.1 billion deemed recoverable was actually collected; in 1977, $700 million of $2.3 billion was brought in; and in 1978, $800 million of $2.7 billion was collected (Varrette et al., 1985). The amounts and percentages that would count as corporate crime, unfortunately, are not revealed in these statistics. A recent self-report study tapping individuals rather than corporations, however, found "a substantial portion" (24 percent) of Canadian taxpayers admitting they evade taxation "at least occasionally" (Brooks and Doob, 1990:154).

Because one victim of tax evasion is government, a powerful actor in its own right, this offence has been somewhat better studied than the bulk of corporate crimes, where the victim is the unorganized public or the relatively powerless employee. Estimating the number of these offences is a difficult and time-consuming task, but once again it has been established through other evidence that offences victimizing the workforce and/or the public are common. A 1984 survey reported that two-thirds of the largest industrial companies on the Fortune 500 list had been involved in illegal behaviour in the previous decade (Etzioni, 1985). Leigh (1989) shows that the most reliable industry fatality data in the United States omit as much as 66 percent of occupationally caused deaths due to contamination by factors such as self-selection bias. Carson's painstaking analysis of 200 firms in Britain found that every firm studied had violated health and safety laws at least twice; the average number of violations per firm, according to the British Factory Inspectorate, was nineteen (Carson, 1970).

More recently the British Factory Inspectorate visited some 4500 construction sites in the summer of 1987. Conditions so dangerous that work had to be immediately halted were found in one of every five sites; 868 prohibition notices were issued (Pearce, 1990b:421). A victimization survey that questioned 889 individuals in Islington (a suburb of London, England) discovered that half of those who had arranged credit in the past year had been victimized, in this case by lenders who violated the conditions of the Consumer Credit Act of 1974. Moreover, 9 percent of respondents said they had been the victims of misleading or false advertising, or false information on the marketplace; 19 percent had been overcharged, and 25 percent had paid for defective goods or services (Pearce, 1990a). In Canada, occupationally induced or related disease is the third leading cause of death, immediately after heart disease and cancer, and at least half of all workplace deaths can be attributed to unsafe and usually illegal working conditions (Reasons et al., 1981; Reasons, 1986; Henry, 1986). Such deaths, then, are caused by corporate crime. It is not unreasonable to assume that thorough studies would reveal victimization rates much higher than those provided by the inadequate statistics presently available.

Additional evidence, albeit conflicting, comes from a series of interviews done with senior executives in Canada's private sector. In this study, everyone in the sample believed that employee theft was a real and omnipresent problem, and all could list numerous offences that cost their respective corporations money: theft of company time, theft of property and computer time, expense account padding, kickbacks, espionage, and other frauds. (The usual sanction was to fire the offending employee; companies were reluctant to waste time by laying official charges and involving the criminal justice system.) However, survey participants were much more reticent when asked about the problem of corporate criminality—the offences they, their companies, and their competitors committed. Despite almost daily revelations of insider trading filling the business pages of newspapers at that time, brokers who were asked about securities offences said their greatest concerns were about the physical security of the stocks they traded (that is, they worried about protecting stocks from thieves who might steal them from their briefcases and automobiles). They showed no comparable concern about protecting these stocks from their own peregrinations. When the researchers sampled the opinions of market regulators, however, they found the latter reporting, not surprisingly, that bribes, conflicts of interest, incompetent executives, and insider knowledge and trading were all serious problems in the industry (Varrette et al., 1985:48–53). Once again, the prevalence and significance of corporate crime vary with the perspective and interests of those whose point of view is solicited.

No discussion of prevalence would be complete, however, without recognizing that the victims of corporate crime frequently do not realize they *are* victims of an offence. When they are aware of their victimization, more often than not there is no official body to whom they can report. In addition, there is unlikely to be any way they can seek or obtain compensation, either financial or psychological, for their suffering. The few, weak, government-sponsored bodies that do provide aid for different kinds of victims are in most countries obscure, underfunded, unpublicized, and known only to lawyers and the knowledgeable elite who read consumer reports or listen, for example, to CBC or Public Network radio. The few victims who have sought satisfaction from such agencies typically report their needs and losses were low-priority items, making the search for redress a highly frustrating one (Moore and Mills, 1990; Pearce, 1990a). Moreover, victims of white-collar offences have been completely excluded from the spate of laws spawned by victims' rights movements in the 1980s (which provided in the United States, for example, an average award of $1869 in 1988 for survivors of such offences as child sexual abuse and other sexual offences, assault, and homicide) (Moore and Mills, 1990).

Ignorance of the fact of victimization is exacerbated by the tendency of victims of white-collar offences to blame themselves for having been victimized (Shover and Mills, 1990). Complex ideological forces shape the social construction of blame in ways that direct attention away from the antisocial acts of the powerful and shift it toward the nasty deeds of the powerless. With complex conditions such as dirty air or degenerative diseases, where there is no equivalent of the "smoking gun" and causality is not immediately obvious, people have to depend on the media, science, or union authorities to alert them to danger and pinpoint sources of harm. The powerful corporate sector works hard to shape this process, and to shift responsibility away from its own activities. Both legal and ideological (public relations) arguments are typically utilized. Companies routinely deny, in courts and media, that there are any dangers inherent in workplace conditions, additives, or toxic discharges. An individual wishing to challenge such arguments will be faced with libel suits and a battery of company lawyers and assorted academic experts all arguing that any problems the complainant has suffered are due to his or her unhealthy lifestyle or carelessness. Faced with the massive resources of the corporation, such unequal battles are unlikely to be attempted, let alone won. The implications of such facts, for those who would gauge the incidence of corporate crime, are that many corporate crimes never appear in statistics of any sort. Estimates of prevalence must therefore understate the extent of criminality by an unknown, but undoubtedly massive, amount.

PROBLEMS WITH MEASUREMENT:
CASE STUDIES OF CORPORATE CRIME

This section examines some case studies of corporate crime, beginning with the pioneering work of Edwin Sutherland, first published in 1956. Sutherland, studying the criminal careers of the seventy largest corporations in the United States since their inception, found that each corporation had at least one offence registered against it. There were a total of 980 adverse decisions, an average of fourteen per corporation. Or, as he put it, "90 percent of the 70 largest corporations in the United States are habitual criminals" (Sutherland, 1977:73). Sutherland also pointed out that such figures understate the actual amount of corporate criminality, because corporations could and did use their power and size to hide violations and block enforcement. Among the violations, Sutherland found offences against the Pure Food and Drug Law, the Federal Trade Commission (mostly misleading, dishonest, or fraudulent advertising), the National Labor Relations Law (offences against employees, violating their right to organize and bargain collectively), and violations of antitrust laws. Such transgressions were frequent and continuous; moreover, even the most fraudulent and unethical activities, as it turned out, cost business leaders no loss of power or prestige (Sutherland, 1977:83). Had they robbed banks, for example, which would have netted them much less, they would have been social pariahs.

This study was updated by Clinard and Yeager some years later. They looked at all legal actions initiated by twenty-four federal agencies against the 582 largest industrial corporations in the United States during 1975 and 1976. They found that 40 percent of the corporations had no legal actions registered against them during this period, while 60 percent had at least one adverse decision. The average number of "crimes" was 4.8 per company. Eighty-three corporations (17.5 percent of the total), logging five or more violations each, qualified for the "habitual offender" label. Large corporations violated laws more often than small ones. The most frequently broken laws (an equally plausible interpretation would describe these as the most frequently enforced ones) were those governing manufacturing, the environment, and labour relations. The automobile, pharmaceutical, and oil refining industries were the most criminogenic sectors; a total of thirty-eight firms accounted for more than half of all reported violations, averaging 23.5 violations each over the two-year period (Clinard and Yeager, 1980:110–21).

Another study, by Wheeler et al. (1988), looked at individuals charged and convicted of felonies in U.S. federal courts in 1976, 1977, and 1978. Eight different offences were examined, representing both occupational offences and corporate crimes. The offences were: (1) criminal violations of securities; (2) criminal violations of antitrust acts; (3) bribery of a public official; (4) bank embezzlement, by officers, directors, or bank employees; (5) mail fraud (an omnibus category including both occupational and traditional crimes as well as the occasional small-scale corporate offence); (6) tax fraud; (7) false claims (to social security, medicaid, etc.); and (8) credit fraud. Wheeler and his team examined pre-sentence reports, filed for almost all federal offenders, which provide a treasury of information on the offender's social and personal characteristics as well as details of the offence. For each offence category, thirty cases were selected at random in a total of seven urban districts (Los Angeles, Atlanta, Chicago, Baltimore, New York City, Dallas, and Seattle). Offenders and their offences were then compared with data on nonviolent traditional crimes.

Obviously, this study cannot provide an accurate assessment of the number of white-collar offences actually occurring, or reveal a great deal about the characteristics of the majority of corporate or occupational criminals, because most of this population is never convicted of a felony offence in federal court. Only the atypical minority of individuals, those who actually suffer criminal charges and get convicted, are included. Moreover, since only individual offenders are sampled, no corporations appear. Whatever its drawbacks, however, the study does provide us with a comprehensive picture of a rarely studied group of people convicted of a variety of white-collar and corporate offences, and the findings are therefore useful and accurate, as long as the biases of the sample are kept in mind.

First, looking at the eight white-collar offences as a group, Wheeler et al. report that white-collar criminals steal much more than traditional offenders. Only 2 percent of the latter steal amounts greater than $100,000, while 30 percent of white-collar crimes are above this threshold (all amounts are in 1976–78 dollars). White-collar cases also take much longer to prosecute, with 50.9 percent of them, versus 7 percent of traditional offences, lasting more than one year. Moreover, despite the fact that offenders in this sample represent the least powerful subset of white-collar criminals, they are still much better educated than either the public at large, or traditional offenders. They are also older, more frequently white, more likely to be steadily employed, and more likely to own their own house than those convicted of traditional offences.

Some variations occur within each offence category. Those convicted of mail fraud, for example, are more likely to be those who victimize organizations than representatives of organizations that victimize the general public. Thus, people who steal from telephone companies through the fraudulent use of long-distance calling privileges are more likely to be charged and convicted than organizations that use the mail to flog unreliable products. Given prevailing patterns of power, this is not surprising. Similarly, those convicted of bank embezzlement are often low-level employees—female and/or black bank tellers—who have stolen the most easily traceable commodity of all, money. Offenders convicted for other offences follow a similar pattern: simple and unsophisticated offences; offenders who are either outsiders trying to defraud corporations or government, or low-level employees. Only those convicted of antitrust or securities offences are different. They are the most affluent, the most likely to have good jobs and stable work histories, and rank higher on the social-class scale. They are also the "biggest" criminals, measured by the amounts stolen. It was reported in 1982 that individual offenders garnered $5279 on average; occupational offenders took $17,106; and organizational or corporate offenders took $117,392 (Wheeler and Rothman, 1982; and Benson, 1989).

There are no comparable Canadian studies. Annual government reports, however, reveal that there have been 278 prosecutions "or other proceedings" commenced from 1965–66 to 1987–88 for offences against Canadian combines laws, an average of twelve per year. Fewer than 100 companies a year are charged with false advertising or deceptive marketing practices, a total of 1666 from 1968–69 to 1987–88, or 83.3 per year on average (Canada, 1989:59 and 60; also Reasons, 1986). Few would argue, however, that such figures present an accurate picture of the number of false advertisements or price-fixers actually "out there." There were, for example, 12,374 allegations of false advertising/deceptive marketing made to the Department of Consumer and Corporate Affairs in 1987–88, which led to 2187 "complete examinations" (case investigations). However, only 113 cases were referred to the attorney general for prosecution that year (Canada, 1989:60).

Whatever the deficiencies of the data, there is much indirect evidence to suggest that corporate crime is becoming increasingly prevalent. The regulatory agencies charged with controlling such crimes have been savaged, which means that the temptation to amass huge profits virtually risk-free is greater than ever. The 1980s saw massive attacks on regulatory agency budgets in Britain, the United States, and Canada (Calavita, 1983; Calavita and Pontell, 1990; Reasons, 1986), and the consequences of this abound. The savings and loan fiasco in the United States, for example, is the most expensive white-collar crime in history (now estimated as costing every American household a minimum of $5000) (*The New York Times,* June 10, 1990; *The Observer,* April 8, 1990). Second, the emphasis on short-term profit maximization, leveraged buyouts, and the like has encouraged companies to pay less attention to ethics; the dominant philosophy became even more growth oriented and pragmatic than in earlier eras. This was seen in the aforementioned survey of Fortune 500 companies, the largest industrial concerns in the United States, from the mid-1970s to the early 1980s, where more than two-thirds were involved in illegal behaviour (Etzioni, 1985). Brenner and Molander (1977), updating an earlier study of business ethics by Baumhart (1961), found the percentage of executives stating that they are unable to be honest in providing information to top management nearly doubled. Over half the respondents in the later time period felt their supervisors did not want to know about illegal acts as long as the desired results were obtained. The executives "frequently complained of supervisors' pressure to support incorrect viewpoints, sign false documents, overlook supervisors' wrongdoing, and do business with supervisors' friends" (1977:70). Or, to cite a typical executive in a typical study: "Once you are given your end [short-run profit], it justifies whatever means you have [to adopt] to reach it" (Dugger, 1988:108).

SUMMARY

This chapter has looked at the incidence, prevalence, and measurement of white-collar crime. Because of the tremendous increase in the size, power, and scope of the corporate sector, and the rise to dominance of the multinational corporation and transnational conglomerate, corporate crime has become harder to monitor, discover, and control. At the same time, its potential effects have become ever more lethal, because the percentage of the world's population directly affected by the activities of corporations has continued to increase. Because large organizations have the power to hide their own transgressions and shelter those of their employees (both occupational and corporate), it is difficult to discover how many offences are really occurring. We have enough information to conclude that such crimes are as damaging as they are common; but we lack the data to hazard more than educated guesses on the "dark figure" of white-collar crime. To some degree this is an unanswerable question, because "crime" increases with the number of crime watchers available, and the "real" amount is never a fixed and knowable number.

Putting aside this epistemological problem, even reasonable approximations of the most blatant and harmful white-collar crimes are hard to come by. As Reiss and Biderman (1980) stated, following an extensive review of administrative records and agency audits of thirty federal agencies in the United States, an inventory of white-collar crime with a uniform statistical reporting system utilizing standard definitions and classification procedures will be necessary before any meaningful pronouncements on prevalence can be made. Since no country is within striking distance of putting such a scheme in place, we are forced to extrapolate on the basis of scattered case studies, estimates, and occasional self-report studies and victimization data. Meanwhile, the bulk of the population, the police forces, and politicians all continue to act as if poor and powerless populations constituted the primary threat to the collective well-being.

In the next chapter the focus will shift somewhat to look at the dominant theoretical approaches to the study of corporate crime. Consensus/pluralist and conflict/Marxist perspectives, each having particular assumptions and biases, will be examined. The aim is to shed light upon the more academic explanations of upperworld criminality.

NOTES

1. A few studies employing self-report methodologies, asking employees directly about their participation in various criminal behaviours on the job, have been done with occupational offenders. The most ambitious of these was completed by Hollinger and Clarke in the early 1980s. They used a combination of questionnaires and interviews to assess employee theft, defined as "unauthorized taking, control, or transfer of money and/or property of the formal work organization that is perpetrated by an employee during the course of occupational activity" (Hollinger and Clarke, 1983:2). Singling out three different sectors of the economy (retail stores, hospitals, and electronics firms), they looked at forty-seven organizations in Minneapolis/St. Paul, Dallas/Fort Worth, and Cleveland; 1372 employees from Minneapolis/St. Paul, 1303 from Dallas/Fort Worth, and 822 from Cleveland submitted completed questionnaires. The information generated by this large sample was supplemented by interviews with 247 key executives in the forty-seven organizations, and 256 randomly selected employees as well.

    The results are interesting, if not surprising. The researchers found, first, that the official statistics on employee crime kept by each organization revealed more about the policing practices of the firm than about the actual amount of criminal behaviour. The statistics gathered by the organizations were wildly varied and diverse; hardly any information was uniformly produced by all forty-seven organizations; and even statistics on inventory shrinkage, necessary for the most basic kinds of organizational records, were not always kept. To examine the crimes employees admitted committing, employees must be differentiated by sector. For those in retail businesses, the most common deviant act admitted was misuse of employee discount privileges (intended only for the employee) through buying discounted goods for others (43 percent admitted this). Seven percent admitted stealing property, and 6 percent said they took pay for time they had not worked; overall, 35 percent admitted involvement in some kind of theft. By comparison, 33 percent of hospital workers and 28 percent of employees in manufacturing admitted illegal acts. The most common "crime" was one Hollinger and Clarke call theft of time: 65.4 percent of retail workers, 69.2 percent of hospital employees, and 82.2 percent of those in manufacturing reported that they had taken long lunches, come in late, or called in sick when they were not. There was no relationship between low incomes and theft; that is, the poorest-paid employees did not steal more (or at least did not admit it if they did). However, people most worried about family finances were more likely to admit theft, and so were younger employees. Also expected were the findings that theft was related to both job dissatisfaction and access. Unhappy employees were more likely to steal, but only where there were opportunities available. Theft levels were highest, then, among dissatisfied employees who controlled scarce resources, but lacked close supervision.

As a check on validity, Hollinger and Clarke chose a subset of the main sample, assessed the security practices of these firms, and compared their statistics on employee theft with the self-report study. Thus, sixteen retail corporations, twenty-one hospitals, and ten electronic manufacturing firms were singled out. Looking at measures such as inventory shrinkage, it was found that employee theft varied widely within each sector: from a low of 19.2 percent of all employees to a high of 76.9 percent in the retail sector; from 17.7 percent to 41.7 percent in hospitals; and from 20 percent to 37.8 percent in manufacturing. This means, as Hollinger and Clarke point out, that less than half the employees steal in most organizations (1983:99); it also means, however, that more than half of them steal in others. Moreover, employees caught stealing suffered very different fates in different workplaces. Retail stores were the most security conscious, the most zealous in policing and prosecuting offenders, and the most concerned about theft. But even they apprehended only 5 percent of the workforce in a given year (while 35 percent of retail employees, as mentioned, admitted some involvement in theft in the self-report study). Fewer than 1 percent of all employees in hospitals or manufacturing were apprehended for theft. The most common sanction for all organizations was to fire the employee. Even retail organizations prosecuted only 40 percent of employee offenders, and prosecution was exceedingly rare in the manufacturing sector or hospitals. Fewer than half of the offenders were required to make restitution to the company (Hollinger and Clarke, 1983). Hollinger and Clarke conclude with this assessment: "A small number [of workers] take a lot; the majority take a little" (1983:6; see also Wheeler et al., 1988). This adds up to a tremendous number of white-collar (occupational) crimes that never become official statistics. The "dark figure," the discrepancy between the amount of deviant behaviour occurring and officially recorded crime, is indeed high.

C   H   A   P   T   E   R   **2**

Dominant Theoretical Approaches

INTRODUCTION

This chapter looks at social theory and the different perspectives
that have been generated about corporations, corporate power,
and corporate criminality. To understand the development of theories about corporate crime, It is necessary to know something
about broader social theory and the assumptions of the various
theoretical schools. This background knowledge is particularly
important because many authors do not spell out their assumptions for the reader. An understanding of these assumptions is
obviously essential in assessing the utility of an author's arguments. Just as it is necessary to know the bottom-level assumptions economists make about human nature or the operation of
market economies to understand economics, or to set out the tru-
isms about the legal system accepted by legal theorists, so in sociology one must be aware of authors' assumptions about the
nature of society and the place humans occupy in it.

Since there is a great diversity of theoretical viewpoints and
assumptions, this chapter focuses initially on two major
approaches: the consensus/pluralist and the conflict/Marxist.
These two perspectives on social order and law have dominated
social theory over the last 200 years. In addition to outlining the
history and primary tenets of these approaches, we look at the
way they have shaped research on corporate crime. Finally, we
examine feminist theory, which extends and challenges both the
traditional approaches, although it has had much less effect on
the literature of corporate crime up to this point.

DOMINANT THEORETICAL APPROACHES: CONSENSUS THEORIES

The consensus approach (also known as the order or functionalist perspective) has its roots in the 18th-century writings of theorists such as Montesquieu and Adam Smith. It was refined and developed by Emile Durkheim in the 19th century, distorted by social Darwinists such as Spencer, and emerged, courtesy of Talcott Parsons and his followers, as structural functionalism in the 20th century. As befits a complex macro-level theory that has drawn adherents of varying ability and sophistication for several centuries, the approach has been applied both well and poorly. Moreover, it has been used to explain virtually every modern institution from the legal structure to the educational system, and has been adapted to every social science discipline from anthropology to psychology. It has also spawned dozens of lower-level theories that apply macro-level ordering principles derived from consensus theory to the organizational (middle) and social psychological (micro) levels of analysis. However, it is the applications to the field of social order and law that concern us here.

The basic assumption of consensus theory is a very simple one: namely, that societies are held together by the consent of their members. People in Western democratic societies are socialized through the family, educational institutions, religion, and the mass media to accept certain core values and play certain social roles. They learn what to value, how one should live, what one should strive for, and the reasons their society has the existing distribution of income, power, and prestige and not a different one. The roles and values people adopt may vary slightly according to gender, class, social position, or ethnicity, but these differences are generally over means, not goals; that is, disagreements revolve around the methods one should use to attain valued goals—goals such as progress, knowledge, or increased status or income for the individual—and not over the validity of the goals themselves. The roles, values, and the institutions that reflect and reinforce these social goals are all interdependent. This means that major goals reinforce each other and bear a certain internal consistency (which is not the same as saying they are rational). Dominant societal institutions in each sector are responsible for particular tasks that reinforce consensus. For example, economic institutions such as corporations are charged with generating sufficient resources to supply people's material needs; schools, the family, and the mass media are responsible for socialization, for ensuring that "desirable" attitudes and behaviours are learned; political and legal institutions set down rules and handle disputes and nonconforming behaviour; and cultural and religious institutions look after spiritual needs.

When applied to law, consensus theorists have interpreted criminal or deviant behaviour as indicative of the failure of the institutions of socialization. Criminals, therefore, become people who need to be resocialized (or, in earlier centuries, punished and prevented from reproducing). Thus, consensus theorists in the 20th century have concentrated on finding out why socialization does not "take" for people in certain environments, and on working out mechanisms to prevent such failures in future generations, by changing the environment, the socialization practices, or both. Those for whom such solutions come too late, present-day criminals, are studied to discover traits that identify them early in life, or are put through programs whose aim is to cure or rehabilitate. This explains consensus theorists' focus on youth, and especially on juvenile offenders. By studying such factors as upbringing, diet, education, the social pathology of the urban slum, class, peers, religiosity, mothers, and pathological disturbances, consensus theorists feel one can discover the roots of criminal behaviour. (All of these factors and more have been studied, through methods ranging from participant observation to the most sophisticated, large-scale statistical techniques.)

Anomie theory was an early adaptation of consensus theory. Developed by Robert Merton (1938, 1957), its central hypothesis, that deviant behaviour is related to the disjunction between goals and means that characterizes American society, attracted much attention and stimulated much research. In societies where all people are taught to value and seek the goal of success, but the aspirations of many are blocked by their social origins, race, or ethnic group (gender was not mentioned), anomie, on both the psychological and social levels, is created. Some people attempt to circumvent the anomie through nonconformity. In short, they innovate, looking for new means to achieve the goals, and criminal acts become an alternative route to the socially valued goal of success. For such a solution to "work" for the individual or group, the dominant social order must stress the end goal, the result, more than the means required to achieve it. The emphasis in American society on money and power, combined with a lack of regard for how these were attained, meant that crime, especially undetected and unsanctioned crime, could indeed lead to success. The visible badges of success, the Porsche, CD player, and conspicuous consumption, could be obtained right away; the prestige, power, and status, if not immediately forthcoming, would happen in five or ten years or, at worst, a single generation. Of course, not all youth or all social groups in anomic positions choose criminal acts as their adaptation of choice. Some continue to struggle against racism or other barriers, collectively through political action or individually. Others conform to dominant values in a ritualistic fashion; they give lip service to the goals, but lack any expectation of personally achieving them. Yet others opt out of the struggle by retreating into behaviours that allow them to escape (subjectively or objectively) the anomic situation, such as drug addiction or monastic life.

Turning to social policy, these perspectives have produced a wide range of prospective solutions to the problem of crime. In the 19th century, children were removed from "inadequate" parents and placed in institutions where they could be "properly" socialized and disciplined. Many parents deemed defective in their roles were sterilized to prevent further procreation. By the middle of the 20th century, consensus theory had taken on a liberal cast, and advocates were arguing that anomie and defects in socialization could be addressed through social programs. Public housing to clean up the slums, the War on Poverty in 1960s America, and initiatives such as Head Start programs (a plan to compensate for defective family backgrounds by providing children from low-income and single-parent homes with special preschool training to bring them "up to speed" academically and socially) were recommended and sometimes put in place.

Such policies were largely preventive measures. For those who had already shown antisocial tendencies (by committing crime), consensus theorists in the 1950s and 1960s advocated a variety of rehabilitative measures in a wide range of institutional settings, ranging from compulsory psychological and medical programs, to free universal education and full civil rights for prisoners. The philosophy underlying all these programs was the belief that human nature was infinitely malleable, and that the knowledge and methods of social and medical science could ultimately solve the problem of nonconformity. In the last two decades, however, this faith has evaporated as dominant society hardened its attitudes to crime and criminals and swung to the right politically. Most of the rehabilitative schemes and social programs were denounced as failures, and disenchantment along with fiscal cutbacks produced a new emphasis on punishment in social theory. Consequently, consensus theorists have increasingly turned their attention to large-scale quantitative studies that seek to identify criminal tendencies at an early age. In addition, attention has shifted to general and specific deterrence, techniques of crime prevention, and the needs and viewpoint of victims of crimes.

All of this is, of course, a long way from corporate crime. Consensus theory did not predict corporate crime and lacked ways of explaining it. As we have seen, it looked for deficiencies in the individual, and then in the opportunity structure, to explain criminal behaviour. Rich, successful, properly socialized people do not commit crimes according to consensus theory. This was why Sutherland's rediscovery of the antisocial acts of the rich was such a bombshell to the criminological community in 1939, and why he went to such pains to point out that "we have no reason to think that General Motors has an inferiority complex or that the Aluminum Company of America has a frustration-aggression complex or that U.S. Steel has an oedipus complex" (Cohen et al., 1956:96). Indeed, consensus theories to this day have been unable to explain, at the macro level, why corporate crime occurs. They have concentrated instead on documenting its occurrence, describing its different forms, and estimating its prevalence, straying into the theoretical realm only at the middle or organizational level of explanation, where the goal was to explain how specific organizational structures affected corporate crime. It is at this level of generality that a more sophisticated version of consensus theory, known as pluralism, has emerged.

PLURALISM

Pluralist theories recognize that, in a highly complex, stratified society characterized by substantial inequalities of income and power, problems will arise concerning the distribution of resources despite an overall general consensus. It is the job of government, the officials responsible for decision-making in the public sector from the municipal to the federal levels (both politicians and civil servants), to ascertain and carry out the wishes of the majority of the electorate. This cannot be done without a certain amount of conflict, as different groups vie to get their particular agendas adopted. However, the purpose of government policies, in a democracy, is to reconcile diverse interests and prevent serious, enduring breaks in the basic consensus. Government policies, then, may require that restrictions be placed upon the rich and powerful to benefit the poor, or vice versa. Government assumes the role of neutral arbitrator, seeking a course acceptable to all; it is a referee that oversees the struggles of conflicting interest groups, which must act ultimately in the interests of all. It, and the legal system that backs it up, is independent of the interests of any particular group, and in the end, losers of particular policy battles are reconciled and consensus re-emerges (Rose, 1967; Dahl, 1961; Bell, 1970; Friedman, 1977).

More sophisticated versions of pluralist theory do not assume that the many diverse groups in the modern democratic state have equal power, or are equally effective in making their voices heard in the councils of government. Some are recognized as more "strategic" than others, and they therefore carry more weight, but only on particular issues. Pluralist theorists strongly maintain that any group of people, if they feel strongly enough about an issue, if there are enough of them, and if they organize efficiently, can be represented in the policy-making process. For them, there are no structural barriers, and certainly nothing inherent in the nature of the capitalist state that renders certain groups and interests powerless; no one group is seen as dominating the political process in a way that is either overwhelming or permanent. To pluralists, government regulations are rules or laws formulated by politicians and civil servants that attempt to resolve or prevent conflicts by redressing the balance of power between different interests in the society (Keller, 1963; Parsons, 1970). Applied to the study of corporate crime, this means that pluralist theorists assume that governments, once they have been properly alerted to the extent and nature of problems posed by corporate wrongdoing and the damage done, can and will respond in an appropriate way; can and will pass and enforce laws designed to eliminate the problem. Government policies on corporate crime, then, will be analogous to those on traditional crime; the effectiveness of these policies will be limited only by inadequate knowledge or resources.

DOMINANT THEORETICAL APPROACHES: CONFLICT THEORIES

Conflict theories have taken a very different approach, both to the problem of explaining social cohesion and order, and eventually to corporate crime. Essentially this perspective sees society as a framework within which different groups with opposing roles and values struggle against each other. If order and cohesion are achieved, it is through power; it is a sign that one faction or group of factions has successfully dominated the others. Conflict theory also has ancient roots, with preliminary concepts appearing in the works of Rousseau, Montesquieu, Saint-Simon, Robert Owen, Beccaria, and William Godwin (McDonald, 1976). Modern conflict theory largely grew out of the 19th-century theories of Karl Marx and Friedrich Engels. Like consensus theory, it has taken many different forms and given rise to both simplistic and sophisticated applications. However, its adherence to the concept of power (as opposed to consensus), as a basic force that explains both social order and social problems, has remained a distinctive and distinguishing characteristic. In the 19th century this led conflict theorists to explain crime in terms of relative deprivation, with poverty seen as a major causal factor. Poverty to conflict theorists meant not that the poor suffered from pathology or degeneracy (as consensus theorists believed), but that they had unequal power. As McDonald has summarized:

> For conflict theorists, the ultimate causal factor lay in the actions of the holders of power—in the pursuit of their advantages. Inequalities in power, economic or political, were ultimately responsible. (McDonald, 1976:22)

MARXISM

Karl Marx was one of the first scholars directly to address the basis and origins of power. He developed a formulation ascribing the roots of social structure to the economic system, the system that produces the material necessities of life. Manipulating the natural environment to produce food and shelter (the definition of an economic system) is essential in every social order to maintain life, and every society develops a division of labour and set of institutions to ensure that these essential tasks are done. Under a capitalist economic system, Marx argues, there is an essential contradiction, a basic fissure between the needs and interests of the class that owns the means of production (the bourgeoisie), and the class that owns only its labour power (the proletariat). The proletariat must sell its labour to the bourgeoisie in order to survive, while the bourgeoisie prospers only by exploiting the labour of the proletariat to its limits. To survive and grow, the bourgeoisie as a class must take from the proletariat far more than it gives back in wages; that is, it must *make a profit* from the labour of the proletariat. This profit is the engine of progress under capitalism, because it allows the entrepreneur/capitalist to expand the means of production, hire more workers, and produce more widgets. (Alternatively, it can be used less productively, for his or her personal aggrandizement.)

Moreover, because the bourgeoisie as a class controls the means of production and therefore the life chances of virtually everyone else in a direct or indirect way, it has enormous power. Its ideas, values, interests, and institutions become dominant in that social order. It is the values of the bourgeoisie, embedded in the legal system, religion, politics, art, and education, that are taught to succeeding generations and accepted as common sense. This process is not unique to capitalism; as Marx explains, "the ruling ideas of each age have been the ideas of the ruling class" (Marx and Engels, 1959:26). However, the class struggle between the bourgeoisie and the proletariat, the fact that the one can thrive only by exploiting the other, and the productive forces this system potentially unleashes all set the capitalist system apart.

These ideas were applied to criminality by Wilhelm Bonger, a Dutch criminologist born in the late 19th century. Bonger set himself the rather ambitious task of explaining the origin of "criminal thought," discovering the forces preventing its execution and their origin, and explaining the causes of criminal acts. To do this, he developed the theory that crimes are immoral acts arising out of the egoism generated by the capitalist economic system. This system, by destroying the economic basis of cooperative behaviour or labour, generates unrestrained competition, destroys community, and encourages every individual to maximize his or her own opportunities, creating "uncertainty of existence for all" (Bonger, 1916:10). Bonger, consistent with the psychologism that dominated this period, proceeded to classify crimes according to the motives that produced them—vengeful, sexual, political, and economic. On this basis, economic crimes were subdivided into poverty, cupidity, and professional crimes; the latter two were typically crimes of the bourgeoisie, the former crime typical of the proletariat. Bonger was one of the first, therefore, to predict and examine what we now call white-collar crimes. However, he also maintained that acts that come to be called crimes are those that harm the interests of the ruling class. Acts that *only* harm the lower classes will not be defined as crimes (and this was an empirically correct observation in his day).

We see here the beginnings of a theory of corporate crime. We also see the basic problem conflict theorists have had to confront in their explanations of corporate crime. For if the dominant classes (ruling elite, bourgeoisie, or whatever one wants to call them) are wholly responsible for generating the dominant ideas of the period, as well as the legal and political machinery to explain and enforce these ideas, there should be no laws that criminalize or even question the validity of upper-class value systems or practices. In the emerging capitalist democracies of the West, this was not the case. To explain this, and take into account other indicators showing that ruling-class power was nowhere near as monolithic as originally hypothesized, Marxist theory began to change. A number of theorists began to look more seriously at the role of government, which led to the development of theories of the capitalist state. Two of these, commonly labelled the instrumentalist and structuralist approaches, are examined on the following pages.

Instrumentalism

Originally, much work in the Marxist school tended to assume that the state was the direct tool of the capitalist class. Its policies were their policies; its laws their laws. This reality, it was argued, was effectively hidden from the working classes, who were conditioned to believe they lived in a free country where every citizen, by virtue of the secret ballot, had an equal voice in determining government policy. This dominant ideology also stressed the existence of an egalitarian, universalistic legal system blind to inequalities of class, race, or gender, which punished all lawbreakers. Those who became identified as instrumentalists were interested in the mechanisms by which the capitalist class shapes the state. It was obviously not the case that prime ministers or presidents phoned up key corporate moguls each day to get their orders. Why, then, were state policies so often slanted to favour the interests of the corporate elite? Why did they so seldom, even under social democratic or labour governments, reflect the opinions or improve the lot of the working classes or poor?

The key was obviously the state, defined here as those who occupy key decision-making posts in the political elite (in Canada, prime ministers and cabinet ministers at the federal and provincial levels, plus municipal officials with key territories or responsibilities), in the civil service, in the military, and in the judiciary (Miliband, 1969:50). The answer to the riddle of state subservience to capital lay, instrumentalists argued, in the fact that the capitalist class and the state elite were one and the same. Indeed, a myriad of studies from a number of countries have demonstrated that the majority of senior civil servants, judges, and top politicians in capitalist democracies came from upper-class families, received private school educations, and enjoyed upper-class club memberships, social networks, and marriage ties with the corporate elite (Miliband, 1969; Clement, 1975, 1979). Small wonder, then, that the state reflected upper-class/corporate interests. The ideas and values of this class would be the common-sense, taken-for-granted beliefs state elites were socialized into, reinforced rather than challenged by their daily social and business contacts as adults.

The instrumentalist formulation, however, has come under attack for oversimplifying the relationship between capital and the state. It overstates the amount of cohesion in the capitalist class, ignoring the diversity of interests and needs that exist within it. Thus, a policy that benefits the interests of some types of capital may not be in the interest of others, as the recent free trade debate in Canada illustrates. Moreover, if the personalities and backgrounds of the main actors in the state really cause its ruling-class bias, how does one explain instances where leaders from the working class, rare as they may be, behave in the same fashion and are similarly unsuccessful in changing the direction and effects of state policy? Similarly, if the main function of the state is to serve capital directly, how does one explain the laws and regulations that do get passed despite the opposition of capital, such as minimum wage, medicare, or employment equity? Such problems forced critical theorists to look more closely at explanations rooted in the structure of capitalism rather than the characteristics of its standard-bearers.

Structuralism

In structuralist theories, the state is seen as structurally dependent on capital in the final analysis. But it also has, and must have, qualified independence from capital under certain circumstances, because this is essential to protect the long-run interests of capital (see, for example, Poulantzas, 1973; Gold, 1975). In capitalist democratic systems, the state must sometimes act against the dominant class, or factions of it, in order to preserve the status quo. For example, where stability is threatened by serious dissent or unrest and there is danger that factories will be attacked by mobs or that governments antithetical to central interests of capital will come to power, the state must put in place measures, often reforms, to prevent this from happening. (It will also use coercion, law, the police, and the military to contain the unrest.) This independence is limited, however, because the state is structurally dependent on capital. It must attract and retain those with capital to invest, because private capital is the major generator of employment opportunities and prosperity in such economies. Thus, a set of conditions under which capital is free to accumulate and control surplus value (the profit that comes from paying employees less than they are worth, less, that is, than the income their labour generates for the employer) must be maintained by the state.

Law plays a central role in persuading workers to accept this inherently exploitative deal. As explained by Antonio Gramsci (1971), the capitalist state is strongest if its citizens believe in the system they live and work under. The state and capital, therefore, foster acceptance of a complex of beliefs and opinions that support the status quo, resulting in a social order known as hegemonic order. Securing hegemony—getting people to accept freely the terms of capitalism—was not easy initially, because capitalism requires an unprecedented level of personal discipline and social control. Moreover, it is riven with contradictions and inequalities. There is, for example, the contradiction between the freedom to elect representatives and call them to account, which characterizes the political sphere, and the economic dictatorship, which prevails in the workplace; or the opposition between the belief that all citizens are equal (as dominant ideologies preach), and the knowledge that some are wealthy beyond belief, while others are so poor that they have to walk the streets without homes, jobs, or sufficient food to eat.

In the United States, much of the consensus that does exist depends on nationalism—the consoling belief that, however poor one may be, one is part of the greatest nation in the world, the envy of citizens of all other countries. In countries such as Canada, where nationalism is more muted, consensus is grudging and depends on the ability of the state to provide a high standard of living, defined in terms of income and social services such as universal medicare, for a sizable proportion of the population. In the final analysis, consent is backstopped by the widespread and ideologically sustained belief that there are no reasonable or workable alternatives to capitalism. The ideological interpretations of the collapse of the socialist economies of Eastern Europe and the former Soviet Union provides a perfect example of this process in operation.

The state and law, then, are conceptualized quite differently than in consensus theories. The state is seen as possessing a limited autonomy from capital, but ultimately state actions are limited by capital and its needs as an economic system (O'Connor, 1973; Panitch, 1977). It is the responsibility of the state to secure the political, social, and economic conditions under which the capitalist class can profitably operate. This means that the state will put in place all kinds of little publicized mechanisms that benefit the capitalist class, ranging from publicly subsidized transportation systems to move goods (such as airports and highways), to government-funded educational systems to train workers, to depletion allowances and tax write-offs. It also means that major social institutions—laws, educational systems, religious beliefs, and so forth—reinforce capitalist values and serve capitalist needs.

Since the majority of the population must accept its place in the class structure for capitalism to work to optimal effect, so the manufacture and reinforcement of consent is crucial. If it appears threatened, the state will put in place reforms that control the excesses of capital, in effect saving capitalism from itself. Unemployment insurance, health and safety regulations in the workplace, old age pensions, welfare, family allowances, and workers' compensation are all examples of measures that can be interpreted in this way. Marxists agree with pluralist and consensus theorists, then, on the importance of consent; they differ, however, on its source and nature. For Marxists, consent is a carefully engineered and ultimately deceptive device that keeps oppressed groups down and manipulates the working and middle classes; for consensus theorists, it is a freely given, intelligently held belief that the social order to which they belong is on balance the best one possible.

Consensus and conflict theorists also differ on the role of coercion. For conflict or Marxist theorists, the repressive forces of the state are always waiting if measures of legitimation fail, if capitalist interests appear to be in danger of losing control. These coercive forces, the police and the criminal justice system internally, and soldiers and armies externally, come into play to repress groups and individuals who have become defined as threatening to the status quo, and ensure that the "will of the people" does not carry the day. However, the use of coercion against its own citizens is a weapon democratic societies must use with caution, because their populations have been socialized to believe these societies run on freely given consent, and that law is only used against criminals, not as a weapon in a political struggle. State authorities therefore try to ensure that populations against whom force is used are discredited, powerless, and invisible. The average person charged with a traditional criminal offence (the classic break and enter case, for example) is a perfectly safe target for coercion—usually young, unemployed, poorly educated, and often from a visible minority as well. The average trade union militant or native leader has become a more risky target, and legitimation might be jeopardized by the use of coercion unless it can be hidden (Ratner, 1986; MacLean, 1986a; Reiman, 1984).

For consensus theorists, on the other hand, force is a necessary and legitimate measure for the state to employ against those who threaten the social order and/or break the law. The very language is different here; the terms coercion or repression are largely replaced by terms such as discipline, control, or law enforcement. This does not mean that consensus theorists are blind to the occasions on which law has been used as a political instrument to repress dissent; merely that they see this as an exception, an aberration to be deplored, not a structurally mandated necessity. Most uses of law and criminal justice, however, are assumed to be beneficial, and the legal system is conceptualized as protecting the social order, discouraging those who would go against the law (which in their view represents freely held consensus), and enabling the individual to enjoy liberty and personal safety.

FEMINIST THEORIES

It is obvious from the discussions above that traditional theories have been gender blind. The various types of consensus theory were written as though they applied equally to men and women, but it is clear that they do not. Anomie theory, for example, is built on the premise that everyone is socialized to go out into the public sphere and attain wealth and power; deviance is related to blockages or failure to succeed. However, women have not been socialized to seek status through money and power (at least, not until very recently); their role models and expectations were based on nurturing, reproduction, and mastering the skills and attitudes to enable them to create and sustain a relationship with a "successful" man. The literature derived from Marxist theory, on the other hand, while recognizing women as an oppressed group (Engels in particular), has nevertheless viewed class, not gender, as the basic explanatory variable.

Feminist theory argues that gender, a differentiation at least as fundamental as class, serves as a necessary precondition for class hierarchy. All classes are gendered, and components of the mode of production affect men and women of the same class in different ways. Gender systems, then, are dialectically co-determined with economic systems (Maroney and Luxton, 1987). In the case of women, control by state forces has been mediated and supplemented by control in the private sphere, especially through the family. The state has supported patriarchy (a system of institutionalized male dominance) in a variety of ways; concepts such as family privacy or the idea that "a man's home is his castle" (but often a woman's prison) have been used to keep women subordinate. It is also argued that state systems have mediated, through law, the extension of control over women by institutional centres of power such as the church and, more recently, the medical profession (Gavigan, 1987; Smart, 1989).

Socialist feminist theory maintains, however, that neither state nor law is all-powerful. Law as a social formation, and as a mixture of ideologies, acts through its claims of universalism, due process, and impartiality to reproduce the social relations of capitalism (Hunt, 1985; Poulantzas, 1978). However, law and legality are not merely derivative; that is, they cannot be "read off" from an *a priori* analysis of the "needs" of capital. In practice laws usually reinforce the dominant relations underlying both capitalism and patriarchy, in form as well as substance. For example, law posits "the reasonable man" as the basis of legislation and decision-making, directing attention away from "the reasonable woman" and transforming conflicts that involve the rights of genders or groups into interpersonal struggles over the rights of individuals (Pashukanis, 1978; Balbus, 1973, 1977). This individualizing potential is built into the formal language and structure of the legal system (Smart, 1989; Howe, 1990;

Lahey, 1988). Feminist theorists have pointed out that key components in dominant ideologies that reinforce patriarchy—beliefs about women's nature and role—are even more central and universal than those that reinforce capitalism. Feminists and other social movements attempt, through collective organization and struggle, through confrontations with law and the state, and through judicious use of media, to challenge such definitions and belief systems.

Attempts to apply feminist perspectives to the analysis of corporate crime, however, are at a very early stage. Partly because women have traditionally been confined to roles in the private sphere, and discouraged if not barred from occupying senior positions in organizations, few women have been accused of corporate offences. There is no disagreement on the fact that women have frequently been victimized by corporate crime. Doctors prescribe more mood-altering drugs for women patients than for men, and women are the prime recipients of birth control devices; hence defects in such products due to improper testing and fraud hurt many more women than men (Dekeseredy and Hinch, 1991; Mintz, 1985; Chenier, 1982; Perry and Dawson, 1985). Moreover, as relatively powerless and vulnerable employees, women have certainly been defrauded by employer violations of minimum wage or benefit laws, and they have long been paid much less than men even when doing the same job. In most jurisdictions this was not illegal; and in many places it is still a prime, and legal, attraction of female labour (Messerschmidt, 1986; Dekeseredy and Hinch, 1991). It seems obvious that traditional attitudes to women lay behind much of this victimization, and that class, gender, and social structure combine to make certain groups of women particularly vulnerable.

Beyond this level, very little is known. It has been suggested that corporate crime is a particularly male offence because men, particularly upwardly mobile male executives, are socialized and rewarded for displaying flexible ethical systems that allow them to use others as means to an end rather than ends in themselves. This willingness to sacrifice particular individuals in the pursuit of long-term goals (be they those of the executive or of his or her employer) and to take risks is rewarded by the typical business organization. However, this willingness to take short cuts to attain goals, and disregard the inconvenience or pain of others, makes this kind of individual more vulnerable, more at risk of committing criminal acts in the pursuit of goals. Messerschmidt posits that the typical corporation is patriarchal in form and structure, reinforcing male socialization patterns and attitudes in a variety of ways, particularly through the "old boy" network. The result is that masculine self-concept and image, as well as self-respect and self-esteem, become bound up with corporate success (Messerschmidt, 1986:118–19). As he says:

> The corporate executive's masculinity, then, is centered around a struggle for success, reward, and recognition in the corporation and community.... This image of work, rooted materially in the corporate executive's gender/class position ... helps to create the conditions for corporate crime. Devotion to achievement and success ... brings about the "need" to engage in such crime. (Messerschmidt, 1986:119)

To link ideas of masculinity and structures of patriarchy to corporate crime does not mean, however, that a managerial class composed entirely of women would behave any differently than men do, particularly if the dominant structures and ideologies now in place were to remain. The fact that women have not in the past been encouraged or allowed to occupy senior positions does not rule out their doing so in the future. Indeed, one of the main goals of liberal (as opposed to the socialist) feminists has been just this: to remove barriers and encourage women to occupy positions that have historically been held by men. No attitudinal or structural changes (other than subsidized day care and similar supportive policy reforms) were deemed necessary. Unless one believes women are inherently more resistant to law violation (that is, more obedient to established authority, or more loath to take risks), it is hard to see why replacing some people with penises with others with vaginas would materially affect the commission of corporate crime. However, if one believes that feminism as a philosophy and movement must necessarily change today's value and belief systems, and the structures of motivation and reward that are presently in place, then one can understand feminist theory postulating that the introduction of women into corporate power structures will change these structures in ways that reduce corporate crime. At this point, however, we await further developments and research.

SUMMARY

This chapter has looked at the theoretical structures and assumptions that have been generated to explain law and the state. Specifically, the two theoretical positions that have spawned virtually all theoretical work on corporate crime were examined: consensus and conflict/Marxism. Consensus theory and its more sophisticated offshoot, pluralism, assume that societies are held together by a complex interrelationship of functions that leads to substantial agreement on the basic rules of the particular social order. Conflict theory and Marxism, on the other hand, assume that power and coercion are the keys to understanding consensus and order, and that an elite minority always benefits at the expense of the majority (although the size and nature of this elite is far from fixed; it varies with a number of other factors). A theoretical newcomer, feminist theory, insists on the primacy of gender as an explanatory variable. However, gender has not been incorporated into most theories, or into specific analyses of corporate crime thus far, despite the fact that criminal behaviours (like all others) are gendered. With these theoretical positions set out, the next chapter will examine specific theories on the causes of corporate crime.

C H A P T E R 3

Theories of Causality

INTRODUCTION

Only in the last fifty years or so has the social science community looked seriously at why employed and comfortable people commit crimes. Until then the dominant theoretical school of consensus/pluralism argued that crime was basically a problem of the poor, and looked to economic and social conditions, or personal pathology, for causal factors. As we have seen, anomie theory postulated that crime was committed by people (men) who lacked the material wealth and success their society had taught them to value. The affluent white middle class, who enjoyed access to success goals through the legitimate means of university education, private clubs, and promotion through the ranks, were labelled conformists. The very term connotes the expected absence of criminality.

Anomie theorists were not alone in overlooking the criminal acts of respectable citizens. The bulk of criminological work to this day focuses upon crimes of the powerless, and citizens and social scientists alike visualize the poor young male (usually black or native) as the quintessential "criminal type." In disciplines ranging from psychiatry to geography, from political science to psychology, crime has been traced to factors such as bad companions, or no companions (a loner); too much aggression, or too little (too easily led); too little intelligence, or too much, insufficiently reined in by conscience; single-parent families (that is, led by mothers); failure at school; eating patterns, such as consuming junk food or foods containing red dye #2 (or other additives or chemicals); lack of identification with legitimate authority figures (such as teachers and ministers); and the presence of crack cocaine (or, in previous decades, alcohol, marijuana, or heroin) in ghetto areas.

However, as discussed in Chapter 2, these theories do not easily explain the behaviour of more than half of the population, females, who are subject to a different range of pressures and influences, and to greater levels of parental and community social control (Hagan, 1991). Nor are they appropriately applied to occupational or corporate criminality, where offenders are well-educated people with good jobs, strong ties to community institutions, and memberships in all the organizations that symbolize conformity (such as churches, service clubs, and political parties). Unlike traditional offenders, white-collar criminals tend to be married, with stable histories of employment, and years of involvement in the community. Their incomes are above average, and their belief systems are traditional and conservative. They most certainly do not think of themselves or their peers as criminals. Why do such people commit crimes?

This is the question addressed in this chapter. There are three levels of generality or analysis from which explanations may be sought. The first is the psychological level. Offences are committed by individuals, but not all individuals are equally susceptible. There may, therefore, be differences between people, or particular personality characteristics that facilitate or inhibit lawbreaking. The second level is organizational. The organization is the tool employed by the white-collar offender; it is either the victim of the offence (as in occupational crime) or the beneficiary (as in corporate crime). Organizations, like individuals, are not equally susceptible; there are wide variations in the nature and amount of criminal behaviour that seemingly identical corporations exhibit. The third or macro level of analysis focuses upon the characteristics of a society or cultural system, because societies are also differentially susceptible to corporate and occupational crime. Within capitalist systems there appear to be wide variations, for example, between the United States and Sweden, or Japan and the Netherlands. Moreover, although comparative data are either unreliable or unavailable, one would expect wide variations in the propensity to offend between capitalist systems, with their reliance on private corporations and profit maximization, and socialist or feudal systems, which operate under different sets of pressures. It is necessary, therefore, to ask whether and how particular political and economic structures, or particular value systems and institutions, relate to white-collar crime.

This chapter will look at causal factors that have been identified at each of these levels, then at illustrative case studies. Finally, it will assess the relative significance of the various causes identified.

THE PSYCHOLOGICAL LEVEL

Asking questions about the differences between individuals, and the ways they vary in their susceptibility to criminal acts, is the most ancient of explanatory levels. Western religions have traditionally traced the fundamental cause of evil to the individual, through the concept of "sin," and prescribed individualistic solutions such as repentance and atonement. Western legal systems, similarly, have focused upon the behaviour and culpability of the individual through the pivotal legal concept of *mens rea*, the guilty mind. It is not surprising, therefore, that early criminologists from the classical tradition, as it has been called, looked first to the character, discipline, and soul of the individual in their attempts to understand criminal behaviour. Consequently, it was predictable that, many decades later when the concept of white-collar crime became the subject of scholarly study, the first focus of interest would be upon individuals and their willingness to commit criminal acts. One of the first studies of embezzlement, for example, asked how those who embezzled differed from their peers who did not, and hypothesized that the concept of the "unshareable problem" allowed one to differentiate between the two groups (Cressey, 1953); that is, individuals who stole had a set of problems they felt unable to discuss, and unable to resolve any other way. Nor has this desire to explain complex phenomena at the individual level gone away. One of the latest and most ambitious attempts to construct a theory of criminal behaviour relies heavily on individual differences, using factors such as the (presumed) greater inability of criminals to delay gratification to explain susceptibility (Gottfredson and Hirschi, 1990).

In this context, then, the most interesting thing about those white-collar offenders who have been studied is their normality, the almost total absence of meaningful differences between the offenders and the general population. The literature tells us again and again that white-collar workers charged with offences are no different in personality, and certainly no more "abnormal," than those who have not been charged. Such generalizations must be interpreted with care, because several methodological problems are inherent in this literature. We cannot confidently say that white-collar workers who have committed occupational or corporate crimes are essentially the same as those who have not, because we have no idea whether the tiny minority who have been caught and charged are typical of the overall universe of white-collar offenders. There is good reason to believe they are not, because they evidently lacked the skill (or luck) to avoid detection and identification, as well as the power or clout to escape official sanctioning. However, a few minor differences have been identified. Several studies (all rather dated) found that white-collar offenders show a greater tendency to "recklessness"—perhaps not surprising considering these are the ones who were caught. Researchers have also found that offenders have a greater desire for power, more personal drive, and higher ambition than their counterparts (Blum, 1972; Selling, 1944; Spencer, 1965). However, the similarities between offenders and peers were far more striking than the differences.

This should not surprise anyone. In a culture where a primary goal is to make money, where those who compete most ruthlessly are held up as cultural models as long as they "win" (and just as ruthlessly destroyed on the pages of tabloids and talk shows should their feet of clay be discovered), the social pressures to become rich and succeed are immense. The dominant culture of capitalism urges all men, and women to an increasing degree, to achieve; it sees poverty as a stigma, a mark of inferiority linked with immoral lifestyles and failure. Traditional manual work is not respected or revered, particularly in North America, and the person whose career goal is "only" to be a carpenter or sales clerk has to fight for both self- and social-esteem. Witness, for example, the dozens of companions ads in the personal columns of newspapers where the sought-after mate must be professional, executive, or affluent; witness also the defensive and apologetic tone of the few advertisements that disclose that the mate-seeker is a truck driver or waiter. Alternately, observe the negative labels and low status that Canadian high school students affix to their peers in vocational or trade school "streams."

The "normal" personality produced by such influences is one that sees rules as barriers imposed by an alien body (government, regulatory agency, or elite), which must be circumvented or avoided on the road to success. One must take risks, with the money, or health, or aspirations of others, to make it big. It is, after all, "a dog eat dog world out there," and those who would deny this are "ivory tower academics" or "theorists who have never had to meet a payroll." Indeed, as the preceding sentence illustrates, the rationales to excuse lawbreaking, especially corporate crimes, are free-floating in the wider business culture, and available inside every organization. Most business people believe their competitors are unethical types who will cheat when the opportunity presents itself (Baumhart, 1961; Lane, 1954). Thus, the omnipresent psychological excuses expressed in forms such as, "If everybody else does it, it must be moral whether it is legal or not," or "I have to cheat to survive," allow lawbreakers to engage in corporate crime with little moral angst.

This is less true of occupational than of corporate crime because dominant ideologies, reinforced by corporate values, are more likely to define crimes against employers as ordinary theft; and theft, like all traditional criminal offences, carries its own ideological baggage, as something done by "punks" and disreputable classes. This social structuring of dominant personality types inside and outside the corporation does provide clues that help explain the essential normality of apprehended white-collar criminals. However, it leaves us with another problem: explaining why some corporate employees, presumably subject to similar cultural and organizational influences, refuse to break the law, and sometimes take great personal and professional risks to control those who do ("whistle-blowers," for example). Research has therefore turned to explaining what prevents people from engaging in particular white-collar offences. The key factors identified thus far are motivation, opportunity, and access.

MOTIVATION

There are still a few stable pockets in North America (more in Britain and Europe) where a solid, geographically rooted, working-class culture centred around fishing or mill or mine work has been maintained. Although such communities are disappearing rapidly, as technology and pollution take away jobs and politicians remove income supports from rural or hinterland communities to force workers to move to cities, they still provide a haven of quasi-oppositional values. This does not mean such communities are crime-free, merely that the pressures to succeed that motivate mainstream white-collar criminality are less intrusive here. Such working-class cultures have their own definitions of acceptable behaviours. On the job, there are a wide range of "fiddles," practices that would be seen as occupational crimes in other contexts (and, under the rationale of global competitiveness, are increasingly being redefined this way by management). In the past, such practices have been accepted as legitimate by workers, and passively tolerated within certain limits by management. Workers' "borrowing" lumber from a mill to complete a recreation room, for example, was traditionally acceptable, and could be seen as compensation for overtime not charged, or inadequate salaries; stockpiling lumber to sell on the open market was typically not. The characteristics and amount of allowable goods were prescribed by a rigid moral code, and workers who overstepped were likely to find themselves stigmatized as thieves (Clarke, 1990; Ditton, 1977). Such subcultures shape the occupational crime that occurs. Because workers can find self-respect, economic survival, and a place in the community by conforming to these limits, they are likely to confine their pilfering to fit these parameters, and feel less need to chase the great god of success in the form of riches and/or middle-class status. To the degree that they value their standing in the community, then, they are less likely to pick up a gun and rob a bank, or take things from the workplace that would violate the norms.

There are other niches, other escape routes from dominant culture. Communes, religious orders, and some ethnic groups, for example, hold up alternative value systems as models for members to emulate, which provide roles and duties conferring self-esteem and identity independent of the systems existing outside the community. However, alternative definitions have become harder to maintain, because mainstream media, the education system, and modern technology are increasingly difficult to avoid. Geographical remoteness can no longer guarantee escape from dominant value systems (if indeed it can be found in the first place), and it is rare for the ideological purity of movements to survive past the first generation. Religious belief no longer provides much of a bulwark against "the bitch goddess of materialism." Consider, for example, fundamentalist Protestant sects flourishing in the United States that have turned God into a white businessman out to maximize converts for fun, profit, and the glory of God. Poverty is no longer blessed, and it is clear that neither the poor nor the meek will inherit the world. The religious rich person must still adhere to certain norms to be accepted. He or she must not behave in an "uppity" manner or think himself or herself better than anybody else; the demeanour must above all be democratic. Large sums must also be donated to the church to help the deserving poor. But the fact that such a person receives "brownie points," extra credit socially, for *not* acting superior is a clear indication of the higher status worldly success bestows. There is little motivational escape here from the necessity to succeed, despite elaborate (and sincerely meant) strictures against dishonesty coming from the pulpits. The real moral devils in these religions are not those who become millionaires through insider trading or violation of labour laws, but communists, atheists, and those seen as moral defectives (such as lesbians, homosexuals, and adulterers).

Having said this, we still know very little about the process by which dominant ideologies of success and power become translated and absorbed into individual personalities, or are rejected by them. We do not know the components that mediate the journey from abstract ideological concept to personal biography; nor why people subjected to apparently identical cultural forces respond differently to them. People construct their own meaning and value systems within the broad framework of cultural beliefs and practices available to them, accepting some and rejecting others. But our inability to reconstruct accurately these mechanisms at the phenomenological level does not alter the fact that dominant cultural pressures demonstrably exert some influence on everyone within their sphere, requiring people to take account of these belief systems, even if this takes the shape of constructing rationales to justify rejecting them. It is empirically evident that the vast majority of "properly" socialized North Americans accept the idea (and the behaviour that derives from it) that material goods are an essential component of the good life. One cannot legitimately attain these without becoming, to some degree or other, a success. Success means getting a good job and lots of money; and personal happiness for many therefore comes to require necessities such as the BMWs, Birkenstocks, and Reeboks (although the actual material goods that confer status are culturally learned, and vary with class level and lifestyle).

Unfortunately, the jobs most people can obtain, assuming they are lucky enough to be employed, offer pay levels that cannot support such affluence even with both partners employed outside the home. Even for the objectively affluent, there are always goods that remain just out of reach, goals beyond one's grasp. People in the upper-middle business classes, where the ideology of success tends to be most virulent, can never rest easy knowing they have "arrived," because the competition could be gaining on them on the personal or professional levels. One can, and should, always strive for more as an individual; concomitantly, one's corporation can never stand still; it must grow or perish. The dominant culture, then, might have been purposively designed to instill in the majority of its members a motivational structure predisposed toward acts giving them a financial advantage over others. The culture provides copious motivation for white-collar (and traditional acquisitive blue-collar) crime. Advertisements, television shows about ideal families, and movie heroes and heroines reinforce the message that in order to be happy and respected one must be rich and young (and preferably an American living in California). Unfortunately, neither corporate nor occupational crime will make one young; it has a much better chance, however, of making one rich and American.

A few case studies illustrate these processes. Although studies of nonapprehended white-collar offenders are rare, Hollinger and Clarke (1983) used a self-report methodology to gather detailed information on large numbers of working- and middle-class employees. Senior officials were not examined, in part because their cooperation had to be obtained to secure access to lower-level employees; they would presumably have resisted being defined by researchers as the objects of study themselves.

Hollinger and Clarke found three factors that predisposed employees to steal. First were external economic pressures, not poverty per se, but the perception of needing more. Employees in similar objective circumstances differed on this variable; moreover, those who reported the need varied in their willingness to translate it into the commission of illegal acts. This finding is reminiscent of the "unshareable problem" complex first identified in Donald Cressey's (1953) study of embezzlers. The employee with mammoth gambling debts, massive medical bills (there being no medicare in the United States), the perceived need to provide an expensive private school education for a child, or amass material goods to impress a girl (boy) friend, is more likely to embezzle, particularly if the employee can see no alternative ways of filling the need and is barred—by shame or lack of access or trust—from discussing it with others.

Age was the second factor identified. Hollinger and Clarke found that younger workers were more likely to offend, and that younger and newly hired employees were apprehended most (1983:7). Punishment per se, if defined as the objective likelihood of prosecution and restitution, was not significant; however, the subjective probability of punishment was. That is, the employees' perception of risk, the likelihood of getting caught *in their minds*, did affect chances of offending; and their assessment of risk was related to the number of employees they knew who had been apprehended and fired. Job dissatisfaction, the third variable identified, is the most significant overall. Employees who did not like their employer, and did not think they were being treated fairly, were more likely to offend regardless of company position or age. This finding has been replicated in a number of studies employing very different methodologies. As British author Michael Clarke concludes, following a lengthy review of European and American literature, there is a direct correlation between management attitudes and theft. Where management is seen as supportive and open, employees seek extra benefits through legitimate channels; where it is distant or perceived as unreasonable, employees feel justified in stealing and sometimes do so just to get revenge (Clarke, 1990:51).

Many of the offenders studied by Hollinger and Clarke were at the lower end of the white-collar occupational scale. Middle-class offenders tend to commit more sophisticated offences. They also have more opportunity and access than those further down the hierarchy, because upper-level employees are scrutinized less closely and trusted more. Michael Clarke (1990:53–55) says middle-class employees are less likely to be detected, but steal larger amounts. Dalton's study of the chemical industry found that items were frequently manufactured for management-level employees using company time and equipment; company funds were also diverted to individual uses. These practices were justified by the employees involved as necessary to "keep the team happy" (Dalton, 1959; see also Benson, 1989; Johnson, 1986). Where there are high-value products and weak control systems (true at the management level of most corporations), there will be high levels of middle-level crime (Clarke, 1990:55).

There are no comparable empirical studies of the motivation of corporate criminals. However, Passas (1990) attempts to spell out why people who seemingly "have it all" engage in illegal acts. He points out that the meaning and content of success goals varies throughout the social structure. Thus, jobs and salaries that would spell success to a ghetto youth confer little respect upon those reared in the upper classes. Because of this relativity of goals, upper-income executives will be pressured toward law-breaking in the pursuit of ever larger market shares and ever greater profits. The goal of corporations, after all, is profit maximization, not "reasonable" profit levels. Top executives have been shown in personality tests to be "ambitious, shrewd, and possessed of a non-demanding moral code" (Gross, 1978:71).

The personality most likely to succeed in the corporate world is not one that is overly fussy about the deleterious ways one's activities affect others. As Presthus has remarked, the favoured social character has superficial charisma and the ability to view decisions in black and white terms. Such people are good at categorizing others into types (necessary versus superfluous, productive versus nonproductive), a useful characteristic when they must be fired, or subjected to high-risk environments in the interests of corporate profits (Presthus, 1978). They also tend to possess what social psychologists designate as type-A personalities, distinguished by traits such as "free floating hostility, competitiveness, a high need for socially approved success, unbridled ambitions, aggressiveness, impatience" (Kanungo, 1982:157). Such tendencies are often reinforced by business school courses that stress success above all else. In one study, 79 percent of business students refused in a simulated situation to withdraw from the market a life-threatening but profitable drug (Braithwaite and Grabosky, 1986).

OPPORTUNITY

The opportunity to commit offences is a second causal factor influencing occurrence, and it refers to the *subjective* availability of the offence. Illegal behaviours are not psychologically available to everyone because some have imbibed ethical or religious values that countermand individualistic and competitive ones, and others have weaker needs to acquire or compete. This may be relevant in explaining differential rates and rationales for male versus female offenders (Daly, 1986). The individual who has learned to value honesty more than success would suffer more—psychologically and socially, through negative reactions of those he or she values—from committing an offence than from refusing. The physical opportunity or access may be present, but the offence is not psychologically available to that person at that time. This factor will only operate if the individual defines the offence in question as dishonest and not, as is frequently the case, as "clever business practice."

It is precisely this former response that leading business schools and corporations are now attempting to put in place, by educating present and future employees on ethical behaviour, establishing courses, and endowing institutions on corporate ethics. Their chances of actually altering motivational and opportunity structures in this way are problematic because of the complexity of the factors involved. It seems unlikely that any one program, however well intentioned and generously funded, can offset the effects of an entire culture dedicated to demonstrating, on the one hand, the rewards of success, and on the other, the "wimpiness" of obeying other people's rules. In this cultural setting, the strictures of ethics are easily dismissed as the dead hand of religion, or the inappropriate stifling mechanisms of a government that has, in mainstream business ideology, no place in the market in the first place. It is probable, then, that many individuals will still be able to convince themselves that the profitable behaviour in question is not "really" wrong. The corporate sector itself, through lobbying and public relations, has sponsored many of the beliefs that "responsible" segments of it are now trying to change, through its attempts to preserve ambiguity about the moral (not to mention legal) status of corporate crime (Simon and Eitzen, 1990; Box, 1983).

Corporate power to define morality is further reinforced in academia, where learned professors argue about whether corporate crimes are "really" criminal, and classify offences as *mala in se* and *mala prohibita*. The former are acts that are morally evil, the traditional offences primarily committed (it is assumed) by the poor and the damaged (such as burglary, assault, or homicide); the latter are "bad" only because they have been declared illegal by legislative fiat (Cranston, 1982). Not surprisingly, most corporate crimes—antitrust, false advertising, predatory pricing, and the like—are classified into this category. Such attitudes are also found among the judiciary: Justice Dickson of the Supreme Court of Canada has actually argued that regulatory and public welfare offences are "not criminal in any real sense, but are prohibited in the public interest" (Sargent, 1990:107). This battle over the moral meaning of corporate crime has not been totally won by business, for there is continual and growing evidence that the general public view corporate crimes much more seriously than corporate executives and their political and academic supporters, and support heavier punishments for offenders and organizations (Goff and Mason-Clark, 1989; Cullen et al., 1982). However, the dominance of currents of thought that promote corporate crimes as harmless peccadilloes does render such offences psychologically available to many who would not dream of committing acts they or their peer group defined as "really" criminal. Such ideologies are therefore important in understanding why corporate crimes are motivationally acceptable to a substantial percentage of the business class.

Thus, it is not surprising that business executives frequently defend their involvement in corporate criminality by saying, apparently in all sincerity, that they did nothing wrong. Senior executives at Revco Drug Stores, who defrauded the Ohio Department of Public Welfare of more than $500,000 by falsifying prescriptions for welfare clients, said the offence was actually the welfare department's fault, because Revco's billing procedures were not effectively policed (Vaughan, 1982). A senior executive at Westinghouse, convicted of a massive price-fixing scheme that cost customers millions of dollars, responded to a question regarding the illegality of his behaviour as follows: "Illegal? Yes, but not criminal ... I thought that we were ... working on a survival basis ... to make enough to keep our plant and employees" (Geis and Meier, 1977:122). Or examine the attitude of senior executives of A.H. Robbins, the company that rushed the Dalkon Shield onto the market despite evidence that the Shield's multifilament tail had the potential to "wick," thereby transmitting deadly bacteria into the uterus. After months of litigation and many deaths, executives of the company survived with individual and corporate reputations apparently unscathed, still denying that the device actually caused harm (Perry and Dawson, 1985). When Vandivier (1992:216), investigating the development and marketing of a faulty aircraft brake at B.F. Goodrich Company, asked a senior executive whether he was worried about injuries that would result from marketing a defective brake, he got this response: "I have no control over this thing.... Why should my conscience bother me?" Or examine the rationale of an official in an asbestos plant where contaminated working conditions caused hundreds of cases of asbestosis in workers and their families, who said (from the lofty perspective of one whose office was far from the source of contamination): "I think we are all willing to have a little bit of crud in our lungs and a full stomach, rather than a whole lot of clean air and nothing to eat" (cited in Michalowski, 1985:334).

Opportunity, then, is facilitated at the individual level by dominant ideologies that define corporate crimes as nothing more than quirks, or see lawbreaking as a necessary part of business, subservient to the "real" goal of business, which is to maximize profits. Sykes and Matza (1957:664–70) coined the term "techniques of neutralization" to describe the generally less successful attempts of traditional criminals to get around or neutralize beliefs that would make lawbreaking psychologically difficult for them. Such rationalizations are much easier for corporate criminals because their beliefs, unlike traditional or occupational offences, are supported and popularized by the most powerful and prestigious groups and institutions in the society. The techniques are, first, the denial of responsibility. For example: "It's not my job; I can do nothing about it; if our company doesn't do it, others will." Denial of injury and denial of victims are the second and third techniques; offenders convince themselves that their acts do not actually hurt anyone. Occupational criminals, for example, maintain that they are not stealing, but "borrowing" money (Cressey, 1953). Fourth, miscreants condemn their condemners, easier for corporate criminals to do because there is strong social support for the idea that laws against corporate crime are illegitimate, representing nothing but government infringement on individual rights (Fisse and Braithwaite, 1983; Stone, 1975; Newman, 1977; Ermann and Lundman, 1982). A fifth technique is the appeal to higher loyalties. We have already seen this in operation, in the comments of executives who argued that unsafe working conditions and price fixing were necessary to stave off bankruptcy and keep people employed.

Rationalizations differ by gender as well as by class and social location. Evidence indicates that women are more likely to choose rationalizations that prioritize the needs of husbands or children. In other words, the higher loyalties they cite to excuse illegal behaviour are to their families (Daly, 1989). Men, on the other hand, are more likely to blame business pressures, the need to succeed, or the necessity of staving off disastrous losses. Over and above this are rationalizations common to all who engage in instrumental criminal acts: the belief that everyone else is doing it too; that the chances of getting caught are small; and that the applicable sanctions are not too great to be borne. The difference for corporate criminals is that *their* rationalizations are likely to be both accurate and accepted (Ermann and Lundman, 1982). Morality and motivation, then, are socially constructed; and excuses are more easily available to some social classes, especially the powerful corporate sector, than to others.

Once the opportunity is psychologically available, the presence or absence of physical opportunity becomes important. A person who has accepted all the above rationalizations will be unlikely to commit an offence if there are no opportunities to do so. Certain jobs expose one to much more temptation than others. The opportunity to steal millions of dollars worth of stocks and bonds is likely to prove more attractive than the opportunity to steal lipstick or screwdrivers. And employees whose jobs provide them with control over scarce resources (purchasing agents, for example), or give them the power to monitor the infractions of others, are more vulnerable to bribes or abuse of power than those lacking such power. Thus, one can expect, and does find, higher rates of offence in certain jobs than in others. All employees are not equally tempted; opportunity and access are clustered at certain positions in organizations.

A recent theory of crime, interestingly enough, takes this approach one step further and maintains that white-collar offenders are no different, in motivation or social characteristics, from traditional criminals. Gottfredson and Hirschi (1990) argue that both types of criminals seek benefits for themselves: the one uses a knife or gun; the other an organization (or the records or computer network that belongs to it). These authors argue that all criminals are active, impulsive, aggressive individuals with low self-control, and there is "no reason to think ... that [white-collar] offenders ... are causally distinct" (1990:190). However, because the occupations of white-collar workers usually require some education, they hypothesize that rates of offending are low, because education requires "persistence, willingness to defer to the interests of others, and attention to conventional appearance" (1990:191). These are all characteristics that "real" criminals do not possess, according to the theory, so rates of offending must therefore be low, and the majority of white-collar crimes must be banal and mundane in nature, demanding little or no sophistication from their perpetrators. The authors conclude that white-collar crime is rare; there is, they assert, an "extraordinarily high level of law-abiding conduct among white-collar workers" (Gottfredson and Hirschi, 1990:198). They also maintain that white-collar crime is not supported by co-workers, and that white-collar criminals, like all others, tend to be young rather than older, black rather than white, and less rather than more intelligent.

Unfortunately, whether this theory can be applied to low-level occupational offences or not (and the empirical evidence is mixed at best), it certainly does not apply to corporate crimes.

These offences are highly sophisticated and complex, they require extensive coordination and planning, and they are typically committed by senior executives who are both white and well into middle age. Offenders frequently participate in elaborate and painstaking conspiracies that require considerable intelligence and determination to plan and execute, necessitating double sets of records, code-names, and elaborate false accounting schemes (see, for example, Gil Geis's 1967 description of the extremely complex scheme to fix prices in the electrical industry). The theory applies to occupational crimes only insofar as it describes which offenders in the United States are most likely to show up in official statistics. It is well documented that people with the least amount of power—the young, black, and ethnic—are most likely to be noticed, processed, and subjected to official and criminal sanctions (Reiman, 1984; Robin, 1967; Simon and Eitzen, 1990). This does not mean that they are the only or most likely groups to *commit* such offences.

Although Gottfredson and Hirschi's theory does not fit the facts known about corporate crime, there have been other more successful attempts to include white-collar offenders in general motivational-level theories of criminal behaviour. Keane (1991), for example, argues that a variant of control theory (Hirschi, 1969) could be so adapted. Control theory predicts that people with weak ties to conventional society are more likely to commit crimes than those with strong ties. Specifically, those who are emotionally attached to conventional authority figures (such as parents or teachers), committed to conventional goals and means, involved in conventional activities, and believers in conventional tenets stressing the importance of law and the immorality of lawbreakers are less likely to become involved in criminal behaviour. While white-collar criminality, on the surface, appears to contradict each of these tenets—offenders are generally the most conventional of people—the theory applies if reconfigured to refer to attachment to a corporation. Individuals who identify too closely with the organization that employs them and with its goals of profit maximization may therefore be, because of the intensity of this bond, more likely to break the law to promote organizational interests. In this instance, attachment to a conventional albeit lawbreaking organization can lead to crime (Keane, 1991:228).

THE ORGANIZATIONAL LEVEL

In occupational crimes, the offender takes advantage of his or her position within an occupation or organization to commit an illegal act, making the organization an enabling factor in the offence. Its presence makes that particular offence possible. One cannot perform unnecessary medical operations unless one is a doctor with hospital privileges, market unsafe goods without a senior position in a manufacturing firm, or alter the bank's computer without insider knowledge of the correct codes. Here, however, the organization is no more than an unwilling tool in such offences. Far more interesting are corporate crimes where the organization benefits from the offence. It is complicit and directly involved.

A few examples will illustrate the nature of this involvement: the falsification of research results on two drugs, Aldactone and Flagyl, by the G.D. Searle Company to make them appear safe when in fact the company's own studies indicated that they were carcinogenic (Clarke, 1990:147); the tampering by coal-mine owners with dust samples sent to federal safety inspectors to avoid being forced to undertake costly clean-up measures, even though workers subjected to high coal-dust levels face increased risk of black lung disease (*The Washington Post,* April 4, 1991:1); the payment of $25 million in bribes to foreign governments by the Lockheed Aircraft Corporation to induce customers to purchase Lockheed planes (Fisse and Braithwaite, 1983); the falsifying of data by the Richardson-Merrell pharmaceutical company to certify a new cholesterol-inhibiting drug as safe when, in fact, company tests showed that experimental animals either died or developed cataracts after the drug was administered (Clarke, 1990:148–49); the marketing of the intrauterine device, the Dalkon Shield, by the A.H. Robbins Company, which killed seventeen women and injured 200,000 more. These are all typical offences. Their commission necessarily involves large vertical slices of the organization itself. Employees and their supervisors up to the vice-presidential level (and often above) are the only people who can make the decision to produce the defective product, pay the bribe, or fudge the data. They are complicit, if not as active participants, then as passive onlookers who failed to take action to correct, stop, or report the illegal acts.

This emphasis on the social structure of the organization as a causal factor is a recent one because of the aforementioned preoccupation with micro or psychological levels. (The 1990 Gottfredson and Hirschi theory is, in this sense, a throwback to an earlier age.) To comprehend how organizations cause criminality, one must understand what makes the organization, as a structure, so unique. Organizations exist not as random creations, but as entities purposefully set up to achieve particular goals. They can be defined as "social structures which coordinate individual effort in the service ... of certain collective goals ... which are established for the explicit purpose of achieving the goals" (Gross, 1980:205).

Thus, the hierarchy of positions, the duties and responsibilities attached to each, and the detailed divisions of labour within organizations all take the form they do because these structures are believed to facilitate goal achievement. Business corporations under a private enterprise system are particular types of organizations, distinguished by their central mandate, which is to generate surplus value (that is, produce profits). Business schools and organizational theorists spend a lot of time, therefore, studying different organizational models to find those that facilitate "efficiency" and "productivity," thus making the corporate organization more likely to achieve its goals. Similarly, those interested in corporate crime study corporate structure and goals to understand where, how, and the degree to which different modes of organization encourage or require the commission of criminal acts.

CORPORATE GOALS

When analyzing corporations, there is some debate about the uniformity of corporate goals. Stone (1975), for example, asserts that maximizing profits is only necessarily a key goal when the corporation is newly established and insecure. Once it has been in existence long enough to secure a certain level of profitability and develop its own history, it can and frequently does develop other priorities. Social responsibility, prestige, and reputation (public image) may then take precedence over "pure" profit maximization. However, this scenario obviously works only for a small and favoured few; the company must be profitable, stable and secure, enjoy market dominance, and be tightly controlled by a small number of like-minded people. It needs to be privately owned because, if its shares are traded on public exchanges, it is likely to be seen as a "cash cow" and forced to fight continual takeover attempts.

Particularly in the rapacious 1980s, enlightened managements and boards of directors controlling profitable, responsible companies were tempting targets for corporate raiders representing conglomerates seeking just such companies to fund further acquisitions. Moreover, as Coleman points out, "unsatisfactory" profit levels are still the most common reason chief executives lose their jobs (1985:222). This does not mean Stone is entirely wrong. Short-run goals other than profit maximization will indeed be pursued—companies may decide to diversify or expand or become more environmentally responsible. But these goals will not be (knowingly) undertaken at the expense of long-term profitability. As Steven Box put it, "these short-run goals are pursued with a green-glinted eye focused on long-run profitability"

(1983:35). At the present time, theorists from both the right and left agree that seeking profits is the major corporate goal, but they differ on whether this is a beneficial or detrimental state of affairs. Barring government bail-outs, corporations cease to exist if they are insufficiently profitable.

Given this, then, we must examine whether and how corporate goals, particularly profit maximization, lead to lawbreaking. Many argue that increased corporate crime is related to low profit levels, and some evidence indicates corporations suffering from declining profit levels commit more offences (Kramer, 1982; Lane, 1954; Simpson, 1986; Clinard and Yeager, 1980). It is reasonable to assume that the pressure on management to break laws will be heavier when the company's profit margin is slim than when profits are healthy (Stone, 1975; Coleman, 1989). However, the generalization does not hold true for all industries or time periods. Falling profits and recessionary conditions do seem to produce more antitrust offences, and more serious ones at that (Simpson, 1986), but the most crime-prone industries—pharmaceutical, oil, and automobile companies—have also been among the most consistently profitable (Clinard and Yeager, 1980). Clearly, just as poverty per se is not the primary cause of traditional crime, declining profits are not the only factors leading to corporate crime.

An interesting attempt to meld corporate goals and crime comes from Steven Box (1983:35–37), who argues that environmental uncertainties always make corporate goals difficult to achieve. Such goals therefore predispose corporate executives to try "alternative means" (such as lawbreaking) to remain profitable. The environmental uncertainties Box sets out are indeed omnipresent; more significantly, they are inseparable and inescapable components of a successful capitalist system. First, companies must cope with competitors who try to take over their markets, undercut them through pricing strategies or novel advertising campaigns, or get a competitive advantage through technological breakthroughs. To get around such pressures, companies may try to secure their markets by bribing potential customers; collaborating with the competition to fix prices at levels high enough to guarantee profits for all; or employing predatory pricing. The latter is an illegal strategy that is only available to large companies. It involves pricing one's products at levels that are below the manufacturing cost in order to drive competitors out of business. When the competitors have been forced into bankruptcy, the victorious party is free to charge whatever the market will bear, and prices rebound to reflect this.

Governments, or more specifically government policies, are a second source of environmental uncertainty for corporations, for they are notoriously likely to upset the investment climate or turn profitable courses of action into unprofitable ones without warning (particularly near election time). Governments do this by increasing (or threatening to increase) taxes, changing laws, or suddenly enforcing regulations heretofore ignored. In response, corporations can and do lobby to influence the state in every conceivable legal way. But corporations may also choose illegal methods, such as covert donations to particular officials or parties, or electoral "dirty tricks" (as in the Watergate burglary and associated blackmail that brought down U.S. President Richard Nixon in 1974). Or they may engage in creative bookkeeping to avoid taxes in a high-tax country by making profits appear, instead, in a low-tax country (Passas, 1990; Simon and Eitzen, 1990).

Employees also cause environmental uncertainties for corporations, by forming unions, demanding higher wages, going on strike, and agitating for safer working conditions. Illegal corporate responses to employees include harassing and firing ringleaders (Pearce, 1976), lying to employees about the safety of substances in the workplace (as in the asbestos industry), or covering themselves by ensuring that posted warnings will not be accessible to employees (as in the Film Recovery Systems case where the English warning labels on the vats of cyanide could not be understood by the non-English-speaking workforce) (Cullen et al., 1987:71).

Consumers constitute a fourth cause of environmental uncertainty for corporations. Consumers can be fickle, turning onto or off products for reasons that are unclear (and, worse, unpredictable). Companies attempt to control consumer tastes legally through market strategies and advertising, but may revert under pressure to false advertising, deception, and the sale of dangerous products. Box cites the unpredictability of the general public as the fifth factor of environmental uncertainty. Various pressure groups and concerned citizens make all kinds of demands (for a clean environment or risk-free chemicals, for example) without a commensurate understanding (in the corporate view) of the costs and consequences of these demands. Companies may react by appearing to comply with environmental requirements while hiring low-cost firms to dump hazardous waste illegally (Szasz, 1986); they may bribe and corrupt governments, either to prevent passage of legislation or escape enforcement (Simon and Eitzen, 1990); or they may dump hazardous or unsafe products in the Third World, thus maintaining profit levels while apparently obeying the law. As Box concludes: "When environmental uncertainties increase so the strain towards corporate criminal activity will increase" (1983:37).

CORPORATE STRUCTURE

A second organizational factor, corporate structure, is every bit as significant as corporate goals. Based on fieldwork in Japan, Braithwaite and Fisse (1983) conducted interviews with thirty top executives in six major corporations, as well as with civil servants involved in corporate regulation in four ministries. They found four distinctive structures of intracorporate responsibility, each with different implications for corporate crime. First is a style they labelled "noblesse oblige," where the titular head of the organization takes symbolic responsibility for all corporate successes, failures, and offences. Second is the "captain of the ship" mode, whereby the senior executive at a particular worksite is held responsible. This means, in decentralized operations, that people who head particular divisions are accountable for everything that takes place in their territory. A third mode is "nominated accountability," whereby particular individuals are designated in advance as the people responsible for certain activities. For example, the advertising manager may be held to account for false advertising or the safety officer for unhealthy conditions in the workplace. This is related to the "Vice-President in charge of going to Jail" style of management often found in the West, where a senior executive is responsible for ensuring compliance with a whole series of statutes. The final mode, the dominant one in North America, is called "fault-based responsibility." Here, fault is imposed on a person (or persons) who is singled out, often after the fact, as causing the offence through intentional, reckless, or negligent behaviour (Braithwaite and Fisse, 1983).

Each structural model affects the frequency of corporate crime, as well as corporate responses to it. Although the data are insufficient to allow a thorough comparison, the first two structures, where people at the top of the organizational chain take responsibility for criminal behaviour regardless of their personal culpability or knowledge, are the most likely to monitor and internally sanction corporate crime. When the person at the top has to "take the heat," both the motivation and the power to ensure compliance exist. Thus, structures that ensure that potentially embarrassing illegal or unethical conditions are caught before they can blow up in the face of the chief executive are likely to be in place. Many North American corporations, on the other hand, have adopted the third or fourth models Braithwaite and Fisse (1983) identify. Under these systems, chief executives have much less reason to concern themselves with corporate crime, provided profit levels are healthy. Structures that provide high levels of monitoring are less likely to be present, and employees may actually be discouraged from reporting problems to supervisors. Operating rules may leave those who "squeal" open to reprisals, and employees may believe that their superiors do not want to hear about possibly illegal short cuts they had to take. Thus, whistle-blowers are likely to be stimatized or fired rather than encouraged, and levels of compliance low.

As this study illustrates, corporate structures can be crime facilitative or crime coercive. Studies of car dealers have demonstrated that major North American automobile manufacturers pressure retail dealers to provide unrealistically high profit levels or else risk losing their franchises. Since dealers are unable to do this through new car sales, where competition to offer low prices is intense, they compensate by performing fraudulent and unnecessary car repairs, charging brand-name prices for cheap generic parts, or charging for repairs that were not made (Braithwaite, 1978; Leonard and Weber, 1970; Needleman and Needleman, 1979). Senior management, in other words, sets up conditions that it knows cannot be met without a certain amount of fraudulent or dishonest practice. It is then able to deny all knowledge and all responsibility when criminal acts are uncovered. Should offences remain hidden, management is happy to claim credit for high profit levels.

Vaughan (1982) argues that the transaction systems of complex organizations—the ways the many and varied components of a modern corporation interact with each other within the corporation—may directly or indirectly encourage illegal behaviour. Transaction systems do this by providing easy access to illicit resources with little risk of discovery, and/or motivating executives to break the law to obtain organizational goals because the transaction system itself impedes the attainment of these goals. Advanced computer networks, she says, further magnify the risk. Denzin (1978) makes a similar argument about the post-Prohibition growth of the Illinois liquor industry. Using historic and ethnographic data, as well as interviews with distillers, distributors, and retailers, he shows that many key elements of the industry's relational structure, such as its circumvention and survival strategies and its legal and extra-legal negotiations, actually promote lawbreaking. Companies that tell the world that occupational safety is their top priority, then set such unrealistic daily production quotas that workers must ignore safety procedures to reach them, provide other examples of criminogenic corporate structures (Walters, 1985).

Returning to the question of culpability, the presence of criminogenic structures does not mean employees have no choice but to break the law, however fervently the offender may believe this. Individuals always have choices, although some may be more palatable than others, and the consequences of refusing to offend may include losing one's status, friends, or livelihood. Corporate structures, then, make criminality easy or difficult; they attach different costs to lawbreaking as opposed to whistle-blowing, and to compliance versus noncompliance. However, modern corporations are not death camps where nonconforming employees are shot at dawn, and no relatives are taken hostage or tortured. Companies that depend on high levels of unethical/illegal behaviour would rather avoid the problem of employees with delicate consciences. This they do, in part, by choosing senior management with care. They are most unlikely to promote people who show signs of being unwilling to put corporate interests first, or to move anyone who shows "dangerous" signs of nonconformity into key senior positions. Box summarizes the dilemma of the ambitious but honest executive in the following way:

> They are required to choose between impairing their career chances or being a loyal organizational person. That the latter seems to be chosen overwhelmingly testifies not to the existence of coercion, but to careful selection procedures for placing persons in corporate positions coupled with successful methods of persuading them that their interests and the corporation's interests happily coincide—or at least, that that is the most sensible, pragmatic way of looking at it. (Box, 1983:42)

Company size has also been identified as a causal factor. The evidence here is contradictory, however. Some studies indicate large firms are more likely to violate regulatory laws than small ones, while others show just the opposite (see, for example, the summary in Coleman, 1989:231–32). No easy resolution is possible, because violations in larger corporations are probably harder for regulators to identify, and such bodies are certainly harder to convict and sanction (a necessary step before their offences can become visible). Acts tend to be hidden in a "vast interorganizational matrix" that impedes surveillance or the attribution of responsibility. Records are hard to find, easy to doctor, and highly manipulable; and few signs of criminality are visible to external observers. Declining stock prices, for example, may be due to many factors; illegality is only one of many, and may indeed cause stock prices to increase (Shapiro, 1990:346–55). Both the size and complexity of the internal structure of corporations make it difficult, then, to identify offences and offenders. This does not necessarily mean that companies themselves, with full command of the internal structure and access to all parts of it, are unable to determine responsibility, however difficult this is for outside investigators. As Braithwaite has observed:

> All corporate actors benefit from the protection afforded by presenting to outsiders an appearance of greatly diffused accountability. Yet when companies for their own purposes want accountability, they can generally get it. (Braithwaite, 1984:138–39)

On the other hand, smaller and less powerful concerns, in every sector of the economy, are more heavily policed, and therefore more likely to show up in official statistics (Snider, 1987; Coleman, 1989). Small businesses are correspondingly easier for regulators to track and sanction than large and powerful multinationals with their political connections, legions of lawyers, and overflowing legal budgets. Because we have little knowledge of the actual amount of corporate crime that occurs, and studies rely on the records of regulatory agencies to establish the frequency of offending, factors that govern the behaviour of regulatory agencies are central to discussions of causality.

Once a set of illegal activities is entrenched in the organization, all the pressures that induce employees to conform become factors that sustain the offence. Organizations produce conformity by holding out rewards on the one hand and sanctions on the other. Rewards may be tangible (promotions, pay raises) or intangible (the approbation of one's peers and supervisors, the feelings of loyalty and commitment to the company, pleasure at having done one's job well). Sanctions are also tangible and intangible, and range from losing one's job or promotion chances to being ostracized and ridiculed. Thus, some employees will participate in (or ignore) illegal behaviours to gain acceptance and rewards; others, to avoid being punished by peers or superiors. Moreover, the extensive division of labour within complex organizations helps employees deny their own culpability. For example, a long list of employees participated for many years in the Lockheed Aircraft Company's scheme to bribe foreign governments to buy its products, but each played only a small role in the crime. One official would negotiate the payment, a clerk would get the money ready for delivery, someone else would put it in an envelope, another would carry the envelope onto the plane and someone else again delivered it to the bribed official. When an illegal act is broken into that many parts, each act can be conceived as innocuous by the person doing it (Fisse and Braithwaite, 1983; Ermann and Lundman, 1978; Blau, 1955). The organization facilitates this process by developing, in the internal corporate culture, its own customized rationalizations. This helps to insulate employees from the judgments of the outside world, and to neutralize certain criminal acts so that employees come to see them as taken-for-granted components of their job.

The third factor at the organizational level to be examined is the immediate organizational environment. Some factors that relate to criminality, such as taxes and the competitive situation, have been discussed above. However, the major external force affecting the propensity of corporations to engage in illegal behaviour is the state, its laws, and particularly its regulatory systems. Because organizations are goal-seeking entities, and the primary goal of corporations is to make profits, the degree to which law-breaking is profitable in a particular society is a key determinant of its likelihood and frequency. What are the costs of lawbreaking? What are the possible sanctions and risks? What are the chances of being caught? How much does the corporation stand to lose if caught? Here, intangible losses to reputation and image may be as important to long-run profitability as immediate dollar losses. Therefore, one must ask how the commission and possible discovery of offences will affect a given corporation's relations with the investment community, its peers in the market, and its future clout with political authorities and regulatory agencies. American corporations are increasingly run by financiers (rather than technical experts) and driven by the rate of capital return (Pearce, 1991:10). Indeed, corporations have been known to take a direct, cost-benefit analysis to corporate crime, balancing the costs of the offence versus the cost of correcting the problem.

The Ford Pinto case is the best documented and most famous example of this strategy. The Pinto was rushed onto the market in September 1970, in an effort to beat Volkswagen and Japanese manufacturers in the small-car market. The president of Ford at that time, Lee Iacocca, instructed designers to come up with a new model car that weighed less than 2000 pounds and cost less than $2000. The Pinto met both these criteria, but at the cost of severe design flaws, the most serious of which was the placement of the gas tank only six inches from the rear bumper. When hit from behind, the bumper was pushed into the gas tank, allowing fuel to spill out. The slightest spark would then make the car explode in flames. Moreover, it appears that Ford executives had run tests showing that the Pinto could not sustain a rear-end collision at speeds as low as twenty-one miles per hour, and as early as January 15, 1971, they knew that the defect could be corrected by lining each gas tank with a rubber bladder. However, this would cost more than $135 million in total. The prospective cost of not fixing the defect (paying damages assessed in lawsuits launched by relatives of the dead and injured) was deemed unlikely to top $50 million. The corporate memo uncovered by an investigative journalist is reproduced below.

BENEFITS

Savings: 180 burn deaths, 180 serious burn injuries,
2100 burned vehicles.
Unit Cost: $200,000 per death, $67,000 per injury,
$700 per vehicle
Total Benefit: (180 x $200,000) + (180 x $67,000) +
(2100 x 700) = $49.5 million

COSTS

Sales: 11 million cars, 1.5 million light trucks
Unit Cost: $11. per car, $11. per truck
Total Cost: (11,000,000 x $11) + (1,500,000 x $11)
= $137 million

Source: Cullen et al., 1987:162.

The result is that some 500 to 900 people lost their lives and thousands of others suffered debilitating and painful burn injuries before the Ford Motor Company, in May 1978, finally recalled 1.5 million 1971–76 Pintos and 1975–76 Mercury Bobcats (Cullen et al., 1987:160–69; Dowie, 1987:13–29).

This gruesome example illustrates the importance of the organizational environment as a causal factor. It underlines the role that strong regulatory sanctions, or in this case their absence, can play in motivating or impeding corporate crime. If the Ford Motor Company had been forced to calculate the results of its negligence—if it knew, for example, that rather than facing a few thousand civil suits by angry consumers with no access to evidence to prove Ford's negligence or complicity, it was likely to face criminal charges and strict regulatory sanctions that would multiply the costs of not fixing the defect by another $100 million—its internal calculations would have been very different. It would then have been more cost efficient to install the rubber bladder and make the gas tank safe. As it happened, Ford's initial calculations went hideously wrong. Largely as a result of Mark Dowie's investigative journalism, which brought the damning memo reproduced above to light, Ford was actually indicted in Indiana for the murder of three young girls who perished in flames on August 10, 1978, when their Pinto was struck from behind. This celebrated case ended with a not-guilty verdict, but did untold public relations damage to Ford nevertheless (Cullen et al., 1987). Similarly, if Ford—or any corporation in the same situation—knew that the chances of getting caught were high (rather than very low, as they actually are), this and similar offences might have been prevented, because under such circumstances a cost-benefit analysis would indicate the offence was not likely to be profitable.

In reality, however, the weaknesses of the regulatory agencies responsible for discovering and sanctioning corporate crime make corporate criminality extremely profitable. While the role of regulatory agencies will be examined in detail in Chapter 5, it is important to note here that regulatory weakness is itself a direct cause of corporate crime. The rewards of lawbreaking in dollar terms are accurately perceived by corporations as very much higher than the combined deterrent effects of the weak sanctions that are likely to be assessed. Furthermore, the odds are high that offences will never be discovered in the first place, because agencies are so dramatically understaffed that they are lucky to investigate 1 percent of target companies in a given year (Calavita, 1983; Coleman, 1989). Inadequate enforcement, then, causes corporate crime because it means such crimes pay, and they pay very well. In fact, even the maximum fines on the books, if assessed, would in most cases represent a minuscule percentage of profits reaped from the offence. In this sense, lawbreaking is rational corporate behaviour, a key part of profit maximization that is itself (as we have seen) the raison d'être of business.

MACRO-LEVEL FACTORS

Macro-level factors refer to social and cultural value systems that encourage and support white-collar crime. Such factors are common in Western capitalist democracies, which accounts for the normal, nonpathological personalities of offenders. Capitalism itself, with its emphasis on maximizing profit and minimizing cost and its insistence that the human costs of production are not important, is criminogenic. Once again it must be stressed that this does not mean that corporate crime is unique to capitalism: feudalism and socialism have distinctive, albeit different, criminogenic features; organizational crime occurs in communist countries; and indeed in nonprofit corporations as well.

Data about organizational crime under socialist systems are hard to come by, and not directly comparable with Western statistics because of the huge differences in the underlying relations of power between state and corporation that prevail in each setting. These factors affect whether or not offences are discovered or, indeed, labelled illegal in the first place. Nevertheless, one would expect that certain offences, such as price fixing and predatory pricing, would be rare because they presuppose the existence of competition and a free market. Crimes against the environment or infringements on workers' health and safety, on the other hand, offences that require countervailing pressure groups such as unions or opposition parties and an active media to alert the public, might well be common. (Preliminary evidence from Eastern Europe indicates such offences were indeed widespread.) Rates would undoubtedly differ greatly between socialist nations. However, much more information is needed before any generalizations can be made.

It is also the case that other characteristics of industrialized societies—the dominance of large-scale organizations, extensive divisions of labour, high levels of population mobility, and bureaucratization—may also be criminogenic. These factors tend to break down intense interpersonal ties (negative as well as positive) that characterized traditional communities; they also prevent the high levels of interpersonal scrutiny on which traditional social control depended. Prevailing low levels of what we now call privacy meant there were fewer opportunities to escape surveillance and therefore to indulge in deviant acts; a situation most unlike that which prevails today, even with advanced technology facilitating surveillance in many settings.

Nevertheless, capitalism does have distinctive criminogenic features, because of its dependence on commodity production. This system has a tendency to transform everything—people, labour, products—into commodities, useful mainly for their potential to be exchanged for other commodities. The value of every "thing" depends not on its intrinsic worth, but on what it can be exchanged for. A beautiful painting, for example, is valuable not for itself or for the aesthetic pleasure it provides, but for the prestige that owning it brings, and its potential to be sold for money. Money, of course, is the quintessential commodity because it is useless in and of itself; it will not feed or clothe or shelter anyone. Its sole value is in exchange. Similarly, labour, which does have intrinsic value, is valued not for its potential to facilitate the survival, comfort, and happiness of people, but because it can be sold for money. Labourers, therefore, are not valuable because they are unique individuals or because they have souls to be redeemed (as in earlier eras), but as instrumental means to a productive end, tools that suit a particular industrial purpose. Those who use the products of labour are not people with needs, but consumers—an evocative word, signifying individuals who can be manipulated, persuaded, and cajoled to buy. Thus, a mindset develops that encourages levels of impersonality and irresponsibility conducive to corporate criminality.

The problem is not that the people who own, run, and manage business organizations are bad, immoral, or dishonest. A few undoubtedly are, but no more than would be found in any occupational group at any social level; and many are responsible, caring, and deeply ethical people by the terms of this social order. Criminogenic tendencies do not originate at the individual level; they are rooted in the structure of capitalism, which is why they are *tendencies* rather than predetermined, immutable rules. The system of exchange described above is related to the capitalist mode of production, where employers hire labourers whose purpose is to produce goods as quickly and cheaply as possible, which the employer can then sell for profit. This enables the employer to get more out of the exchange than he or she originally put into it; that is, by paying workers less than the value of the work they produce, and thereby realizing a profit, the employer benefits.

The capitalist system, then, rests upon a relationship between employer and employee that is at its base exploitative. The one group uses the other to make a profit. The word exploitative here is not a value judgment; workers may believe they are receiving fair rewards for their labour. Indeed, the responsibilities and risks undertaken by those who put their money at risk may be seen as "entitling" them to profits. But the basis of the bargain, and the foundation of capitalism, is an unequal exchange where one party benefits from using the other (and presumably the entire social order benefits in turn). The force that promotes growth under capitalism is the ability to extract more surplus value than one's competitors. This is what becoming more "efficient" means. Companies, under pressure to realize ever higher rates of return, naturally view their plants and personnel as physical and human capital, and seek to maximize the productivity of both (Marx, 1973). Should they fail to do so, they face bankruptcy or takeovers by competitors who are more efficient, perhaps because they are more ruthless.

This means that capitalist systems encourage a level of impersonality and ruthlessness that is conducive to both corporate and occupational crime (and, for that matter, to traditional offences as well). We saw how this relates to individual motivation, through the virulent "culture of competitiveness" (Coleman 1989:204–10), in the first section of this chapter. The worship of success and stigmatization of failure produces a social stratification where everyone, however ill-equipped for the struggle, enters an unforgiving race from birth on, for the prizes of prestige, ego gratification, power, and material rewards. Women are now pushed by economic pressures and liberal feminist philosophies to seek the same goals as men. Those people who cannot make it to the finish line (the great majority) experience degrees of material and psychological deprivation that vary according to reference group, age, sex, occupation, and class. Businessmen and women are likely to feel these pressures more than most, as it is necessary for them both to *be* successful, rich, and powerful, and to *appear* this way. Because the culture of competitiveness instills insecurity, one can never stop competing. There are always new goals to reach, new territories to be conquered. One is never "there."

Such an ethos is directly related to the structure of capitalism, since the extraction of surplus value (profit), necessary for expansion, technological development, research, and wage increases, fuels the entire economic system. It also influences every part of the society—socialization patterns, religion, education, the mass media, and the criminal justice system. This is not to say that economic forces determine the content and nature of other institutions in any simple or direct fashion. They interact with many other factors, and the shape of any particular policy struggle reflects the outcome of a series of ongoing struggles among various groups within each nation-state, with a history fashioned over decades or even centuries. As Pearce has phrased it: "How the state operates ... is not determined in advance by the needs of capital but depends upon the struggles engaged in by different groups upon its terrain and, indeed, in constituting its terrain" (Pearce, 1991:6).

Nevertheless, religion, education, politics, and the family have all undergone changes that reflect the influence of competitiveness, individualism, and consumerism. None of these institutions has survived unscathed (though some would argue the changes are on balance positive ones), and all are vastly different than in pre-capitalist, pre-industrial eras. Such forces create a climate in which widespread white-collar crime is inevitable. However, they are also responsible, in large part, for the high standard of living citizens in capitalist democracies enjoy. The resulting moral equation, then, is complex and contradictory. The most efficient way yet devised to produce large numbers of consumer goods that a fair proportion of the population can afford also produces people and organizations with strong reasons for breaking the law and harming fellow citizens.

SUMMARY

This chapter has examined the causes of corporate crime in capitalist societies at the social-psychological, organizational, and macro levels. It has become clear that both corporate and occupational crime are deeply rooted in the social relations of capitalism, although they can and do occur in other economic and social systems. The factors that create and encourage organizations and individuals to seek goal maximization without worrying too much about legality were outlined in some detail. Both formal levels of social control (law and regulatory systems) and informal levels (subcultures that sanction by disapproval or ostracism) were found to be weak for corporate offences. Because of this, white-collar crime is widespread and likely to remain so. The next chapter will examine the struggle, on the ideological and legal/institutional levels, to establish controls against corporate criminality.

The Struggle to Secure Legal Regulation

INTRODUCTION

The history of laws defining and regulating crimes of business is one of fierce struggle. The business class resisted the notion that any of its profit-seeking activities could be immoral or criminal; it also balked at the principle of government overseeing business practices through law.

One of the most dramatic results of the Industrial Revolution has been the expansion of social control. In every part of the social order, every activity from labouring to playing has been "rationalized"; that is, broken down into its smallest components and analyzed, scrutinized, and regulated (Foucault, 1979). This development was spurred in the first instance by the bourgeoisie's fear of the so-called dangerous classes. In eras when mob riots were not infrequent, state-funded police unknown, and large sections of urban areas "out of bounds" after dark, the propertied classes began to worry about their ability to maintain social order and control crime. Efforts to find more effective means of inducing conformity led to the abandonment of control by terror tactics of the 18th century, where public torture and capital punishment were prescribed (if not always implemented) for every offence from the servant-girl's theft of leftover food to highway robbery. In their place came the workhouse and later the penitentiary, institutions designed to hold people and change their behaviour. This emphasis on changing and controlling people's minds rather than punishing their bodies, the switch from revenge to redemption and rehabilitation, was revolutionary in every sense of the word.

Allied movements arose in the workplace, with the aim of transforming a rural peasantry into an efficient proletariat, a disciplined working class that could be relied upon to show up every day and commit both mind and body to industrial production (Thompson, 1963, 1975). This larger problem—how to create a disciplined workforce out of pre-industrial peoples—has been confronted whenever industrial development and capitalism have occurred. In every country industrial elites, in collaboration with political authorities, have resorted to tactics ranging from penalties (head taxes and coerced labour) to incentives (rewards for low absenteeism and bonuses for consecutive days of service) to persuade people to engage in the arduous, disciplined, and often dangerous labour industrial production demands (Melossi, 1980). Typically both carrot and stick have been employed. We forget too easily that the capitalist/industrial mode of production requires a way of thinking and acting and being that was entirely foreign to the land-based peasantry in 18th-century Europe; moreover, it is a largely unattractive alternative for tribal peoples accustomed to lives dominated by custom, the seasons, and the land.

Gradually, however, modes of social control and concomitant habits of mental discipline spread throughout industrialized societies and rose up the social order. No class today is entirely free from scrutiny or surveillance in the workplace or private sphere; nor does any escape cultural demands for social discipline, uniformity, predictability, and accountability in patterns of thought and action. As employees, consumers, patients, professionals, and taxpayers, individuals are the beneficiaries (or victims) of elaborate, carefully studied techniques of socialization designed to produce internalized control mechanisms. This is supplemented and reinforced at every stage by institutions (such as schools) and external forces (such as law) that reward certain behaviours and discourage spontaneous, undisciplined, or unpredictable ones. Everything from leisure patterns to driving habits has come under the aegis of this new mode, one made possible by technological innovation, universal education, and the rise of professions that specialize in bringing rationality and predictability to whatever corner of human behaviour their specialty is designed to regulate (Smart, 1989). The external, formal face of social control, expressed through legal systems, is the component that concerns us here.

Every developed country has seen a proliferation of new laws, and a massive increase in the number of professionals (such as lawyers, barristers, judges, advisers, and counsellors) who make a living by interpreting law and providing advice to interested parties. The vast majority of laws on the books today were unheard of 100 years ago. Offences punishable by criminal law in England before the Industrial Revolution were limited to a few acts specifically defined as theft, plus murder and treason.

Offences against morality (predominantly sexual behaviours) were found in church law, along with meticulous restrictions prohibiting deeds and even thoughts defined by the church as sinful or heretical. Laws against "substance abuse" (heroin, alcohol, marijuana) were unheard of, and inebriation was socially acceptable over a wide range of classes (Denzin, 1978). Drunkenness became increasingly common following the discovery of distillation, which allowed potent alcohol brews (predominantly gin) to supplement the traditional beers of England and Germany, and the wines of France and Italy. An entire range of laws were not in existence because the technologies they govern had not yet been invented; traffic offences, computer crime, or aircraft hijacking are obvious examples.

Personal expressions of anger were virtually unregulated unless they led to death (and even then, laws were class biased and only enforced against selected populations at particular historical periods and in specific places). There were no laws against wife or child "abuse." Women and children were the property of the male "head of the house," and men did much as they wished in the household, subject only to religious strictures and informal community standards of acceptable behaviour. High levels of interpersonal "violence" (as we would now call it) and other "undisciplined" or licentious behaviours do not appear to have been prohibited or even disapproved. Interpersonal conflicts were usually seen as private matters best settled by the families, clans, or communities involved.

At some periods and in some areas there were laws that do not exist today, such as bans on usury (the payment of interest on borrowed funds), or trade restraints (prohibiting competition between tradespeople, for example). There were also vagrancy statutes, laws forbidding certain peoples from leaving their home parishes or counties to seek work (and therefore, it was hoped, preventing rootless desperate people from becoming either crime or charity problems to a new community) (Rothman, 1971, 1980). Overall, however, the number of laws was minuscule compared to modern times, and more importantly, even these were only sporadically enforced. The public spectacles of torture and the draconian nature of the penalties were supposed to control by example, through fear, so only a few such spectacles were believed necessary to have the desired deterrent effect (Foucault, 1979). Efficient social control as we know it today was simply impossible. The machinery of surveillance and detection, the basic technologies, did not exist; effective social control was largely a product of small, close-knit, stratified communities where everyone was able to monitor the behaviour of everyone else. When this system began to break down under the pressures of industrialization and mobility, there were few alternatives available. No federal salaried agents dedicated to law enforcement were in existence until 1829, when the first police force was formed in England. Moreover, record-keeping and communication between parishes even a few miles apart was rudimentary; it was nonexistent over larger distances and spheres.

Laws against corporate crime, not surprisingly, are one of the most recent categories of offence. Most are less than 100 years old; indeed, the majority have been passed in the period since the end of World War II. In this chapter the history of particular laws, specifically those regulating the quality of food, the nature of the workplace, and the shape of the marketplace, will be examined. The aim is to understand the long and arduous struggle, a struggle that continues to this day, to regulate, criminalize, and ultimately control the acquisitive acts of privileged classes.

HISTORY OF ATTEMPTS TO CONTROL CORPORATE CRIME

Conflict and resistance accompany the passage of just about every law, provided the people who will be affected know about its impending passage. Whether or not resistance is visible and overt, however, or invisible (to ruling classes and the state) and covert, depends largely on the power of the parties in question. Thus, it has only recently become obvious, thanks to the labour of historians who painstakingly pieced together fragments of information from many sources, that the English working classes of the 18th and 19th centuries were diametrically opposed to the passage of laws that took away their access to deer and other game, disallowed their traditional rights to pasturage on common lands or to "glean" crops left on the lord's land after harvest, and to the establishment of a central police force (Thompson, 1963; Hay, Linebaugh, Thompson, and Winslow, 1975; Phillips, 1977). However, their unhappiness was generally unknown and unremarked at the time. Since rural peasants and the emerging proletariat were not allowed to vote and were generally illiterate, the only way their resistance could be registered was through riots and rebellions; lesser measures were unlikely to merit a passing glance from the ruling classes. However, the combined weight of traditions and laws requiring conformity to the existing order, along with the long odds against success and the stiff punishments for disobedience, made rioting a very last resort indeed. The balance of power was so unequal that, after the uprising was put down and the rioters tried and hanged, the episode was likely to be interpreted in the discourse of criminality rather than that of political protest (Thompson, 1975; Hay, Linebaugh, Thompson, and Winslow, 1975). Revoking or suspending the offensive legal changes was, to say the least, uncommon.

Today, universal suffrage has given every adult the vote, and this, along with near-universal literacy, mass means of communication, and new organizing techniques, has greatly increased the power of the lower and working classes. It is now possible, though not common, for protest and resistance from below to change government policy. The 180-degree shift of the Mulroney Conservative government in May 1985, when it reinstituted full indexing for old age pensions (which the budget had previously removed), and the 1990 defeat of the Meech Lake Accord provide recent illustrations demonstrating that the monolithic capitalist state is neither monolithic nor impenetrable. The working and lower middle classes have become more visible over the last 100 years and can exert real influence when allied with dissident factions from other classes. Thus, we hear now a good deal about popular resistance to the Goods and Services Tax (GST) or the Canada–U.S. Free Trade Agreement, price supports for farmers, and the need for stronger laws against drinking drivers or rapists. Feminist groups have been particularly successful in forcing particular nation-states to change public policy by passing laws against the sexual abuse of children or wife battering: a striking example of such success is the inclusion of women in the equality provisions of the Canadian Charter of Rights and Freedoms. These controversies all exemplify attempts by people and groups outside the structure of the government to influence the content and passage of laws.

However, these successes must not be overstated. While groups outside the dominant consensus have occasionally succeeded in influencing the state on issues of manners and morals, securing laws that constrain the activities of powerful organizations and dominant classes has been much more difficult. Here the resistance from economic vested interests is palpable, because laws against corporate crime, symbolically and sometimes in practice, challenge the dominance and threaten the interests of corporate elites and the organizations they control, organizations that have made them rich beyond measure. Moreover, getting laws passed was made more difficult by the fact that the people who owned and controlled the corporations often controlled the state and the machinery of law passage and enforcement as well (Clement, 1975; Palmer, 1983). Furthermore, when they were not the same people, the political elite almost always came from the same class background as the corporate elite. Even today there are few senior politicians who rose from working-class roots and retain a working-class perspective

(Clement, 1975), and there were fewer still in the 19th- and early-20th-century parliaments when the struggles to criminalize corporate excesses began (Smandych, 1991). Elected politicians usually shared the same values, belonged to the same clubs, and even intermarried with corporate elites. Their experience with and sympathy for the working class was limited by their backgrounds, and by the fact that they usually accepted dominant ideologies of the time, which saw capitalism as the engine of prosperity and the invisible hand of the marketplace as an "objective" mechanism that could not be tampered with. Moreover, businessmen (and they were all men at this time) were not meant to be criminalized; they were still very much lionized as nation-builders (Yeager, 1991; Bliss, 1974).

Thus, when working- and middle-class groups began to complain about abuses by the corporate elite in the late 19th century (and began to be heard, because they now had means of protest at their disposal), those who ran the machinery of government were in a quandary. Their general policy had been to ignore the predatory acts of business and to focus instead on the crimes, licentiousness, and lawlessness of powerless groups. The alleged abuse of opium or marijuana by "inferior races" and the sexual degradation this produced, the ignorant youths, especially immigrants and natives, running wild on the streets, and the weak-minded and genetically inferior offspring created by immorality and rampant overbreeding among the lower classes were all popular moral crusades at the time. However, a combination of events eventually forced political elites, in North America and elsewhere, to reconsider.

First and most important of these were the series of crises, accidents, swindles, and frauds that caused much loss of life and property. Among the earliest regulatory laws were the Passenger Acts, which prescribed minimum standards of sanitation and space for companies in the British Isles in the business of transporting people from one place to another. The genesis of these laws lay in the deplorable conditions those travelling to the far-flung reaches of the British Empire were originally forced to endure. In the absence of regulation, shipowners, adhering strictly to the principles of profit maximization, paid little attention to the health or safety of their clientele, particularly those at the bottom of the fee structure in steerage. As many customers as possible were crammed into each ship, insufficient food was provided, sanitation was minimal, rats overran both cargo and passenger areas (if the two were differentiated), resulting in frequent epidemics, and endemic dehydration and scurvy. Such conditions endangered the rich in first-class compartments as well as the poor in the holds, since both were susceptible to drowning if the ship sank or to disease if it did not. In consequence, large numbers of people never arrived at their destinations (Macdonagh, 1961). Moreover, colonial authorities and prospective employees in the New World, who needed settlers who were alive and healthy to populate the country and reproduce, began to complain.

Similarly, the conditions of the English working class in the 19th century were so bad that they threatened the very survival of the capitalist system. As documented by Marx and Engels, men, women, and children laboured from dawn to dusk in unheated, unventilated, and unlit factories that were both unhealthy (bad air, fumes, no leisure or exercise time), and dangerous, for industrial machinery frequently lacked safety switches or guards, and frequently amputated limbs. Those who survived such conditions emerged broken and diseased. Life outside the factory gate was little better, because the new industrial cities suffered from polluted air (caused largely by the widespread use of coal as a heat and energy source), unclean water, and contaminated food (Marcus, 1974). There were no safe, efficient systems to transport food from country to city or to preserve it for long periods of time. Adequate sewage and waste disposal systems were not yet available. This produced an unhealthy, unmotivated, and unstable workforce who were ultimately unproductive. Moreover, having the majority of the population living in such conditions was politically dangerous for the upper classes because of the omnipresent risk of rebellion. It also put them physically in peril because, in the absence of penicillin and antibiotics, such conditions spawned epidemics that claimed the lives of the privileged as well as the underprivileged (although the latter died at much higher rates than the former) (Marcus, 1974).

Thus, by the end of the 19th century, it was becoming apparent to enlightened members of the privileged classes that certain kinds of reforms were in their interest. On top of this, protest and pressure from other segments of the population was increasing, as knowledge of working-class conditions grew. Compassion for the suffering of the labouring classes was awakened among the intelligentsia by novelists and playwrights such as Charles Dickens and later George Bernard Shaw; some members of the clergy, liberal politicians, and the nascent feminist movement were all calling for various reforms. This finally produced legislative change. A series of factory laws were passed in Britain between 1819 and 1853 that provided limited protection for workers. They limited the length of the workday, eliminated child labour, and made rudimentary provisions for ventilation systems and meal breaks (Carson, 1980a, 1980b; Hutchins and Harrison, 1962). Other laws forced the new industrial cities to engage in public works to provide safe drinking water, clean up the air, and provide facilities for sanitary waste disposal (Lambert, 1963; Yeager, 1991). Laws regulating the safety of foodstuffs and drugs that could be offered on the marketplace were also passed during this period.

None of these improvements came easily; nor did they result from the high ethical standards or tender consciences of the business sector. Historically, the state had to be forced to move against business interests. Let us look, for example, at the struggle to regulate the quality of food (Paulus, 1974, 1978). Despite the fact that adulterated food and drug products were regularly offered for sale on the English marketplace in the 19th century, and regularly resulted in injuries and deaths, resistance to legislation was fierce. The first laws, passed in 1851, required only that the names of those whose wares were found to be adulterated be published. Since most of the population at risk was illiterate, and methods of mass communication were still rudimentary, the putative power of publicity was not a massive deterrent and conditions did not improve. In 1855 a parliamentary inquiry into abuses in the manufacture and sale of food and drugs was launched, and testimony on the damage such products had caused was produced. In 1857 a bill was drafted by a private member that provided punishment for negligent manufacturers without requiring the prosecution to prove intent (since this had proved a major impediment to securing convictions; it was in practice impossible to demonstrate intention in court at a level that would satisfy a judge). The measure was so hotly contested that it was never even debated.

Then, in 1858, 200 people were poisoned and seventeen died from eating adulterated lozenges. This crisis finally forced the British government to act and resulted, in 1860, in the Food and Drink Act. The act allowed a public analyst's certificate testifying that a product was contaminated to be used as *prima facie* evidence for conviction, thus getting around the need to prove intent and setting the stage for effective enforcement. However, the act provided no officials to conduct investigations; individual citizens had to take the initiative, pay the fees, and conduct their own prosecutions. Moreover, local (as opposed to national) authorities had to be persuaded to lay a summons in the first place, an act that required them to excite the enmity of the manufacturer, who was almost always an influential and highly respected person with whom the putative enforcer shared class membership, common financial interests, and often kinship ties. This system, then, still had its drawbacks. Moreover, the prosecution still had to prove culpability, even though the standards for establishing liability were now weaker.

The results were predictable—no convictions were registered between 1860 and 1872. However, continuing pressure led to further changes, and in 1872 public inspectors were provided, and local authorities were required to appoint analysts. In 1875 the necessity of proving intent was totally removed and adulteration became a "strict liability" offence, whereby proof of contamination constituted sufficient evidence for conviction. By this time, the government agents responsible for enforcement had developed into a group with vested interests of their own, a stake in effective control, and their own ties to powerful politicians. By the end of the century, even the business community had come to see these laws as beneficial to their long-range interests, since allowing companies to produce products that poison the potential market is not notably good for business (Paulus, 1974, 1978).

Thus, it took a series of deaths, injuries, accidents, and investigations before meaningful laws governing the manufacture of food were secured. Before this could happen a whole set of beliefs had to be contested. It was argued, for example, that businessmen were not criminals, and their activities were intrinsically "good" for society. Corporations were seen as private property; therefore, whatever took place inside them was the business of the owner alone, whatever the cost to employees, the community, or the environment. Those arguing against the regulation of working conditions frequently maintained that workers were there of their own free will; if they didn't like the conditions, they could leave (Bliss, 1974; Carson, 1970). This was errant nonsense, of course, for workers' "free choice" amounted to taking whatever job they were lucky enough to secure or facing starvation. In an era without welfare, unemployment insurance, medicare, or workers' compensation, with access to rural land or game restricted to landowners, theft or vagrancy were the only alternative means of subsistence, should starvation not appeal.

A similar picture emerges from Carson's review of the history of British laws on the factory from 1819 to 1853 (Carson, 1970, 1980a). He looks at the struggle to attain laws to limit the length of the working day, limit the hours women and children were employed, stipulate the number of breaks, and legislate a minimum wage. Initial resistance from business was massive, as the need for cheap labour in this stage of laissez-faire capitalism was intense. Business owners felt pressured to make ever higher returns on their investment, which meant that overworking their human capital was an economically rational thing for them to do. Regulations were also resisted because they interposed the power of the state (still rudimentary at that stage) between the worker and the factory owner, and set the stage for outsiders to monitor and question the "private" pact between the owner and "his" workforce. Regulations also made careful record-keeping a necessity, which further raised the owner's costs. However, it was ultimately recognized by some that state action was necessary to break the vicious cycle of competitiveness, for only by forcing all employers to provide healthier working conditions would it be possible for any to do this without sacrificing their relative economic position.

A similar process has been traced in North America. The rise of gigantic trusts in the United States following the Civil War ushered in the era of the "robber-barons," men who built up fabulous fortunes and gigantic business empires through business genius combined with the judicious use of fraud, theft, bribery, corruption, and sometimes even murder. Around the beginning of the 20th century, a series of exposés were published by the newly popular mass magazines and newspapers. The stories documented, in careful and readable prose, the role of the Standard Oil Company in corrupting the Pennsylvania legislature, the purchase of the entire legislature of Montana in 1899 by two copper companies and their subsequent attempts to bribe the Montana Supreme Court, and the hiring of thugs and killers by major corporations to "discourage" union organizers (Weinberg and Weinberg, 1961). Upton Sinclair's *The Jungle*, originally published in 1906 and typical of this publishing genre, documented in meticulous detail the conditions that employees in meat-packing companies were forced to endure as well as cost-cutting practices the industry employed, which involved using diseased carcasses and putting everything from rodent droppings to sawdust into packaged meats. Predictably, the largely middle-class readers reacted first and foremost to the news that they were being sold unsafe meat products, not to the inhuman working conditions. However, such exposés served an important ideological function by alerting the middle classes to the social costs of capitalism and publicizing the antisocial acts of the capitalist class which had hitherto been regarded an unalloyed benefactor to mankind.

In Canada, where the ties between the corporate sector and the state have traditionally been even stronger than in the United States, the struggle for regulation has been lengthy and bitter. The corporate elite here shared with the nation-state a common interest in the establishment of a strong British presence on the northern half of the continent, and in the protection of both the British and French heritages from powerful American influence, and equally powerful American competition. As Laxer has commented: "The CPR and the Conservative government of Sir John A. Macdonald were so close that it was once observed at the time that 'the day the CPR goes bust, the Conservative party goes bust the day after'" (Laxer, 1973:32). He notes:

It was the financial capitalists with their money in railways, grain elevators and merchandising who dominated Canadian policy during the period. The Canadian State was their state and it served them well in subsidizing the CPR and in using the powers of the federal government to protect and promote the trading system. (Laxer, 1973:31)

Moreover, Canada has historically been ruled by its elites to a greater extent than the Americans, who were, in the early 20th century, substantially more democratic and liberal in ideology and politics than Canadians.

In fact there is evidence that the corporate sector in Canada has exercised direct control over the nature and content of laws that affected its interests. We are not alone in this, as Kolko (1962, 1969) and Domhoff (1967, 1970) have documented in areas as diverse as meat packing, railways, child labour, and minimum wage provisions; but a particularly cozy flavour characterizes the relations here. As Bliss has pointed out, "manufacturers did not oppose factory legislation, having realized from the beginning ... that ... it would be both inevitable and useful as the regulator and balance wheel of the industrial system" (Bliss, 1974:67). In another segment of the economy, "the regular breakdown of voluntary agreements led businessmen to ask for government intervention in the form of early closing by-laws which would restrict hours of business at the request of a certain percentage of merchants in a given trade" (Bliss, 1974:37). Similarly, in yet another sphere, Bliss notes:

Pressure from urban Boards of Trade led to the establishment of the Royal Commission on Railways in 1886 at which many Manitoba and Ontario shippers called for a railway commission to regulate the systems; when the Canadian Board of Railway Commissioners was finally established in 1902 the Canadian Manufacturers' Association proudly took credit for leading the movement on behalf of government intervention. (Bliss, 1974:41).

The benefits of such regulation for business, given a compliant political elite and nation-state, are many. First, regulations may be in the direct interests of business. The need to protect trade, not concern for human health, led to the passage of the first laws against water pollution in the United States, because the swill of industrial wastes and human wastes was threatening to block up certain rivers, essential commercial passageways in the era before automobiles (Yeager, 1991:54). Second, regulation may be necessary to control competitors and stabilize the market. Because regulations increase the cost of doing business, smaller and weaker concerns may be driven out of business, since a generous profit margin or capital cushion is necessary to absorb the higher costs unless these can be passed on directly to customers (which is not the case in competitive industries). Third, regulation may improve the quality of a product (as with meat packing after Sinclair's exposé), potentially increasing public demand for it and expanding the market. Fourth, it allows firms to escape the more drastic consequences of the ethic of competition. For example, firms that did not want to employ child labour or subject workers to dangerous conditions had no real options in a highly competitive unregulated market, because more ruthless rivals would drive them out of business. However, if all firms were forced by government fiat to behave ethically, not hire children, or provide safe environments, manufacturers would be able to be socially responsible without suffering economically. An exact parallel exists today in the passage of environmental legislation, albeit on an international scale. For example, the European Common Market will not impose a new energy tax to combat global warming unless the United States and Japan do the same, lest their industries be put at a competitive disadvantage (*The Globe and Mail*, Monday, June 1, 1992: A6).

On a different level of analysis, regulations can serve valuable functions for the business sector by staving off more basic demands for change. Getting regulatory laws passed may pacify labour unions and other critics, while interfering with company business, procedures, or profits to a minimal degree. They can be written to appear tough, for example, when both industry and government insiders know they will be unenforceable in real life. However, the business class did not easily acquire more long-term and sanguine views of regulation; the first and most sustained response was one of unremitting opposition. The struggle to force companies to compete freely in the Canadian marketplace illustrates all of these processes.

COMBINES LAW IN CANADA

Laws to facilitate competitive behaviour—the Combines Investigation Act in Canada in 1889, and the Sherman Act in the United States in 1890—were among the earliest regulations passed by federal states in North America. Many of these were written in close collaboration with the corporate elite they were meant to restrain. The Combines Investigation Act is a case in point. In the mid-1880s, a group of wholesale grocers agreed to monopolize the supply of certain commodities, particularly sugar, to corner the market and make higher profits. This strategy, perfectly legal at the time, annoyed two competing businessmen who were excluded from the combine. Their complaint to the federal government resulted in the formation of a select committee of the House of Commons to investigate the charges. The committee, in turn, recommended laws that would make it illegal to conspire to lessen competition or enhance prices. This recommendation led to the passage of the Combines Investigation Act in 1889 (Snider, 1977; Stanbury, 1977; Goff and Reasons, 1978; Bliss, 1974).

The act as it was first written, however, made it a misdemeanour to *unlawfully* conspire to lessen competition *unduly*, or to *unreasonably* enhance prices. These three qualifiers, whether there by accident or design, rendered the Act unenforceable. The initiator of the legislation, a Member of Parliament named Clarke Wallace, tried unsuccessfully in 1890 and again in 1891 to get the "unduly" and "unreasonably" deleted; a Senator Read tried again in 1894; and a Liberal MP by the name of Sproule argued for changes in 1896 and 1898. Sproule finally succeeded in 1899, but a year later both of the qualifiers were put back in. Finally, the Senate was persuaded to delete the "unlawfully" clause, and in 1900, a mere eleven years after its original passage, the law was actually made enforceable. This does not mean, however, that a flurry of enforcement activity followed. Between 1900 and 1910, an era marked by trusts and combines, there were nine prosecutions launched, resulting in a total of seven convictions. As Bliss has said:

> Outrage at the price-fixing arrangements entered into ... was a major cause of Canada's first investigation of combinations in restraint of trade.... Neither the investigation nor the ensuing anti-combines legislation ... had the slightest effect on the Wholesale Grocers' Guild's price-fixing arrangements. Old agreements stayed in effect; new agreements on woodenware, rice, starch, and molasses were reached in 1890 and 1891.... The only change ... was that the press was no longer supplied with the details ... although the trade press still had inside information. (Bliss, 1974:34 and 39)

Meanwhile, mergers were becoming increasingly problematic, as small firms continued to be gobbled up at an alarming pace. Between 1900 and 1910, seventy-two mergers were recorded, most involving elite firms taking over smaller ones to reduce competition (Weldon, 1966:233; Stanbury, 1977). In 1910 William Lyon Mackenzie King, then Minister of Labour under whose auspices the Combines Act fell and under heavy pressure from consumers and farmers' groups, responded by forbidding certain competition-reducing mergers and monopolies through the Combines Investigation Act. Wheat farmers in the West, in particular, resented being forced to sell their product cheaply on the open market, but buy their machinery, seed, and foodstuffs from a cabal of eastern businessmen who had banished competition on the retail side. At the same time, King set up an elaborate process to initiate investigations. The act stipulated that any six Canadian citizens could lay complaints by applying to a provincial judge for an investigation. If the complaint was deemed worthy, a board of three commissioners would be appointed by the Ministry of Labour to investigate the charges, and the results of the investigation would be published in the *Gazette* (a federal news sheet). Offenders were expected to cease their illegal behaviours ten days after publication. There were no formal sanctions; as with the 1851 English food and drink laws, publicity alone was deemed both punishment and deterrent. This has led some to conclude that King "had no serious intentions about mergers" (Phillips, 1964:80). Indeed, from 1910 to 1919 (a time when the Canadian government relied heavily on the cooperation of the business sector for the war effort), only one investigation was completed.

After World War I, however, a recession combined with working-class pressure led to the establishment of a permanent tribunal of investigation and prosecution, set up in 1919. This would have allowed the government to enforce the act meaningfully for the first time since its inception. However, the act was immediately challenged by business, declared by the judiciary to infringe on provincial spheres of authority as set out in the British North America Act of 1867, and declared *ultra vires* in 1921. In 1923 the act was reintroduced, this time with a more elaborate separation of civil and criminal powers. A registrar would recommend charges to the Minister of Labour; if the latter deemed a formal investigation necessary, either the registrar or an appointed commissioner would undertake it. The onus of prosecuting was still on the provincial attorneys general, but the wording of the act was widened to allow more successful prosecutions. It was not until 1935, when Canada was buried in the worst depression ever to hit the country, that the government bowed to pressure and widened the act to prohibit predatory pricing, discriminatory discounts, and retail price discrimination.

However, once again the powerful business community challenged the government in court, and once again it was successful: these new powers were also declared *ultra vires*. The seesaw battles continued, with a weak act and little enforcement activity, until a new crisis arose in 1951–52. At this time, the commissioner responsible for the act resigned in protest when the government refused to prosecute flour milling companies for a blatant price-fixing scheme that had been in place since 1936. With pressure from the Co-operative Commonwealth Federation (CCF; precursor of the New Democratic Party) and elsewhere, the government was forced to appoint the MacQuarrie Committee to investigate the state of business in Canada. The committee's recommendations led to the creation of a body with powers to investigate and recommend sanctions against price fixing and other acts that restricted competition or defrauded competitors, customers, or consumers. Although the act has been tinkered with and altered many times since, this set the stage for the post–World War II era. It was not until the 1980s, when the political pendulum swung wildly back to the business side, that the act was totally overhauled once again (as discussed below) (Snider, 1977:239–43; Canada, 1989:5–23).

To sum up, then, every time the Canadian government moved to make regulations effective and tighten control over the anticompetitive or fraudulent behaviours of business, it was flooded with submissions, oppositional briefs, and court challenges. Usually it responded to business pressure by amending the act, watering down key reforms, or eliminating sections that business found offensive. Sometimes it went so far as to fire the minister who had introduced the changes in the House of Commons. Other times, it set up a royal commission or a judicial or parliamentary inquiry to investigate (and further delay) much-needed reforms. However, changes in the ideological climate and in government–business relations are clearly visible in this history. Recommendations arising from such inquiries often opposed business interests, with investigators in the early days frequently suggesting excess-profit taxes on business and urging the government to appoint "impartial" commissioners to enforce the act (Goff and Reasons, 1978). The recommendations were often ignored by government when this occurred.

However, the protracted debate and discussion may well have convinced at least part of the business community that regulation was inevitable; it may also have shaped the ethics and opinions of the up-and-coming generation of business leaders, thus turning total opposition, eventually, into reluctant accommodation. Business hates an unpredictable environment, and uncertainty eventually becomes more worrisome than regulation. Laws have been written and passed, even though they do far less than need would dictate or activists would wish. This kind of checkered history, a scenario of legislative advances followed by retreats and defeats, is typical when regulation of the rich and powerful is attempted in a democratic state (see also Smandych, 1991; Sargent, 1990; Casey, 1985.

Another example is illustrated by the passage of the Factory Act in Ontario. Ontario experienced rapid industrial growth from

1870 to 1900, with concomitant increases in the size of firms and the length of the workday. Work weeks of sixty hours and more became common, and many workers felt they had no control over the pace of their work or the many risks they were required to undergo in the course of a working day. Women and children were widely used as cheap labour. There was little redress when injuries occurred, although employees had the legal right to sue employers for negligence and damages. Few cases were pressed, however, because the legal system was (and remains) too expensive for the average disabled worker, and workers perceived quite accurately that their chances of success were poor; unsympathetic judges frequently ruled that they had voluntarily chosen the job and therefore the risks that went with it.

In the 1880s, however, several factors came together that led to the passage of legislation, Ontario's Factory Act, in 1884. First, a moral entrepreneur and Conservative MP named Dr. D. Bergin became concerned about the employment of women and children in factories, arguing that this caused a decline in their morals and health. Working-class organizations became more vocal and powerful during this period, their militancy fuelled by immigrants from the British Isles and recent successes there. Most important of all, the united front of employer resistance was crumbling. The Canadian Manufacturers Association told its members in 1882 that some kind of legislation was inevitable, but assured them they were unlikely to suffer financially because the National Policy (with its tariff imposed on all imported goods) would protect profit margins and keep prices high. Business resistance changed, then, from the earlier virulent opposition and took gentler forms. Delaying tactics and (generally successful) attempts to shape the legislation in the interests of factory owners became the strategies of choice.

When the Factory Act came into being, it was not a progressive piece of legislation, even by the standards of 1884. As the name implies, it applied only to factories, not shops or other workplaces. Hours of labour were limited to a ten-hour day and a sixty-hour week, a maximum was set on the amount of overtime that could be required, and workers were henceforth to be allowed one hour (unpaid) for lunch, and provided with a room in which to eat it. The act also prohibited the employment of boys under 12 or girls under 14, and banned girls aged 14 to 18 from jobs where their health was likely to suffer permanent injury. (Presumably it was all right for the health of boys to be permanently injured.) Part II of the act set standards for the health and safety of workers, requiring ventilation, toilets, and guards on machines; and Part III provided inspectors to oversee and enforce the act. Public pressure caused three inspectors to be hired initially, (instead of the one originally planned): an ex-manufacturer, an ex-politician, and a mechanic and ex-labour activist. Not surprisingly, the working-class labour activist laid more charges, by far, than the other two combined (Tucker, 1987).

We can see in these capsule histories, then, the beginnings of a pattern. Business did not support initial efforts at reform and regulation. Small entrepreneurs and retailers objected violently to laws that they saw as increasing their costs and threatening their competitive position. Sizable segments of the business class were opposed on principle to any and all interference with their ability to determine the conditions and rewards of employment, seeing regulations as a threat to their power and status and "the thin edge of the wedge." As Bliss has summarized: "Employers felt that virtually the whole legislative programme put forward by organized labour and any favourable political response to it represented an attack on business interests" (Bliss, 1974:123). "When Parliament began to make highly visible responses to labour pressure after 1900—establishing a Department of Labour, founding the 'Labour Gazette,' introducing fair wage provisions into federal work contracts, and giving a friendly hearing to bills to institute the eight-hour day on Dominion public works—employers were outraged at how politicians had abandoned impartiality for fear of offending organized labour and in order to secure patronage" (Bliss, 1974:120). Impartiality in government, then, was defined as any act that supported the interests of business; partiality was any act that did not. Every concession to employees or consumers was seen as an unwarranted intrusion into the rights of business, a step certain to lead to the downfall of the great capitalist class that produced the country's wealth.

Victories, then, were fragile and partial, and the power of the working and middle classes, when faced with the concerted opposition of business, was minimal in the early years. It is too easy to forget, when looking at successful struggles, that public agitation and crises were frequently not enough to secure regulation. As Sutherland points out in the American context: "Between 1879 and 1906, 140 pure food and drug bills were presented in Congress and all failed because of the importance of the persons who would be affected" (1977:45). However, decades of struggle and publicity did have an effect over time. They educated not only business leaders, who slowly and reluctantly changed their view of minimally acceptable standards for First World workers; they also educated the broader public, who learned much from muckrakers, royal commissions, and union leaders. The knowledge that corporations could and did commit acts as antisocial and destructive as those of the common murderer began to take hold (although it took at least another fifty years before the academic community officially acknowledged it). This "folk" knowledge remains, however dormant or submerged by the constant stream of media stories and advertisements promoting the glories of the rich and powerful, and provides a basis for ongoing resistance and struggle today.

CURRENT DEVELOPMENTS IN THE REGULATORY STRUGGLE

Thus far this chapter has discussed struggles over the legality and morality of various business behaviours. This kind of debate has been largely absent with regard to occupational offences committed against the organization, a fact that illustrates the role of power in defining morality and law. Because corporate elites benefit from corporate crime and not from occupational crime, it is very much in the interests of business to promote the belief that employee crime is serious and wrong, while maintaining that corporate crime is an essential cost of a prosperous private sector. However, while corporate elites have experienced considerable success in persuading legislators and judges to accept this view of the world, they have been less successful in the public arena. Thus, laws on corporate crime are considerably more lax than they would be if public opinion directly shaped their content.

Because of the heavy stake corporations have in persuading the public that their acquisitive behaviours are not "really" criminal, the morality of corporate crime continues to be extensively debated, although more than 100 years have passed since the first statutes became law. Continuous attempts to shape the opinions of various publics are deemed worthwhile because of their potential to prevent, head off, or redirect public outrage after the occurrence of a particularly egregious corporate crime (such as the Ford Pinto case, or the *Exxon Valdez* oil spill). To the degree that corporate public relations campaigns are successful, pressure on the political elite to pass or enforce stringent new laws will be less intense. The battle for the hearts and minds of citizens in democratic countries, therefore, is ongoing. Both directly, through public relations, and indirectly, through sponsorship and advertising, the viewpoints of capital are put forth. In the mass media, on television stations and cable outlets, the mammoth financial resources of the corporate sector are seldom if ever employed to produce programs (be they fiction or documentaries) with viewpoints opposed to basic business interests and/or value

systems. Apparently apolitical programs such as situation come-
dies and cartoons extol, in the most obvious fashion, a style of life
and level of consumption that promotes accumulation, materialism, and the superiority of the Western way of life. Corporations
use their considerable financial clout, which frequently spells the
difference between survival and bankruptcy for newspapers,
magazines, and radio and television outlets, to reward certain
points of view and discourage others. This is not censorship; all
they have to do is decline to put their advertising dollars into outlets that are seen as critical.

This is not to suggest that the various factions of capital have
identical points of view on every public issue. But there are
areas—those involving the free movement of capital, the minimi-
zation of corporate taxes, and restrictions on labour, for example—where the interests of all who own or control businesses are
similar. Thus, we have seen a consortium of business groups
sponsoring campaigns pointing out the negative effects of government spending, promoting the value of free trade with the United
States throughout the 1988 election campaign, and trumpeting
the dangers of state ownership in earlier battles over the privati-
zation of Petro-Canada (Hurtig, 1991; see also Simon and Eitzen,
1986:16–24; Randall et al., 1988). In Ontario at the present time
(early 1992) a series of advertisements appearing on a wide range
of media warn the public that the NDP government's proposed
changes to the labour code will be disastrous for the province.
Sponsored by a coalition of business interests, the ads argue that
legislation increasing the power of unions to organize and measures preventing the use of strike-breakers by business will lead
to the loss of hundreds of thousands of jobs. Other groups can and
do resist such campaigns; however the economic and political
dominance of capital ensures that its voice, on issues that
threaten its interests, is among the strongest and loudest.

And yet, large sections of the public continue to view the
offences of the corporate sector with a very jaundiced eye. Indeed,
there is evidence that disapproval is growing over time. A
National Survey of Crime Severity in 1978 in the United States
asked a large sample of individuals to rank the relative severity
of particular crimes. High levels of concern were found, and in
several cases corporate crimes were seen as considerably more
serious than comparable traditional offences. For example, politicians taking a bribe of $10,000 was seen as more serious than
bank robbers stealing $10,000 (the seriousness scores were 370
and 339 respectively); price fixing by retail outlets was deemed
more serious than a mugger holding a lead pipe (201 versus 197);
and factory pollution causing one person to become ill was seen
as considerably more serious than a break and enter theft with a

$100 loss (151 versus 69) (Wolfgang, 1980; Clinard and Yeager, 1980). In the early 1980s a 1972 study was replicated to investigate attitudinal change. Investigators found that public condemnation of white-collar crime, as measured by indices of seriousness, had actually increased more than any other category of offence. The change was particularly marked for corporate crimes involving violence or loss of life (Cullen et al., 1982; and, in Canada, Goff and Mason-Clark, 1989). Public attitudes today regard corporate crimes that lead to injury or death, then, as seriously as traditional offences such as rape or armed robbery (Rossi et al., 1974; Reed and Reed, 1975; Gibbons, 1969; Hartung, 1953).

However, this has not led to the passage of laws comparable in severity to those employed against traditional offences. The corporate sector has enjoyed much more success in persuading lawmakers and government of the innocuous nature of its acquisitive acts than it has in the court of public opinion. This is not surprising. Political elites, be they elected or appointed, receive the views of business in a myriad of ways. They frequently have interpersonal and social class ties with the corporate sector; they are key members of institutions that embody capitalist interests; they are exposed to direct advertising campaigns as members of the public; and they are routinely subjected to intense, highly funded, and highly organized corporate lobbies. Through dozens of lawyers, experts, and specially commissioned studies, representatives of the corporate sector argue their positions on all manner of issues in every conceivable public and private forum, in cabinet as well as in country clubs (Stanbury, 1977; Schrecker, 1989), and for most corporate offences, they are seldom in positions vulnerable enough to allow them to be victimized by these offences. The long-term viability of the state as well as the election chances of the party in power are also dependent on continued investment and wealth generation by the corporate sector, a fact that in no way impairs its lobbying power (Panitch, 1977; Gough, 1979).

COMBINES LAW REVISITED

Some of corporate Canada's most spectacular successes in shaping laws in their own interests are not products of the "bad old days" of the 19th century; they came in the 1980s. The recent history of the Combines Investigation Act (now the Competition Act) stands as a case in point. Business power was able to stall amendments to the totally moribund mergers and monopoly provisions of the act for nearly twenty years, from 1969 to 1986, and in the end corporate interests were given carte blanche to write their own revisions. It is instructive to examine the lawmaking process over this period. The ineffectiveness of the statutes on merger and monopoly in effect in 1969 was originally signalled in the *Interim Report on Competition Policy*, published by the Ministry of Consumer and Corporate Affairs. This was superseded by a White Paper (another discussion stage), out of which came sample legislation in 1970. To say that business did not like the reforms suggested would be a severe understatement. More accurately, "all hell broke loose," according to Ian Clark, Deputy Minister of Consumer and Corporate Affairs (Clark, 1989). The Liberal government of Pierre Trudeau, responsible for the legislation, was blasted in the editorials and boardrooms of the nation, and took the heat from disaffected corporate officers on informal levels as well. Three Ministers of Consumer and Corporate Affairs were appointed and deposed in short order; several versions of the bill were put forth, each weaker than its predecessor, but in the end business resistance proved impossible to overcome.

The result was that the Liberal government admitted defeat by declaring victory. It divided the proposed legislation in half, dropping the proposed changes to mergers and monopolies and retaining those in less sensitive areas. Thus, Stage 1 Amendments, as they were called, passed into law on January 1, 1976. They called for increased maximum fines for false advertising, extended price-fixing regulations to cover services as well as products, and prohibited a range of new sales practices such as bid-rigging, pyramid selling, and bait and switch techniques. Stage II Amendments, on the other hand, had a more onerous "rite de passage." Several more versions of the act and a change of government, from the Liberals to the Progressive Conservatives under Brian Mulroney, were necessary before a revised act was passed in 1986. However, the new act bore little resemblance to the original 1969 proposals, for the officially stated aim in 1969 was to restrain monopolistic practices through law to better protect the consuming public. The 1986 regulations were part of a very different agenda.

To overcome the roadblocks that had bedevilled the Liberals, the Conservative government, on its election in 1984, set up a committee to recommend revisions in the law on mergers and monopolies. The committee was composed largely of members of the corporate elite; the Canadian Manufacturers Association, the Canadian Chamber of Commerce, and the Business Council on National Issues all had their delegates. One of its first acts was to cease holding public inquiries. (It was feared that consumers and workers' groups, aided and abetted by the Canadian media, might cause trouble or lead the government to abandon its newfound "objectivity" and "impartiality.") Politically, the government had a lot of credibility riding on the success of these efforts, since its ability to cooperate with business and run the country efficiently had been a central election promise. Committee members, a blue-ribbon group of business people, proceeded to meet with senior officials of the Department of Consumer and Corporate Affairs on a weekly basis to work out a new competition policy. Representatives of the Grocery Products Manufacturers of Canada and the Canadian Bar Association were added to the original group at a later stage, but representatives of labour and consumer interests were kept off the committee. As the deputy minister phrased it: "The Consumers Association of Canada and interested academics were also consulted" (Clark, 1989:9). The committee never made any pretence of being truly representative.

The resulting legislation, which became law in June 1986, took the form of a Competition Act. It was expressly and explicitly designed not to control business offences, but to improve and facilitate corporate operations. Criminal sanctions were taken out of the merger/monopoly sections, for business argued that the stigma of criminality was inappropriate to handle the well-meaning but occasionally unfortunate acts of corporations and their executives. The public interest, as a criterion for assessing a particular merger or monopoly, was exorcised. The new act adopted an explicitly compliance-centred approach (Goldman, 1989:3). It focused on the provision of a stable and predictable climate for business; business prosperity was its major goal; and meaningful punishment for offenders was virtually removed. Such results, of course, are exactly what one would expect from this kind of legislative process. If committees of armed robbers were routinely appointed to devise criminal laws, one would expect that they too would design legislation to advance their own interests.

This process of shaping political action in the interests of the corporate sector, however, is merely the modern extension of practices and philosophies that are centuries old, as discussed in the first part of this chapter. In 1900 railway managers tried to convince the Royal Labour Commission that running along the tops of moving freight cars to apply brakes by hand was only dangerous in bad weather and "not where the men are looking where they are going." Furthermore, "where men take the responsibility on themselves [to apply brakes] the railway companies are not to blame" (cited in Bliss, 1974:59). Similarly, "it was standard testimony ... that machinery was not in itself dangerous, that the men's own carelessness brought on accidents, or that they had known of the hazards when they took the job" (Bliss, 1974:59). Corporate representatives still tell us that mine workers over age

55 who have death rates more than three times greater than the Canadian average merely "smoke too much" (Deverell, 1975). Corporations consistently argue, despite considerable evidence to the contrary (Green, 1972; Fellmeth, 1973), that combines and monopolies that cause high costs for customers and high profits for manufacturers are inconsequential because of the self-regulating capacity of the marketplace. In other words, if prices become too high, new competitors will enter the market and correct the situation. Unfortunately, this is not the case in most sectors of the economy. It may require initial investments of millions of dollars, as well as decades of court battles, to break the dominant companies' stranglehold on supplies, equipment, patents, and markets.

Business leaders themselves, then, tend to think their antisocial and predatory acts do not merit government attention. Manufacturers, for example, have successfully argued that the test to determine when advertising is false should be the "reasonable man" rather than the "credulous person" standard. In other words, they claim that it should not be against the law (and it is not) to make exaggerated and false claims on behalf of products being sold as long as the average middle-class and middle-aged male (the quintessential reasonable man to advertisers and courts) would realize these claims engage in hyperbole and are not meant to be taken seriously. Similarly, industry representatives have maintained (also successfully) that selling 100 packages of biscuits weighing only 240 grams when they are labelled as containing 250 grams or promising 100 vitamin pills and packaging only ninety-seven in each bottle are not criminal acts. However, entering a grocery store and stealing 1000 grams of biscuits or taking three vitamin pills out of every bottle is theft, punishable by fines and imprisonment. Shoplifting offences such as these, it is argued, committed by criminal low-life characters incapable of earning an honest living, drive up the price of goods. Such people must be controlled if our civilization and way of life are to survive. Fraudulently deceiving the public by providing fewer vitamin pills or biscuits than promised, even though the amount stolen is exactly the same, is an oversight by responsible, upstanding corporate citizens meriting, at most, a notice mailed by government regulators informing the company of its inadvertent error.

That business has such self-serving beliefs is not surprising. Few drunk drivers, child abusers, or embezzlers see their crimes the way their victims do, or the way that law conceptualizes them. The significant factor to remember here is that business, almost uniquely, has the power to shape policy so that laws regularly reflect its points of view. Few other groups enjoy this degree of insider access and overall clout. This is not to say that corporations manipulate government in some mysterious or conspiratorial way. Business opinion is not unanimous on all issues, splits develop, mistakes occur, representations to government sometimes fail, and policies that business intensely dislike do become law. However, that the corporate sector has historically manipulated the actions and opinions of the political elite, and largely shaped the content of laws that govern it, cannot be denied.

SUMMARY

This chapter, has looked at the mechanisms by which definitions of deviance are constructed. Specifically, it examined the efforts of business to ensure that particular profitable business practices do not become the subject of criminal sanctions, against the struggle of other groups to secure effective regulatory legislation. The battles to secure pure food, workplace health and safety laws, and to prohibit various business practices such as price fixing, false advertising, and monopolies were traced in some detail. Despite the fact that corporate crime is increasingly recognized by the broader public as serious antisocial behaviour, the struggle to secure meaningful sanctions has not yet been won, and many efforts have failed to make significant headway against the overwhelming power of the corporate sector. However, more than a century of struggle has produced in the developed world a very different business climate from that which existed in the 19th century, and people on the whole have benefited from this. The next chapter examines the role of regulatory agencies, the bodies in charge of enforcing regulatory laws once they have become law.

CHAPTER 5

The Regulatory Agency

INTRODUCTION

It is impossible to understand the enforcement and sanctioning process for corporate crime without looking at the typical enforcement vehicle, the regulatory agency. It is this agency, in concert with the business sector it is charged with policing, that shapes the enforcement process. In this chapter, the history and characteristics of the regulatory agency will be examined, including the debate about its overall effectiveness.

Historically, regulatory agencies in Anglo-American democracies evolved out of common law principles based upon early court decisions around issues of corporate behaviour and liability. As we have seen, the first modern corporation, the Dutch East India Company, was founded in 1602 (Coleman, 1985:12). With the privilege of limited liability, the corporate form quickly became common. As the potential of this newly invented organizational form for harm (as well as good) became apparent, political authorities began to supplement existing common law doctrines, for these specified only that masters had "vicarious" liability for the wrongful actions of their servants (a doctrine first established in 12th-century Europe) (Bernard, 1984). Direct statutory control through law was then attempted, but its defects quickly became apparent as policing agencies, only recently in existence themselves, had neither the expertise, interest, or power to scrutinize the corporate sector. In time, then, the inspector and regulatory agency were brought into being to fill this gap and make the new regulatory laws politically and socially viable (Mitnick, 1980:28–30).

CHARACTERISTICS OF REGULATORY AGENCIES

POWERS AND SANCTIONS

Regulatory agencies are typically equipped by law with a wide array of powers and sanctions. Initially, agents may choose to invoke the formal regulatory process (by laying charges or filing official complaints, for example), or adopt an informal, educational role, counselling the offenders on problems inspectors have discovered and offering friendly advice. If agencies opt for the formal route, they can usually choose one or more civil, administrative, or criminal charges. If culpability is established, civil and administrative penalties may be assessed, such as awarding victims double or treble damages or allowing judges to impose new standards on the industry, altering the conditions of a firm's licence to operate, or the methods of production it uses. Criminal remedies range from the imposition of prison sentences and punitive fines, to injunctions, consent decrees, and orders of prohibition; the latter two allow the offender to evade responsibility for the crime as the decree or order itself is deemed sufficient punishment.

Attempts to control business by means of regulation have been increasing, although it is not yet clear whether the deregulatory movement of the 1980s has slowed or reversed this trend. (It seems unlikely, because governments pass laws for a variety of reasons, many of which are unrelated to their effectiveness as regulatory devices.) Fels (1982:30) presents figures showing that the number of regulatory acts passed by the Australian federal and state governments doubled from 1960–69 to 1970–79, yielding in the latter period some 9703 acts and 20,131 regulations. In addition, the percentage of total legislation that was regulatory in nature doubled, from 15 to 30 percent. The United Kingdom shows similar tendencies. It has on its books more than 7000 criminal offences; nearly half of these require no proof of intent (which means they are probably regulatory in nature). Indeed, more than half of the offences (4386 to be exact) were passed in the fourteen-year period between 1961 and 1975 (Clarke, 1990:205–6). This trend underlines increases in overall social control noted in the last chapter.

MODELS OF REGULATORY AGENCIES

Due to a myriad of studies, much is now known about regulatory agencies and those who staff and run them. Like all organizations, their functioning is shaped by the external environment, their organizational structure, and the goals and tasks that comprise their mandate. Agencies have been classified into two "ideal types," one known as the expert, the other as the legal model. Under the expert model, regulatory officials are encouraged to exercise maximum flexibility in deciding what action to take with target firms. Few fixed legal rules are used as *a priori* guides to behaviour, although the legal structure determines the overall boundaries of regulatory tactics employed. On the other hand, those employing the legal model, as the name implies, emphasize law obedience above all. Officials are directed to enforce regulatory legislation with paramount attention to the requirements of the legislation (Kagan, 1978:13–15). However, because regulatory laws are typically worded in an ambiguous rather than clear-cut fashion, the agency has to formulate "approved" versions of the "real" meaning of each clause. The primary effect of the legal model, then, is to take discretionary power from officials such as inspectors located in the field, and vest it in their superiors situated in centralized offices.

Normally, each regulatory agency specializes in one type or subset of violations, such as securities, environmental protection, or worker health and safety. Regulatory agencies are officially both proactive and reactive; that is, they seek out violations on their own, as well as responding to complaints from the public. With offences such as false advertising, agents can pick up suspected infractions by reading newspapers and watching television; for others they are largely dependent on investigations by consumer groups or complaints from competing businesses if on-site inspections do not reveal problems. For still others, such as price fixing or securities violations, complex, costly, in-depth investigations are necessary. With such offences, only insiders are in a position to know what is really going on, although companies excluded from a particular scam may report their suspicions to regulators. In such cases, to be proactive requires a great deal of skill, tact, education, and knowledge of the particular industry. Being an effective regulatory officer, then, requires a variety of characteristics and talents that can differ substantially from sector to sector.

PERSONNEL

Such findings direct one to examine the people who staff regulatory agencies. As argued above, regulators need a high level of education and a wide array of skills to do their jobs well. They also need some acquaintance with regulatory philosophies and issues. One study of appointments to two key American agencies, the Federal Commerce Commission (FCC) and the Federal Trade

Commission (FTC), during the period 1949 to 1974 found only ten of the total 108 appointees came from backgrounds with ties to pro-consumer or pro-regulatory groups. Sixty-four percent came from law backgrounds, often entering government service immediately after articling (Graham and Kramer, 1976). However, while pro-consumer activist backgrounds were rare, pro-business activism was often found. One study found that more than half of those appointed to regulatory jobs had experience in the industry they were now asked to regulate (Parenti, 1983). Indeed, the Reagan administration was notorious for the frequency with which it took former lobbyists for industry and placed them in top jobs in regulatory agencies; the appointments of Ann Gorsuch and Rita Lavell to the Environmental Protection Agency are cases in point (Messerschmidt, 1986:123).[1]

Even during the 1949 to 1974 period, a full one-third of regulation appointees went into the business sector when they left government service, frequently taking jobs in the industry they had previously regulated (Graham and Kramer, 1976; also found by Parenti, 1983). Since positions in business typically pay much better and carry more prestige than those in government, especially in the United States where the tradition of a disinterested, dedicated public service is weak, such exit jobs would appear to be important benefits for employees in the regulatory sector. Such career patterns are obviously not going to be open to regulators who take their jobs seriously and are labelled as "uncooperative" or "zealous" by industry.

Another study, this one by the U.S. Senate Committee on Government Affairs (1977), reported that regulatory officials in federal agencies, on average, receive salaries that are lower than comparable ranks in the private sector. They are higher, however, than public sector salaries at state or municipal levels. Personnel at the top of such agencies (deemed commissioners and appointed by the party in power rather than the civil service) seldom serve out their five- or seven-year terms, and they are very unlikely to be reappointed. However, long-term, experienced regulators are found below this level in the civil service. This combination of inexperienced political appointees and relatively experienced civil servants is practically the norm in democratic institutions. As early as 1936, law and public service were the primary former occupations of those going into regulatory agencies (Herring 1936), although the percentage with law degrees had consistently increased (up to 59 percent by 1965) (Stanley, Mann, and Doig, 1967). Local and state agencies frequently serve as stepping-stones to the better paid, more prestigious federal agencies, but increasingly smaller percentages of appointees go into the civil service from business, or with elite backgrounds (as measured by attendance at elite schools). All of these factors illustrate the decreasing influence and prestige of government service as a career option, and the increasing dominance of business both ideologically and practically.

ENVIRONMENTAL EFFECTS ON REGULATORY AGENCIES

The effects of the immediate environment on regulatory agencies are also important. To maintain their existence, all federal, provincial/state, and local government agencies have certain maintenance needs they must meet. For example, they must secure resources, negotiate adequate (preferably increasing) budgets, weaken opposing forces, and line up political support for their existence and mandate. On a day-to-day basis they must successfully handle management problems, cope with case overloads (or the reverse), set priorities, and designate criteria for prosecution (Thomas, 1982).

Many academics have, therefore, tried to specify the characteristics of "effective" agencies, defining effectiveness in terms of successful fulfilment of a given legislative mandate. However, such efforts have met with limited success. Many now argue that long-term effectiveness is not possible. Instead, regulatory agencies may exhibit parasitic growth, historically displaying a pattern of expansion that, however irregular and cyclical, comes to outstrip the growth of the industry being regulated (Stigler, 1975; Meier and Plumlee, 1978; Noll, 1978). Such expansion is most likely where the criteria and standards of regulation are imprecise, where its specific aim is to improve industry performance, and where regulators are free to correct unanticipated loopholes with additional regulations without returning to Parliament or Congress for permission (Wilson, 1974). Moreover, as regulatory agencies grow, they become more rigid in their decision-making, with the result that the highly mobile, innovative and ambitious officers who staffed them at their inception are replaced by (or turn into) conservative bureaucrats who seek only the comfort and safety of a long-term position (Downs, 1967).

Since evidence indicates that political bodies that establish regulatory agencies initially allocate little in the way of resources and staff, regulatory expansion may not be entirely negative. However, from the standpoint of those who view regulation as anathema (a particularly powerful philosophy in academic and business circles in the United States), growth in regulatory agencies indicates inefficiency and mismanagement (while growth in private industry is a sign of efficiency and proper management).

Theories posit that regulatory agencies have life cycles that extend from birth to immobility and paralysis rather than death. After an initial policy-creation stage, agencies may enter a middle period marked by power consolidation and policy implementation, then proceed to a rigid old age where administrative procedures are emphasized at the expense of substance, and policy agendas are dictated by the industry they are regulating, a phenomenon known as capture (Anderson, 1975; Cobb and Elder, 1972; Cobb, Ross, and Ross, 1976; Bernstein, 1955; Glaeser, 1957). Sabatier (1975, 1977) argues that rigidification and capture can be prevented, or at least postponed, if active public groups intervene and monitor agency performance. Such groups, by keeping agencies honest and forcing them to live up to their mandate, can forestall capture.

Hopkins (1978, 1979), in his studies of the origin and life cycle of several Australian agencies, points out there are inter- and intranational variations in the degree to which capture occurs, implying that the political economy of the nation-state is an important factor in shaping capture. Wilson (1974, 1980) suggests capture will be most likely where the regulatory issues at stake are crucial to the target industry, but not to opposing organized forces (or where such forces are absent). Stigler (1975) and Peltzman (1976) take a different tack, arguing that capture is structurally inevitable. Regulation, they argue, is designed and operated for the benefit of the regulated industry, not in "the public interest" at all. Industries, they maintain, need the powers of the state to attain subsidies, control market entry by rivals, regularize the market, and enhance public confidence in themselves and their products. The state, through the regulatory agency, needs the resources (votes, campaign donations, good will, and corporate legitimacy) that industry can provide. The shape regulation takes, then, is determined by the interaction of these two symbiotic needs (see also Cranston, 1982).

As this discussion illustrates, the literature on regulation, and most of the controversies within it, rests on value judgments about the desirability of government regulation of business. The concept of capture, which reflects a negative evaluation of the regulatory agency's adoption of the perspective of the industry it regulates, dominated the postwar literature. Recently, however, it has been seen as ideological and outdated, a relic of 1960s New Left movements. Theorists on the right now eschew these negative value judgments and openly advocate a more thoroughgoing, intense, and cooperative relationship between agency and industry. Indeed, as will be discussed in Chapter 7, many favour outright deregulation, the removal of all agency or government control over business. The left, however, has continued to denounce capture as a sellout, and keeps looking for ways to help agencies avoid this fate.

Whatever position one takes in this debate, it is not possible to assess the impact of regulation or the effectiveness of a particular agency unless one can unequivocally state the purpose of the legislation in the first place. Multifarious purposes exist for each and every interest group that is promoting or opposing each and every legislative proposal. If the original purpose of the legislation was symbolic, to demonstrate concern for the public or prevent electoral losses by passing a law, then the agency has filled its purpose by merely existing. It does not have to "do" anything to be effective from this perspective. If it is captured by industry, so much the better, as long as the broader public does not know the truth. Moreover, because regulatory activity is not easily monitored and not regularly covered in dominant media, or raised by parliamentary oppositions or ongoing committees, the ineffectiveness of regulatory agencies usually goes unremarked. The recent ascendance of the law and economics movement, with its belief in the corrective powers of the marketplace and deregulation, has sharpened this debate. Adherents argue that workers who are willing to take risky jobs get paid high wages, which makes government restrictions on health and safety in the workplace financially and structurally superfluous (Leigh, 1989:823). Others produce sophisticated economic calculations that show, for example, that current laws protecting workers' health cost more to administer and enforce than an individual human life is worth, according to its value on the labour market. Such laws, and the regulatory structure they require, are therefore wasteful and inefficient, and should be repealed (see, for example, Dewees and Daniels, 1986).

Other studies support the argument that regulation is important; that properly constituted agencies have the potential to safeguard the environment, to protect the public, and to save the lives of workers and consumers. A study on federal occupational health and safety laws in the United States, for example, found a statistically significant negative relationship between penalties and violations, but no relation between violations and injuries. Translated, this suggests that assessment of penalties by regulatory agencies may lead to fewer violations, even though an increase in the number of injuries registered does not necessarily mean that more violations are occurring (Bartel and Thomas, 1985). Other studies show that rates of compliance with water quality standards showed marked improvements in the 1980s when industry began to take the issue seriously, resulting in reduced levels of lead, cyanide, cadmium, arsenic, and PCBs being discharged into watercourses. A 40 percent drop in lead-poisoning cases and 50 percent declines in crib deaths resulting from strangulation were reported after regulations were enacted to control lead emissions and regulate the space between bars in infant cribs (after crises and attendant publicity). Following the passage of clean water acts and stricter enforcement procedures, fish are gradually returning to rivers in the United States and the United Kingdom (Pearce, 1990a). Tabb (1980) argues that the benefits of regulation in the United States in the areas of auto and worker safety, and air and water pollution, are five times greater than the costs (while Ackerman et al., 1974, Smith, 1979, and Sands, 1968, argue the opposite position; see summaries in Braithwaite, 1985a; and Coleman, 1989). Examining the longer term, fatalities in coal mining in the United States, the United Kingdom, Australia, France, and Japan are less than 10 percent of the levels they were 100 years ago, and Paulus (1974) showed that the adulteration of food and drugs in Britain dropped dramatically from 1878 onward after a regulatory agency with inspectors and public analysts developed vested interests in effective control. Underpaid and understaffed inspectors managed, despite the ineffectual wording of the Pure Food and Drugs Act, to choose their cases carefully enough to make the legislation effective.

Because there are always more factors influencing outcomes than just the regulatory agency, it is difficult to assess its effect in isolation. All the same, given the absence of meaningful alternative strategies, it is much too early to conclude that regulatory agencies have failed in their purpose, or that they are structurally incapable of accomplishing societally worthwhile goals.

CHARACTERISTICS OF THE ENFORCEMENT PROCESS

Having reviewed the literature on regulatory agencies, it is necessary to examine the specifics and flavour of enforcement efforts. Enforcing regulations, after all, is the official raison d'être of agencies. Enforcement vigour varies greatly over time and place, as one would expect. Nevertheless, a few generalizations are possible. It is known, first of all, that nonenforcement is the most salient, obvious, and frequently found characteristic of regulatory agencies. Summarizing his extensive survey of the American, British, and Australian literatures, Cranston concludes: "There is clear evidence of regulatory agencies failing to function in the manner expected" (Cranston, 1982:11). Faced with a choice between taking formal regulatory action as opposed to counselling, advising, educating, or even mollifying the offending organization, officials overwhelmingly choose the latter.

This is not surprising, because regulatory agencies are creatures of government, and governments, as we know, have good reasons to be lenient toward corporate criminality. Politicians require the money, power, approval, and confidence of the corporate sector to get elected and stay in power; as political appointees, those at the top of regulatory agencies must either have enormous political clout *or* the support of the industry they are regulating. Moreover, the fact that politicians and regulators frequently share similar ideological perspectives—both parties tend to agree that businesses have to cut corners to survive, that profit maximization is the ultimate goal, and that applying the law to corporations may constitute "government interference"—is also important. The current belief in the magic power of market forces to correct all ills has now become an article of faith for regulators and politicians in many arenas, although these philosophies do vary in strength. They are most visible in countries where capitalist ideologies are strongest, where they have been least challenged historically by notions of social responsibility, or by acceptance of the idea that collective or community rights should take precedence over individual ones. Nevertheless, these beliefs are found throughout the capitalist world and, with the collapse of the Soviet empire, in a high percentage of the remaining countries. At the level of the regulatory agency, this means that getting along with business, not taking formal enforcement actions against it, is the easiest avenue for agency officials to follow.

There is not always a perfect fit, however, between the employees of regulatory agencies who do the day-to-day regulating, and their superiors in the agency or outside it in government. Conflict between top administrators and the rank and file does exist, but it can go both ways ideologically. If those running the agencies were appointed by reformist or left-wing regimes, they may be more anxious to enforce the laws formally than their bosses want them to be. This state of affairs is temporary, however, because bosses are quick to replace subordinates who are not in line with their way of thinking with others who are. Conversely, lower-level regulatory agents may feel there should be higher levels of enforcement than their bosses permit.

Since both groups have been socialized and educated in mainstream institutions, and those with visible connections to antibusiness activist groups are unlikely to be hired in the first place, deep-seated philosophical conflicts between them are uncommon (Stigler, 1975; Schrecker, 1989). What one usually sees are differences of emphasis based on the different on-the-job pressures each group faces. At the deepest ideological level, both regulatory personnel and their superiors are likely to accept the dominant ideas of their gender, class, and era, and with few exceptions, these ideas tell them that corporations are a good thing, that governments (and government regulators) are a mixed blessing at best, and that only poor people and people of colour commit really criminal acts that require serious punitive activity.

We thus find that regulators generally adopt a gentle and educative attitude toward those they are regulating, often to the point of identifying with the industry and its problems. Even in the aftermath of the Watergate scandal, in an era much more suspicious of corporate activity than the present one, an American study found that the bosses of regulatory agencies typically believed the problem of corporate crime could be solved by "the development of a more sympathetic attitude toward business problems on the part of the administration" (Lane, 1977:114). Their view was that purposive infractions are committed only by the atypical business person, the "bad apple in the barrel."

Since bad apples are more likely to be found at the bottom of the barrel, the second characteristic of enforcement activity, not surprisingly, is a tendency to focus on the smallest and weakest individuals and organizations. Thus, the most intensive investigative efforts are directed toward the smaller business units, and the heaviest sanctions meted out against them. The largest and most powerful organizations (typically multinational corporations) enjoy the best relations with regulatory officials. Not coincidentally, they are also the most likely to challenge legally any investigation or sanction. This emphasis on the peripheral and weak has been extensively documented for a wide range of corporate activity: for food and drug laws, false advertising, and combines law (in Canada) (Snider, 1978; Goff and Reasons, 1978); for tax violations (Long, 1979); for coal mining (Lynxwiler et al. 1983); for securities regulation (Shapiro, 1985); and for a host of miscellaneous regulatory sectors (Thomas, 1982; Diver, 1980; Benson, 1989; Ermann and Lundman, 1978).

Such differential treatment can be understood when one looks at the advantages small and unincorporated parties hold for regulators. They are ideal targets politically: they lack the power to block investigations; they do not have the complexity and resources to conceal crimes well; they can be investigated, sanctioned, and written off in a relatively short time; and they are unlikely to have the clout to visit political repercussions back upon the agency or its staff. Each and every one of these downsides is involved in the prosecution of a large and central corporation. In an environment where the resources of business can dwarf those of regulatory agencies, causing cases to drag on for five or ten expensive and draining years, only to be lost or dropped when a new administration takes power, such weaknesses are important factors to the agency.

The power of big business is not apocryphal. The Federal Trade Commission in the United States, for example, devoted 12 to 14 percent of its annual budget and an even heavier percentage of its staff complement to an investigation of illegal combinations and price fixing in the oil industry in the early 1970s. Regulators suspected that the great oil crisis, which culminated in the oil shortage of 1973, the 55 mph speed limit on all federal highways in the United States, and a doubling and tripling of the price of a gallon of gasoline, was artificially created by a price-fixing, supply-restricting cartel among the major oil companies. However, after more than eight years of investigation, the case was abandoned—but not because agency suspicions were groundless. On the contrary. The FTC, one of the strongest and best-funded regulatory agencies in the world, simply proved no match for the oil companies with their far-reaching political networks and bottomless resources (Sampson, 1975).

Similar fates befell regulatory agencies after the election of Ronald Reagan in 1980, when dozens of hotly contested cases against powerful corporations in a wide range of spheres were dropped because of political intervention by the new regime on behalf of its friends and corporate allies (Coleman, 1989; Calavita, 1983; Yeager, 1991). As can be imagined, this does not do wonders for morale; nor does it inspire staff with regulatory vigour—one soon learns not to take regulation too seriously if one is interested in longevity.

The concentration of regulatory agency staff on small concerns in peripheral parts of the economy, then, is as understandable as it is ill-advised. Unfortunately, the extent and degree of corporate crime found today would not be possible if the only instigators were tiny fly-by-night organizations or unethical and maladjusted individuals. As C. Wright Mills observed some years ago, if only one business person or company exhibits criminality, the cause may be an individual one, lodged in the particular pathology or circumstances of one person or company. But where there are hundreds of thousands of companies involved, and many of the largest, most prestigious corporations turn up as habitual offenders, as Sutherland (1961, 1973), Clinard and Yeager (1980), and others have discovered, concentrating on the aberrant individual or the two-person business makes no sense at all.

Indeed, given the increasing dominance of megacorporations, and the high profitability of corporate crime, the most logical inference is that larger and more successful organizations will be the most rather than least likely to offend. Even when the small and weak do break the law, concentrating on them, in an economy dominated by giants, means that one is, almost by definition, singling out those with the least chance of causing a major disaster, and with the smallest number of victims. Moreover, there are certain offences where the concentration associated with the creation of a small number of large successful firms is itself criminogenic; four big companies who control 95 percent of the market are much better placed to engage in price-fixing conspiracies than 250 smaller concerns who must do battle with each other for their share of the market. Other things being equal, price-fixing could be better curbed by breaking up the oligopoly enjoyed by the four than by chasing after the peripheral operations (Green, 1972; Barnett, 1982; Nader and Green, 1973).

Thus far we have examined two characteristics of regulatory enforcement: the tendency to prefer nonenforcement or informal measures over official sanctions, and the focus of enforcement activity on the smallest and weakest operators and operations. The third characteristic is that the sanctions actually assessed are very light. Over and over, the literature tells us that the fines and assorted criminal and civil penalties typically handed out are minuscule, and that they do not deter offenders (Pearce, 1976; Johnson, 1986; Carson, 1982; Clinard and Yeager, 1980; Levi, 1981, 1984; and others). No wonder: it has been calculated that average fines for the typical corporate crime represent, for large organizations, less than a fraction of company profits for a single hour of operation (Ermann and Lundman, 1978). The empirical evidence for this assertion will be examined in the next chapter; for the moment, it is sufficient to observe that the penalties the typical regulatory agency imposes or recommends are extremely light, both in terms of the profits made on the particular offence, and in light of the overall company profits.

CASE STUDIES FROM THE UNITED STATES

These characteristics can be illustrated by looking at the saga of the Beech-Nut Company and its adulterated apple juice. From 1977 to 1983, Beech-Nut, a major manufacturer of baby food in the United States, sold as "100% fruit juice, no sugar added" a liquid that was essentially apple-flavoured water according to chemical analyses. When the U.S. Food and Drug Administration discovered, quite accidentally, substantial quantities of adulterated juice on the market, it immediately notified Beech-Nut and other manufacturers on the assumption that the major companies were innocent victims of some fly-by-night supplier. When the company reacted in a hostile and uncooperative fashion, and no peripheral supplier could be found, the FDA slowly became suspicious. While it prevaricated, however, Beech-Nut launched a cover-up operation, ordering executives inside every plant to destroy incriminating evidence. Then, not wanting to lose one penny of potential profits, it shipped the remaining stocks of "apple juice" to Third World countries, specifically the Dominican Republic, Puerto Rico, and the Virgin Islands, and sold it as pure apple juice in these markets. The company, which realized profits of $60 million or more from this operation, was eventually taken to court in 1987. It was convicted and assessed an extraordinarily large penalty (for this kind of offence) of $2 million. Although the fine was larger than the firm could reasonably have expected, given the precedents, the return on investment was still substantial, provided one leaves the health of infants out of the equation (*Consumer Reports* 29 May 1989:294–96).

It is easy to find examples illustrative of the fate of regulatory agencies when they become too zealous for the liking of the industries they regulate and/or of pro-business politicians. Agencies are always prime targets for government cutbacks, whenever deficits look too high or pro-business regimes take power. Although agencies have always been understaffed and underbudgeted by "normal" enforcement standards (if the level of enforcement provided against traditional crime was applied to corporate crime, there would be a hundredfold increase in the number of inspectors and budgets would quadruple), regulatory agencies were among the first victims of the Reagan regime in the United States. The Environmental Protection Agency lost 25 percent of its staff between 1980 and 1983 (Coleman, 1985); the staff working under the Occupational Safety and Health Act (OSHA), which had 2800 inspectors for 4 million workplaces in 1978, was cut by 18 percent in 1980–81, resulting in a 37 percent decline in the number of citations issued and a 65 percent reduction in fines assessed (Calavita, 1983). The Federal Trade Commission, which launched eight antitrust actions and negotiated twenty-five consent orders per year between 1977 and 1981 (not an impressive record in the first place), instigated only three antitrust actions and eleven consent orders after the Reagan administration came to power, a drop of more than 50 percent from 1981–83 (Coleman, 1985:163). It was also forced to drop all structural cases against major industries that it had been investigating.

The OSHA example is particularly instructive. This was an agency that had strong union support. It flexed its muscle in the 1970s, resulting in a number of minor successes. However, because of these limited successes, and because it directly challenged capital's dominance in the workplace, OSHA was widely despised by powerful elites in the manufacturing and industrial sector. OSHA was responsible in large part for the 1972 ban on asbestos in the workplace, which prevented an estimated 630 to 2300 deaths a year. In 1974 it limited the use of vinyl chloride, again saving approximately 2000 lives per year.

All of this cost industries a great deal, both in money and negative publicity. However, OSHA's most egregious sin, from industry's perspective, was its official encouragement to workers to form health and safety groups in the workplace. The agency's policy was to help workers become knowledgeable and informed about workplace dangers, simultaneously focusing media attention on worker health and safety problems. Eventually there were well-publicized protests against the policies of several major multinationals. Indeed, OSHA had American Cyanamid fined $10,000 for its response to the publicity on reproductive hazards faced by female employees working with hazardous substances when it forced employees it could not fire or remove to undergo sterilization. All of this, as Calavita (1983) points out, sent an important symbolic message to workers that they had a right to know the dangers they were asked to confront, and a related right to refuse dangerous work. OSHA, and labour, would pay for such insolence.

One of the first acts of the Reagan administration, through a new Secretary of Labor (Ray Donovan) and a newly appointed director of OSHA, was to withdraw and then kill seven regulatory standards that were due to be implemented (or had already been implemented). The abandoned standards, none of them revolutionary, would have required that all hazardous chemicals be labelled; that substances found to pose a "significant risk" of being carcinogenic be regulated; that an annual list of suspected carcinogens be published and made available to workers; and that maximum legal exposure levels for lead be established. New standards of allowable cotton dust-levels (aimed at reducing the number of workers contracting brown lung disease, which kills at least 21,000 a year) were rescinded, as were regulations to protect workers' hearing from excessive noise, and "walk-around pay," monies paid to workers for time spent monitoring workplace conditions. OSHA also withdrew at least nine films, pamphlets, and slide shows on various workplace dangers from circulation, going so far as actually burning 100,000 copies of a pamphlet on cotton dust and brown lung disease because it was "not neutral" (Calavita, 1983:442). The policy of responding to every worker-reported complaint (if only with a phone call) was discontinued. To replace all of this, a system of voluntary compliance, which allowed 73 percent of the manufacturing firms in the United

States to avoid regular inspections if their record of worker injuries was low, was put in place.

One of this 73 percent was the aforementioned Film Recovery Systems corporation. Three of its managers were subsequently charged and convicted of homicide and fourteen counts of reckless conduct for the cyanide poisoning of a 61-year-old Polish immigrant who could not read the small English-language warning labels on the vats of cyanide he, and all the other immigrant workers in the plant, handled every day (Cullen, Maakestad, and Cavender, 1987:70–71). The incident ably, if tragically, illustrates the folly of assuming that the records compiled and kept by companies reflect their "real" accident rates and of believing that corporations just "naturally" want workers to have a safe workplace (Pearce, 1990a,1990b; Tombs, 1990). (The incident also illustrates the inability of legal systems to make criminal charges against powerful individuals stick—the convictions were overturned on appeal.) The cuts and policy changes produced predictable results at OSHA, where the number of inspections dropped dramatically in 1981—serious citations declined by 37 percent, fines by 65 percent, and follow-up inspections by 73 percent. In 1982 OSHA's budget was cut again, this time by 40 percent (Calavita, 1983).

The fallout from these and similar cuts can be seen today in a range of industrial settings. Examine, for example, the recent history of the petrochemical industry in Texas. Oil refining is a complex and dangerous operation, requiring a workforce both skilled and carefully trained. The potential for accidents has always been present, but recently there has been an epidemic of them in the 220 oil refineries and chemical plants (the greatest concentration in the world) that lie along the Gulf coast from Texas to Louisiana. In the past six years, "87 serious fires, leaks and explosions in the oil-refining and chemical industry have killed 159 people, injured at least 2200 others, and caused more than $3 billion in property damage" (Selcraig, 1992:62).

Investigations have revealed a combination of factors behind these tragedies. The plunge in the price of oil in the 1980s and a series of leveraged buyouts resulted in workforces being chopped, with the most senior and experienced workers (who were the most expensive) going first (Selcraig, 1992:64). Cutbacks in OSHA meant that plants are inspected less frequently. Workers who remain have less leverage, are less able to refuse dangerous work, and are increasingly forced to work long, exhausting hours of overtime, for the power of the union (the Oil, Chemical and Atomic Workers Union International) has been dramatically reduced. Most significantly, one-third to one-half of the workforce is now made up of contract workers. Often poorly educated, given minimal training, frequently illiterate or unable to speak

English, these workers have several key advantages for management. They are cheap, nonunionized, and totally dependent on the company. Moreover, because they are contract workers, their injuries are not counted against the petro-chemical industry; they are classified by the U.S. Department of Labor as "construction" workers. Because industry-generated injury rates are now the key factor in determining whether or not a plant will be inspected by OSHA, this is a significant advantage (Selcraig, 1992).

As the above example illustrates, the regulatory environment in North America has not become more consumer or worker friendly in the 1990s. A further example is provided in the story of the "Environmental Consumer's Handbook," issued by the U.S. Environmental Protection Agency in October 1990. The purpose of the booklet was to teach consumers ways to reduce household waste by recycling, and to encourage them to buy more "environmentally friendly" products. Companies that manufacture disposable products immediately took umbrage, and by February 1991 the handbook was recalled from circulation. The series of letters reproduced below (obtained under the Freedom of Information Act by a Washington environmental lobby group, "Environmental Action Foundation") illustrates the tightrope regulatory agencies must walk. It also shows the importance of external lobbying groups in the regulatory process. While such groups may be unable to stiffen the backbone of regulatory agencies in every case, they can at least make the degree of agency subservience to business known.

Disposable Policy at the EPA

December 20, 1990

Peggy Knight
Director
External Relations and Education
U.S. Environmental Protection
Agency

Dear Peggy:

Pursuant to our conversation yesterday, I enclose comments from both the Foodservice and Packaging Institute (FPI) and the American Paper Institute (API) [both of which are represented by this letter's author] concerning the EPA's publication "The Environmental Consumer's Handbook." I know that FPI is extremely concerned about this and that Joseph Bow [the president of FPI] would like to have distribution stopped and the publication recalled.

From my personal perspective, the publication appears to be one-sided. Much of the material appears to represent the views of environmental activists, but apparently little or no consideration has been given to the positions of the industries whose products are discussed in the publication—particularly the foodservice disposables industry and the paper and plastics industries.

For example, on page three: "Products and packaging designed to be thrown away after a single use can increase disposal costs, deplete our natural resources, contribute to litter, and add to our nation's waste disposal difficulties." How do these items increase disposal costs? How do paper items deplete natural resources when more trees are planted than harvested? How do these items contribute to litter when it is the users who litter, not the items?

Page ten: "Instead of using disposable cups, take a ceramic mug or glass to work that can be washed and reused. Carry your own cup to meetings or on breaks. At home, use reusable and durable plates, cups, silverware, and food containers." This statement fails to consider the safety, health, and sanitation benefits of disposables. It is suggested that the statement be eliminated or modified to say that reusables be considered when proper sanitation standards can be observed. It must also state that paper, plastic, and aluminum foodservice disposables can be recycled or composted.

May I suggest that we arrange a meeting very soon to discuss this?

Sincerely,
Ronald A. Duchin
Mongoven, Biscoe, & Duchin

January 14, 1991
Don [Clay, assistant administrator, EPA]:

Just a note to let you know of some of the activity that a recent OSW [Office of Solid Waste] document has generated. Last fall, OSW published "The Environmental Consumer's Handbook," a forty-page booklet on what the consumer can do to be less wasteful in the course of his/her routine activities. The brochure has become one of OSW's most requested documents. Numerous companies and organizations have made very favorable comments about the document and have requested multiple copies for their own distribution.

At the same time, EPA has recently received strongly critical letters from Ronald Duchin, an attorney on behalf of the Foodservice and Packaging Institute (FPI) and the American Paper Institute (API). The criticism centers around product packaging and the use of reusable products instead of their disposable equivalents. The specific comments appear to be little more than attempts to defend the continued use of disposable and single-use products.

The handbook was carefully and thoroughly reviewed within EPA. OSW went to great lengths to maintain neutrality in this booklet. I suspect that there will always be something in documents promoting source reduction that will upset particular interests. However, I am convinced that the criticisms to which the booklet has been subject so far are a reflection of various self-interests and not a burning desire to improve the handbook's effectiveness.

I understand that FPI and API are attempting to drum up support among their single-service industry colleagues. I think we'll confront more of this as we increase source-reduction efforts. I will soon meet with FPI and API to hear their criticisms. I'll let you know the results of the meeting; it may heat up, since I have no intention of pulling this publication.

Sylvia Lowrance
[Director of the Office of Solid Waste]

February 14, 1991

Donald Clay
U.S. Environmental Protection Agency

Dear Mr. Clay:

There are a great number of excellent ideas presented in "The Environmental Consumer's Handbook." As a result of reading the book, my wife and I now reuse our plastic peanut butter containers as freezer containers for soup, spaghetti sauce, and the like. But there are a fair number of suggestions to which we at Scott Paper Company take serious exception.

The handbook positions disposables as unnecessary and the use of same as bordering on sinful. Yet there is almost no product, disposable or durable, that does not have a negative environmental impact. Before exhorting people to replace disposable cups with ceramic mugs and glasses, one should consider all the externalities. The suggestion seems simple, neat, and right until you consider the impact of the manufacturing process, the water, energy, and chemicals required to clean the utensils, and the potential hygiene problems.

We would ask that industry's views be reflected in the develop-ment of future publications. We would welcome the opportunity to work with you and your staff on this matter.

Sincerely,
Steve Conway
Scott Paper Company

February 15, 1991

Bruce Weddle
Office of Solid Waste
U.S. Environmental Protection Agency

Dear Mr. Weddle:

Sweetheart Cup Company is the nation's largest manufacturer of single-use paper and plastic products. We believe that disposable foodservice products occupy a useful and legitimate place in modern society, and that the statements made about disposables in this booklet are both unfair and based largely on misinformation rather than fact.

The handbook makes disparaging references to the "Throwaway Society," and implies that disposable products are unnecessary and frivolous uses of raw material. Yet the truth is that foodservice disposables possess a number of advantages over their reusable counterparts, particularly in the area of sanitation. For example, scientific studies have shown that single-service cups and plates have an average bacteria load of only 2.0 colonies per utensil, compared with 410 colonies for permanentware.

In addition, using disposables saves a great deal of water and electricity that would otherwise be used to operate dishwashers—an average of 71 gallons of water saved for every 100 cafeteria customers served. Foodservice disposables—when used and disposed of properly—are as environmentally responsible as they are useful.

Very truly yours,
Sandie J. Preiss
Sweetheart Cup Company

February 28, 1991

SUBJECT: "The Environmental Consumer's Handbook
FROM: Don R. Clay, Assistant Administrator
TO: Regional Administrators

Recently, you received copies of "The Environmental Consumer's Handbook." Unfortunately, this booklet contains incorrect information. Because of our obligation to provide information to the public that is factually correct, it is necessary to suspend distribution at this time.

In view of the importance and popularity of this document, we plan to move ahead quickly to develop a revised edition. We intend to include a cross-section of interested parties in an effort to develop a more comprehensive review process. We will be back in touch as revised drafts are ready for your comments.

Thank you for your help on this matter.

(Reproduced with permission of *Harper's* magazine, July 1991:23–26.)

THE SITUATION IN CANADA

The backlash against regulation, which became most visible in the 1980s under the stimulus of declining corporate profits, increased international competition for business. The political swing to the right was not restricted to the United States and Britain, even though Reagan and Thatcher emerged as symbols of it. Canada, not atypically, entered this phase a little later than the United States and Britain, but with equal vigour. When the Conservatives under Brian Mulroney were elected in 1984, the prime minister's first statement was to declare that, henceforth, the country was "open for business." The federal government, which has responsibility for the most significant Canadian regulatory laws, began catching up with a vengeance. The government took steps to bring corporate leaders directly into the legislative process (as illustrated by the development of the Competition Act discussed in Chapter 4), while simultaneously cutting back radically on public sector spending and directly hitting regulatory agencies' staff and budgets.

The result was an even more permissive and lenient regulatory process than existed heretofore, with official emphasis increasingly put on cooperating with business. As the deputy minister of Health and Welfare Canada said in a discussion of the new governmental philosophy: "Most regulatory regimes in the government are in a state of flux" (Regush, 1991:63). The same official publicly defended this shift. Referring to the fact that her department no longer sent out "Alerts," bulletins that used to go to doctors and hospitals when particular medical devices and machines were found to be dangerous or defective, she observed: "They [Alerts] are old hat … a product of bygone days when consumer crusades were in fashion, the days when much of government's regulatory machinery was put in place, when it was assumed that the private sector, in pursuit of the bottom line, would often cut corners" (Regush, 1991:62). This new philosophy would have us assume that corporations will put the public interest first, since profits have become so much less important in the 1980s and 1990s!

The philosophical and behavioural shift in the Department of Health and Welfare has had some interesting results. It is not as if the Department has ever been a thorn in the side of business, or to put it another way, it has never had a sterling record in protecting the public. Take for example its Bureau of Medical Devices, a regulatory agency set up in the wake of the Dalkon Shield scandal in 1973 to protect the public, particularly patients, from the new medical products (from heart valves to incubators) that have become the mainstays of modern medicine.

The manufacture and distribution of such devices is a $2 billion business: there are more than 300,000 medical devices on the Canadian market, produced by some 6595 manufacturing companies. Only 471 of these companies are located in Canada, and few of these devices have been adequately screened or tested (Regush, 1991:16). Indeed, there have long been fears in government and the medical community that foreign manufacturers were dumping unsafe devices on the Canadian market. However, despite the fact that 100,000 Canadians a year have eye surgery to remove cataracts, implant artificial lenses, or get corneas or retinas repaired, and despite the fact that the bureau received evidence in 1987 indicating that many gels and implants are unsafe and cause damage to the cornea, no official action has been taken. Manufacturers are not forced to prove their products are safe; they are required only to notify the bureau that their product is for sale in Canada. The result, as one investigative journalist says, is to "put federal regulation [in that sector] on a par with bandages and tongue depressors" (Regush, 1991:18). Similarly, the bureau failed to inform hospitals and the medical community that more than half of the latex medical and surgical gloves on the market were found in a scientific study to have failed quality tests. Such findings are significant, particularly because gloves are medical workers' first line of defence against the Hepatitis B or HIV viruses.

More recently the Department of Health and Welfare fired an internationally known physical chemist, Dr. Pierre Blais, who persistently lobbied to make his concerns about the health hazards of the Même breast implant known. This device, introduced onto the market in the early 1980s, is made of silicone gel coated with a polyurethane foam. It is planted in the breast by plastic surgeons to enhance breast size or correct disfigurement. When Dr. Blais found that the foam used in the Même was originally developed for use in industry—for carburetors and air conditioners—and that experiments showed it would decompose under certain laboratory conditions to produce an even more dangerous chemical, he became convinced that it posed real dangers to Canadian women. From 1986 onward, he sought its removal from the marketplace, campaigning first inside the department and then, when his efforts proved futile, outside it in the public domain.

His reward was to be identified as a maverick and troublemaker, and on July 17, 1989, he was fired. However, it was not until April 17, 1991, following a highly critical story in *Saturday Night* magazine documenting the evidence against the Même, that the Department of Health and Welfare withdrew the device from the Canadian market for further tests—and even then it blamed "bad publicity" rather than product deficiencies for its decision (*Saturday Night,* June 1991). Indeed, the devices were not removed from the market for good until January 1992, two days after the U.S. Food and Drug Administration announced its prohibition on breast implants.

THE ROLE OF THE REGULATORY AGENCY: CRIMINALIZATION VERSUS COMPLIANCE

CRIMINALIZATION

All this has led to a debate over the "proper" role of the regulatory agency. Given that an enormous number of studies—from Sutherland in 1938, Clinard and Yeager in the late 1970s, Braithwaite throughout the 1980s, to Clarke, Levi, and Yeager in the 1990s—have all documented the minuscule use of criminal sanctions in controlling corporate crime, some have called for a greater use by regulatory agencies of penalties involving criminal law. As we have seen, regulators have typically preferred persuasion and education to laying charges; and their official legislative mandate has usually directed them to balance the benefits of enforcement against the drawbacks, assessing whether or not enforcement is in "the public interest." Will it, for example, have negative consequences such as loss of jobs in a community, or loss of votes for a particular incumbent or party?

Identifying this reluctance to "get tough" with corporate offenders as the problem, some scholars have seen increased use of imprisonment and higher criminal fines as the remedy. They argue that the stigma of criminality is the heaviest moral sanction a society can employ, and the only one the corporate sector will take seriously (Hawkins, 1984; Levi, 1984). Criminalization has practical advantages as well. Laws against corporate crime have to be struggled for, and are typically passed only after an environmental crisis or major disaster has aroused public outrage (Snider, 1987). In this situation, with the pressure on politicians to take immediate remedial action, criminalizing techniques represent the perfect response. They are visible, they appear tough, and they symbolize moral opprobrium. The fact that increasing the number and severity of criminal laws has not provided better control over corporate crime is explained by focusing on insufficient utilization. If criminal sanctions were to be deployed regularly, if corporations knew their chances of escaping criminal conviction were slight, if fines commensurate with the size of the firm and the profitability of the crime were imposed, if jail sentences were given, if these procedures were coupled with more enforcement personnel and more punitive laws, backed by civil and administrative remedies where appropriate, then criminalization and deterrence would be effective (Elkins, 1976; Watkins, 1977; Coffee, 1984; Glasbeek, 1989; Pearce, 1990a, 1990b, 1990c).

In recent years, however, with increasingly sophisticated studies of regulatory agencies, criminalization models have come under heavy attack. The first and most serious charge has been simply that criminal law does not work against corporate offenders. Regulatory law is different from traditional crime because its goal is not to punish, but to secure compliance and educate. Corporate offenders may lack the technical competence required for compliance, they may be ignorant of the law, or unintentional organizational (system) failures may lead them to offend. Moreover, charging corporations and executives and pursuing them through the criminal courts creates antagonism, threatening the cooperation and good will that are crucial to the effectiveness of regulation because so many areas of corporate misbehaviour are beyond the purview of law (Stone 1975).

A second charge is that criminalization actually increases the amount of harm corporate crime does. The strict evidentiary requirements of the criminal courts mean that a regulatory agency, rather than stepping in when it first hears of an offence, has to allow it to continue long enough to gather evidence. The high cost of utilizing criminal justice procedures is also an issue.

Since there is by all accounts even more corporate crime than traditional, and its damage to the society in terms of lives taken and money lost is much higher (see summary in Braithwaite, 1985a:12–13), reliance on the criminal justice system to control corporate crime, if anything close to full enforcement were attempted, would be fiscally impossible. The result would leave the poor not better off, but worse, "in more dangerous factories, marketplaces and environments" (Braithwaite, 1985a:11; see also Fisse and Braithwaite, 1983; Thomas, 1982:100; Shapiro, 1985; Smith, 1976; Kagan and Scholz, 1984).

Empirical studies support such criticisms. For example, Shapiro's examination of the Securities and Exchange Commission (SEC) in the United States argues: "Criminal prosecution is associated with regulatory failure. It is a response to offences that are discovered too late to prevent substantial harm" (1985:199). It is used only when the SEC has failed to discover an offence in its initial stages, when the damage has become significant, and when the administrative or civil remedies that would have contained the offence at an earlier stage are no longer practical. Or it is used on individuals who cannot be punished any other way because they lack corporate connections and ongoing relationships with the agency (small fly-by-night outfits, for example). Shapiro also points out that the success rate is much higher for civil and administrative actions, and that the fines assessed under criminal law are consistently lower than administrative or civil fines, not higher (Shapiro, 1985:202; see also King, 1985:15–16; Levi, 1984; Hopkins, 1978).

Rankin and Brown compared two agencies in the province of British Columbia, one of which used administrative penalties, the other criminal sanctions. The Waste Management Branch, using criminal law, filed an average of forty-four charges annually from 1984 to 1986, and convicted an average of sixteen per year. Those convicted were assessed an average fine of $565 each. Taking 1986 alone, the agency registered nine convictions with a mean fine of $500. The Workmen's Compensation Board, in contrast, issued 300 administrative penalties with a mean fine of $5000 in the first half of 1986, $3100 in 1985 (Rankin and Brown, 1988:6). Jamieson's study of British factory regulation identified four assumptions inspectors make that render them unlikely to use punitive measures: industry is powerful enough to resist regulations it defines as overly restrictive; regulations that threaten economic viability will not be passed in the first place; society only wants the harmful side-effects of industry restricted, as it approves of the corporate sector in general; and societal consent for the regulatory function would be withdrawn if policing were seen as overzealous (Jamieson, 1985).

Increasingly detailed studies on the nature of the regulatory agency also weaken the case for criminalization. As outlined earlier in this chapter, we can now delineate factors that create and nourish regulatory agencies (theories of origins), and specify the various constituencies, from the general public to producers, competitors, and government itself, to which they report (Kagan, 1978:13–15; Fels, 1982:32; Mitnick, 1980). The more we find out, the more limited the ability of the typical regulatory agency to employ a criminalization strategy appears to be. Many regulators argue that criminalization and effectiveness are not compatible. If they hope to protect their constituencies in the most efficient way—that is, using the fewest resources to accomplish goals in the speediest fashion—they cannot rely on criminal law. It is too slow, too expensive, and there are too many legal protections for powerful corporations to exploit to circumvent compliance.

COOPERATION

In light of such studies, scholars have begun looking at cooperative models: those that either renounce criminalization, or invoke it only in the final analysis. Indeed, in the popular and business press cooperative models (specifically models eschewing criminalization entirely) have been heralded as the solution to the vexing problem of government "fetters" on business. Two proposals typify the more scholarly versions of cooperative models. John Braithwaite has been seeking an effective sanctioning mechanism to surmount the weaknesses of criminalization strategies for some time. In 1982 he suggested government-enforced self-regulation, a scheme whereby organizations would be required to file, and have approved, their own proposals for policing potentially troublesome areas of operation such as pollution control or worker health and safety. Strict minimum standards for such plans would be provided by legislation, and the companies' suggested regulations would have to meet specific criteria in each industrial sector. After formulation, each plan would be checked, approved if satisfactory, and monitored periodically thereafter. The monitoring function would remain in government hands.

Such a system, Braithwaite argued, would have several key advantages over a reliance on criminal law. Those primarily responsible for enforcing each company's plan would be insiders, company employees, not agents of an outside regulatory body. As employees, they would have access to all kinds of formal and informal sources of information denied to outsiders. They would also have the technical knowledge of plant and industry processes that effective regulation requires. They would be less likely to be perceived as "the enemy" by fellow employees, since they would interact daily with staff and management. Because firms would draw up their own regulations, they could ensure that the rules fitted their particular organizational structure, something that universalistic criminal laws or even quasi-universalistic external regulatory standards cannot possibly accomplish. Standards and procedures could be adjusted in accord with technological changes in the means of production. Moreover, because the regulated organization would pay most of the costs of the scheme, governments would realize savings.

Braithwaite is not unaware of the potential hazards of such schemes: he concedes that company inspectors would be even more subject to capture than the externally hired present-day inspectors are; and he recognizes that getting companies to formulate rules that potentially sacrifice profitability to corporate responsibility would be difficult. However, on balance he concludes that such problems could be overcome by strict monitoring before the initial approval of company-generated plans, and by laws requiring a public report whenever management in a particular company overruled inspectors' recommendations (Braithwaite, 1982).

Building on these ideas, Braithwaite along with Fisse came up with a model to maximize what they designate as "informal social control," defined as "behavioural restraint by means other than those formally directed by a court or administrative agency" (Braithwaite and Fisse, 1983:1). Informal social control of corporate crime would rely heavily on stigma and adverse publicity as disincentives to antisocial behaviour. They argue that there should be mechanisms to increase public access to and knowledge of corporate crimes, because public criticism could then be a useful deterrent to potential corporate criminality. To demonstrate the potential of public opprobrium to bring corporations in line, they cite the complete about-face on the asbestos issue of James Hardie, formerly a major asbestos manufacturer in Australia. Under intense public pressure, the company progressed from the official position that asbestos was benign, with no potential for causing disease if properly used, to a recognition that it was sufficiently hazardous to require the company to phase it out of production.

Braithwaite and Fisse do, however, recognize the limitations of informal social control as a regulatory mechanism. In fact, they admit that other, equally persuasive reasons for James Hardie's about-face were technological and financial, as markets for asbestos gradually disappeared, and substitutes for asbestos became available. Their conclusion recognizes these realities: "Perhaps the real lesson ... is that informal social control can work when structural realities make it possible" (Braithwaite and Fisse, 1983:76).

Braithwaite (1988, 1985b) then advocated a pyramidal approach based on a hierarchy of penalties. Beginning with the assumption that industrial self-regulation, Braithwaite's ideal starting point, is either absent or has failed, the scheme sets out a series of steps the regulatory agency would be required to pursue from that point on. When it suspects infractions have occurred, the first mechanism to be employed is persuasion: the agency will contact the offending organization and try to convince its officers to comply with the legislation. Should that fail, the agency would next issue an official warning. The third step requires it to assess compulsory civil charges leading to mandatory monetary penalties if investigations confirm the offence. Criminalization is the final option. If all of the above fail, the regulatory agency would then (and only then) initiate criminal charges.

If found guilty, the organization and its executives would face sanctions ranging from prison sentences and fines to the mandatory removal of operating licences, possibly resulting in complete plant shutdowns. To reduce interference from "captured" regulators or politicians, the agency would have no discretion to halt or change this chain of events; each step would automatically lead to the next one until the problem was resolved. The system as Braithwaite conceptualizes it would overcome problems he attributes to excessive reliance on any one regulatory device, be it civil/administrative measures, criminal laws, or persuasion and education.

A variation based on the "prisoner's dilemma" logic game seeks to use mathematics and logic to demonstrate that cooperative strategies offer maximum advantage to both regulators and regulated (Scholz, 1984a, 1984b). Scholz begins with the reasonable assumption that both sides have an interest in minimizing costs, but only one, the regulated corporation, has an interest in minimizing sanctions. Thus, cooperative strategies, because they normally cost and punish less, offer maximum benefits to both sides. However, this truism holds only if both sides play by the same rules. The minute one player defects, the other must also if it would avoid playing the sucker. Thus, if a regulated organization ceases operating in a cooperative mode, the regulatory agency should instantly abandon persuasion/education mechanisms and move to a deterrence strategy by calling up appropriate legal sanctions. On the other hand, if the regulatory agency abandons the cooperative mode, the firm should move toward avoidance/evasion strategies. Under this model it is possible to demonstrate, in theory at least, that the corporation will derive less benefit from cheating than from cooperating; and that the regulatory agency will also benefit, being "suckered" at most one time before it adopts a punitive position. Scholz argues that the criminal law/deterrence strategies now used by regulatory agencies make law evasion a rational strategy for corporations to adopt.

This particular scheme dramatically illustrates the appeal of what has come to be called the law and economics movement. First, the arguments are grounded in mathematical symbols rather than words, and numbers carry a legitimacy all their own, with an aura of objectivity and hard science that make them hard to argue against. Second, the scheme implies that regulation is a morally neutral game with only two "sides," each seeking to maximize its benefits. A rough equality between the sides is also assumed, because an ongoing game is impossible if one side possesses all the chips. In symbolic terms this language conveys a very different set of assumptions about regulation than the discourse of criminality, with its message that regulatory offences are criminal acts; that respect for the law is an essential component of a civilized society; and that corporate crimes are antisocial behaviours that require societal intervention through criminal law to expiate damage done to the social fabric as well as to the lives of individuals. The language of barter and games reduces corporate crime to an ill-advised chess move. Third, the model purports to demonstrate that moving to a policy of cooperation is an economic and not a political strategy. The imperatives are therefore dictated by the hard laws of economic rationality.

Since rationality based on the economics of the marketplace is now widely believed to constitute the definitive, and only, version of truth, this is a much more persuasive argument than one based on "soft" concepts such as the needs of consumers or the moral obligations of business. Cooperative models such as these, then, try to get around the demonstrated pitfalls of criminalization by advocating economically rational schemes that are, purportedly, in the interests of both the regulated and the regulators. For many, they represent the perfect embodiment of the philosophical and ideological changes that have transformed regulatory law and practice in the 1980s and 1990s.

CONTRADICTIONS IN REGULATORY EFFECTIVENESS

Neither criminalization nor cooperative models, however, capture the essence of the regulatory contradiction. For neither takes into account the broader socioeconomic realities of capitalist systems (Gough, 1979), specifically the power of capital and its ramifications. Advocates of criminalization call for stricter enforcement, higher fines, and longer prison sentences while criminal laws on the books sit ignored, their sanctions underutilized. Since regulators, courts, and judges choose not to enforce the considerable arsenal of sanctions they already possess, how can securing even more punitive laws (that evidence suggests will be ignored in a similar fashion) represent an improvement? Moreover, since many of these crimes represent offences against women, is the patriarchal nature of corporate capitalism not also an explanatory factor of note (Dekeseredy and Hinch, 1991; Messerschmidt, 1986)? The sources of the resistance to criminalization cannot be overcome by clarion calls from academics.

Advocates of cooperative models also fail to deal with the implications of class-based power. While they recognize, correctly, that the overwhelming opposition of the corporate sector has consistently vitiated state or regulatory efforts to use criminal law effectively, they miss the fact that it will have precisely the same effect, or a more severe one, on cooperative models. The basic conflict of interest between industry's need for quick, high, stable profits and society's need for safe workplaces and products and humane operating procedures has been overlooked. It is corporate power that makes regulatory agencies and remedial measures ineffective, not some mysterious defect in the measures themselves. The same measures do, after all, function quite adequately in equally complex spheres of social control.

It is corporate resistance to effective regulation, to any and all measures that increase business costs and provide outside agents with a right to intervene in corporate affairs, that will make cooperative models equally futile. Indeed, we might expect such approaches to be considerably less effective than criminalization, although the extreme modesty of the typical cooperative system's regulatory goals may hide this because evaluators typically compare goals with results. Cooperative models offer business a considerable advantage, then, because they tilt the regulatory struggle strongly in its direction.

Indeed, this fatal flaw is the secret of their instant popularity among corporate analysts, the business press, and allied politicians. The reception accorded the law and economics movement in the public arena must be understood in ideological terms. With the decline of liberalism and the dramatic renaissance of the New Right, conservative forces that had been quiescent during the prosperous 1960s and 1970s came into their own. The capitalist class and its allies in the governments of major Western democracies such as the United States and Britain have promoted an economic agenda that favours austerity capitalism and monetarism.

A key component of this agenda has been the establishment of belief systems that make it appear both legitimate and inevitable that the share of national wealth received by working and lower classes be decreased. Concomitantly, in the interests of global competition and national survival, a larger share must go to the corporate sector. To compete successfully in the global marketplace, it is argued, business must lower costs by jettisoning labour, destroying unions, decreasing the corporate tax rate, and getting rid of government regulations that, from this perspective, serve only to increase costs and decrease efficiency (Horton, 1981; Comack, 1988).

Corporate activity, therefore, must be de-regulated, and all government "fetters" over business removed. Government stimulation of business, however, and massive direct and indirect subsidies are acceptable. Representatives of the New Right herald scholarly critiques of criminalization as confirming their ideologically based position. They see arguments such as those advanced by the law and economics groups (Smith, 1976, 1979; Sands, 1968; Scholz, 1984a, 1984b), as conferring scholarly blessings on their attempts to represent the corporate sector as the beleaguered scapegoat of social democracy in the postwar period. Regulation is too expensive, while the overwhelming importance of business to the development of the capitalist economy, they would argue, warrants overlooking any minor "mistakes" it might commit in its legitimate pursuit of profit. The congruence between this movement, then, and the academic critiques of criminalization explains much more about the popularity of cooperative models than any "objective" examination of the evidence can provide.

In fact, as the next chapter examines, the emphasis these models place on cooperation is nothing new. Virtually every regulatory agency studied has attempted, in the first instance, to cooperate with the business sector it is regulating. When the regulatory target is large and powerful rather than small and isolated, cooperation is mandatory, however strict and unbending the directives of the enabling legislation. Indeed, as noted earlier, every law requires those who would control to negotiate some minimal level of consent from their target groups (Pearce, 1991).

The limits of this negotiation, its starting and ending points, are the crucial factors. Limits are shaped by a number of variables, including the enabling legislation and precedents; the power of the groups targeted (meaning their political and economic clout as well as their ability to resist); the powers of the enforcement body (again, both politically and economically); and various structural variables such as the interests that will be served by nonenforcement or the relevant policies of the nation-state. Obviously, this process grants considerably more negotiating leverage to the multinational corporation than the armed robber. But since cooperative regulation in lieu of criminal sanctions is the norm and not the exception, it is obvious that, if there is evidence that criminalization does not work (which there is), there is equally compelling evidence that cooperation does not either.

Regulatory ineffectiveness, then, results from the structural constraints of regulatory agencies and the ideological, political, and economic consequences of these constraints. An instance of ideological power is seen in the fact that regulatory officials themselves frequently "buy into" dominant perspectives that view corporations and executives as essentially incapable of "real" criminality. Political and economic power are seen in the disparity in resources between regulatory agencies and the corporate sector; a disparity that makes it necessary for regulators to employ strategies that will not annoy the targets of regulation. The less powerful are particularly dependent upon the good will of the more powerful, since they lack the clout to be effective in its absence. They must therefore negotiate their path very carefully. Regulators need evidence that they are fulfilling some meaningful social role to continue in operation; however, they must not be too effective, or they will create a powerful group of enemies.

From the regulators' point of view, then, cooperative strategies make eminently good sense. Because they require less of the regulatory agency, they do not force agents continually to measure themselves and their performance against an impossibly high set of goals (that were frequently set during a political crisis to save the constituency of a particular politician or party). Paradoxically, however, from a social benefit point of view it is essential that regulatory agents and agencies continue to struggle with competing and conflicting objectives and even unrealistic and utopian goals. If, because of the political and structural realities of regulation, agents can typically enforce no more than 30 percent of their mandate, then it is essential that this represents 30 percent of a worthwhile, meaningful standard of control. To advance a third of the way toward a goal cooperatively negotiated with industry that would not deliver cleaner air or safer workplaces were it enforced at the 100 percent level is futile. At the risk of oversimplification, the entire agenda of regulation depends on a struggle between the forces opposing regulation (typically the corporate sector and its allies) and the much weaker forces supporting it.

The risk of cooperative models is that they allow the goals of regulation to be set too low. Such models treat the status quo, the existing balance of power between regulators and the corporate sector, as a basic social fact, a starting point, a reality that determines the ability of government to regulate corporate crime once and for all (Pearce and Tombs, 1988). However, if we are to approach the goal of regulatory effectiveness, the status quo ought to be viewed, instead, as a moving target, and those who wish to obtain more effective control over corporate crime must therefore force corporations and regulatory agencies, through ideological, political, and economic struggle, to move closer to this objective. Making the dominance of the corporate sector the starting point for regulators, rather than a barrier that must be challenged and overcome, sets very low standards for regulation.

SUMMARY

This chapter has examined the characteristics of the regulatory agency, its political fragility, and the debate over the adoption of cooperative approaches versus criminalization. At this point we have much more knowledge about what does not work to control corporate crime than about what does. However, a great deal is known about various types of regulatory agencies, the difficulties regulators face, and the solutions they tend to prefer. Because there is intense pressure from the targets of regulation in addition to that from political bosses, citizens, and sometimes external pressure groups as well, regulating corporate crime is very different from traditional policing.

Politicians are likely to intervene to protest against lenience when the target of enforcement is a traditional criminal suspected of low-level theft, fraud, or homicide; for corporate crime, politicians are more likely to intervene to *secure* lenience. The corporate offender's control over precious social resources such as jobs, prestige, and power makes regulation a continuing intellectual and political challenge. As this chapter has argued, regulation by its very nature requires a balancing act between different and frequently conflicting needs. Resolutions will always be tentative, unless and until one side gains total control over the other. However, given the very high costs of corporate crime—the staggering numbers of lives lost, injuries sustained, and mammoth economic costs—the struggle to achieve more effective regulation is a critically important one. The next chapter looks at sanctions, the negative measures actually enforced against particular corporate crimes. The analysis sets out the empirical basis of many of the generalizations about regulatory weaknesses made here and allows further examination of their implications.

NOTES

1. The Reagan administration carried this process even further, frequently appointing executives from regulated industries directly to regulatory positions in that sector (Yeager, 1991; Simon and Eitzen, 1990).

C H A P T E R 6

Sanctions

INTRODUCTION

This chapter examines the sanctions that have actually been imposed for corporate crime, focusing initially on several pieces of Canadian legislation, particularly the Combines Investigation Act. In most cases, this means examining the record and procedures of regulatory agencies, since these are the bodies responsible for calling businesses to account when they disobey a particular piece of legislation. Some of the international literature on the sanctioning process will also be examined.

As discussed earlier, the imposition of meaningful sanctions on the corporate sector has a lengthy history. For decades business resisted the idea that any of its activities could be labelled criminal, as well as the principle that governments have a right to intervene in the internal affairs of business, whether cloaked in the guise of public interest or not. On the behavioural level this has translated into lengthy and intense resistance to the imposition of any kind of sanctions, civil, administrative, or criminal, but particularly the latter. A hundred years later this general opposition persists. This does not mean that every regulatory action is always and everywhere resisted. At lower levels of particular organizations, a wide variety of regulatory regimes in a number of business settings have been routinized, with players on both sides accepting a certain level of enforcement activity as legitimate. Day-to-day relations between regulatory agents and relevant corporate officials, then, can be quite cordial. Nonetheless, generalized resistance remains, and regulatory agencies have to examine all but the most routine sanctioning activities with some care, particularly against large and powerful corporations, although smaller organizations with strong regional power bases and good political connections have also been known to be resistant. Does this level of opposition reflect a particular history? Does it mean that regulatory regimes have been harsh and overzealous in the past? There is certainly no evidence that business has ever been subject to the harsh, arbitrary, and often racist enforcement practices that have too often characterized criminal justice agencies (particularly, though not exclusively, police forces) (Silberman, 1980; Ericson, 1981, 1982; Ericson and Baranek, 1982). This chapter, therefore, will examine more recent enforcement history to determine, essentially, what business is complaining about.

CANADIAN FEDERAL AGENCIES

At first glance, it appears that, with few and temporary exceptions, sanctions have been very light. There is no regulatory agency that could be characterized as punitive in its practices by the standards of law enforcement used against traditional criminals. Indeed, by these standards agencies and laws are absurdly permissive. Compared to the Canadian Criminal Code, regulatory acts are full of loopholes.

Canada's Hazardous Products Act, for example, allows action to be taken only after the product is on the market, and therefore after damage has been done. The Food and Drugs Act allows manufacturers to do their own tests of the safety of their products, and accepts these tests as proof. Occupational Health and Safety Acts, both federal and provincial, in Canada and elsewhere, are worded in such a way that safe working conditions must be provided only if doing so will not seriously affect the profitability of the company. The Canadian Environmental Protection Act imposes emissions standards only after a "significant danger" to human health has been demonstrated (Schrecker, 1989:83). Examples of lenience in the written law (as opposed to law as it is actually enforced) abound. Nevertheless, because few regulatory agencies are completely moribund, enforcement at some level is ongoing.

Arguably the most important piece of federal legislation in the area of corporate crime is the Canadian Competition Act, formerly the Combines Investigation Act. Chapter 4 examined the struggle to create the original act in 1889. The act at that time covered only conspiracies, defined as horizontal combinations formed to restrict trade. Horizontal or vertical mergers were banned in 1910, and monopolies (and monopolization) in 1935. Monopolies were actually forbidden in the 1910 and 1923 acts, but since the word was not given an operational definition until 1935, prosecutions were impossible. (After it was defined, they were merely scarce and unsuccessful; see Canada, 1989:13 and 61.) Predatory pricing and price discrimination were added in 1935, and resale price maintenance and refusal to supply were introduced in 1951. The latter, somewhat technical terms, refer to sales practices that attempt to destroy competition by selling goods at a loss until competing firms have been driven into bankruptcy; or to wholesalers refusing to supply products to retail outlets that "deep discount" prices below a certain level.

Misleading or deceptive sales practices, such as false advertising, exaggerated claims, or bait and switch techniques, all used to entice the consumer to spend more and receive less for purchased goods, were introduced in 1960 and fine-tuned in the revisions of 1969 and 1976. A ban on bid-rigging was also introduced in 1976. Bid-rigging refers to agreements between apparent business competitors whereby organizations seeking a particular contract will all, except one, submit inflated and nearly identical cost estimates for undertaking a particular job, agreeing in advance to take turns submitting the lowest bid. The company whose "turn" it is to get a particular contract will submit the lowest bid in that round, but it will still be high enough to guarantee a comfortable profit margin to the company. The organization that called for the bids (for example, a Ministry of Transportation seeking competitive bids for the construction or repaving of highways), unaware of the conspiracy, may think it is getting a fair and honest price, when the price is actually artificially inflated.

Maximum sanctions vary widely between particular sections; moreover, they are amended in every major and most minor revisions of the act. In 1986, maximum penalties of $10 million or five years in prison were put in place for conspiracies to restrict trade. Sanctions for unfair trade practices such as false advertising were increased to allow maximum prison terms of five years, or up to $25,000 in fines. Mergers, monopolies, and all issues pertaining to them, on the other hand, became "reviewable matters"; criminal sanctions can no longer be applied to them. Indeed, most sections of the act, old and new, allow the Attorney General of Canada to decide whether charges will be laid, and the nature of the charges. Summary charges, with a summons to appear for a court hearing at a later date, are supposed to be laid for "minor" infractions; indictable charges, with the possibility of arrest and preliminary hearing, are reserved for "serious" ones. The attorney general is expected to consult with the relevant regulatory officials before doing this, but retains the right not to do so. A sanction that has survived all revisions thus far, one found only in the regulatory sphere, is the ubiquitous "order of prohibition." This is a "punishment" by which an offending company and/or its officers are ordered to cease breaking the law. If the company is so ungrateful as to defy this request, and such defiance is later discovered (an unlikely event), company officers can be sentenced to a maximum of two years in prison. Although the order of prohibition is commonly employed, the prison sanction has never been used.

For comparative purposes we will look at the sanctions imposed under the old Combines Investigation Act during the postwar period. The level of enforcement provided during this period, particularly the "activist" 1970s, has been criticized by corporate spokespeople as excessively stringent (Canada, 1989). One study looked at sanctions imposed under the Combines Investigation Act from 1952 to 1975. Excluding for the moment the section of the act dealing with misleading or deceptive sales practices (where different enforcement practices are involved), a total of eighty-nine prosecutions were completed during the twenty-three-year period. Of these, fifty-two were under section 32 (conspiracy to combine and/or restrict trade); twenty-nine were under sections 34 and 38 (resale price maintenance and predatory pricing); and eight were under section 33 (mergers and monopolies). This works out to an average of four completed cases per year. By comparison, in an analogous twenty-two-year period between 1949 and 1972 there were 300,771 cases successfully prosecuted for theft alone (Snider, 1977).

Of the eighty-nine cases under the Combines Investigation Act, eight were acquitted on all charges; two others were discharged at a preliminary hearing and never made it into court. The other seventy-nine were convicted. Twenty-two of them "got off" with nothing more than an order of prohibition, the legal equivalent of the biblical injunction to "go forth and sin no more." No one was sentenced to prison; indeed, as mentioned, this sanction has never been used for these offences, despite its inclusion in the act since the early days. In the remaining fifty-seven cases, the offending individuals and/or organizations were assessed fines. Fines varied from $300 to $50,000, but averaged $7000 to $8000 per company. In the vast majority of cases fines actually assessed were much smaller than the maximums allowed by the act at that time. Thus, only fifty-seven cases over a twenty-two-year period were deemed serious enough to merit tangible sanctions of any sort, and the sanctions employed were lenient overall (Snider and West, 1980).

This less than impressive enforcement record was compounded by the excessively conservative role played by the Department of Justice. The Restrictive Trade Practices Commission (RTPC), the agency responsible for discovering and investigating offences under the relevant sections of the act at that time, was not allowed, for a variety of bureaucratic, legal, and political reasons, to prosecute cases itself. Thus, in order to launch criminal charges, RTPC officials had to convince other officials, namely lawyers in the Department of Justice, that charges were warranted. Given that RTPC officials had done all the preliminary investigation in each case, and had special expertise in this area, one would expect their recommendations to be routinely followed. This was not the case. Over the period at issue, the Department of Justice refused to prosecute in more than 10 percent of the cases brought before it; eleven cases in all. The RTPC could never be described as an aggressive or recklessly punitive agency; indeed, excessive conservatism in recommending the laying of charges would more accurately describe its leanings. This is borne out by attrition rates. Of all the complaints received by agency officials from 1952 to 1975, an average of fewer than 2 percent were investigated. RTPC officials actually recommended charges for a minute percentage of the original 2 percent. It stands to reason that they did so only when they were convinced the issue was serious, the evidence overwhelming, and the case winnable (Snider, 1977:179–80; 1978:149).

THE 1986 REVISIONS

On June 19, 1986, the Competition Act and the Competition Tribunal Act came into force. The Competition Act combines criminal and noncriminal law provisions, and represents a major change in the philosophy and composition of regulation in Canada. Many components of the former Combines Act, particularly the provisions on mergers and monopolies, were thoroughly overhauled. The most significant change is the division of offences into two categories: criminal offences and "reviewable matters," and the establishment of a special regulatory court, the Competition Tribunal.

At the time of writing, only the following can be prosecuted criminally: bid-rigging, agreements among banks (to set identical service charges or interest rates, for example), conspiracy, discriminatory and predatory pricing, resale price maintenance, and a series of misleading or deceptive trade practices. Of course, charges do not *have* to be laid under these sections, any more than they did under the old act, where counselling and education were always the dominant enforcement strategies. All remaining behaviours—mergers, refusal to supply or deal, abuse of dominant position (which has replaced monopoly), tied selling, market restrictions, and the application of foreign laws and judgments for Canadian companies—have become "reviewable matters," subject to adjudication by the new Competition Tribunal under administrative law standards (Canada, 1989:27–28).

The Director of Investigation and Research retains the ultimate responsibility for enforcement of the Competition Act. For behaviours still subject to criminalization, this senior civil servant decides whether charges should be laid in a particular investigation, or whether "the promotion of continuing voluntary compliance" should be maintained (Canada, 1989:28). A "compliance-oriented approach" (Canada, 1989:28), now officially adopted, applies to all offences including those subject to criminalization.

The revisions have dramatically altered the language of the act. Instead of launching investigations, the director "initiates information contacts." In place of the adage that ignorance of the law is no excuse, the "information contacts" can be launched when the director thinks a person or corporation may be "unaware of a particular provision of the Competition Act" (Canada, 1989:29). Instead of forbidding offences, the act now seeks to investigate business climates and assess competitive opportunities.

The policy implications of this shift have been made explicit—officials of the regulatory agency, the Bureau of Competition Policy, are now responsible for communication and education, giving advisory opinions, providing information contacts and advance ruling certificates, monitoring compliance, and last and decidedly least, responding to possible violations. The primary criterion for assessing corporate behaviour, particularly prospective corporate mergers, has become the competitiveness of the businesses involved. Unlike the majority of Anglo-American countries, including Britain (Howe, 1989; Baxt, 1989), the criterion Canada will now employ is definitely *not* one that puts public interest first. Indeed, there is no instruction to the director or the tribunal to consider in any way the needs of regions or workers, employees, or communities. The director does not have the power to ask whether prices presently charged are excessive, let alone the authority to roll them back.

However, if the needs of consumers and workers are not taken into account in the Competition Act, the needs of industry certainly are. To avoid being "surprised" by officious regulatory actions, an industry can now approach the agency and obtain, free, advance opinions from regulatory officials about the legality of particular courses of action it is contemplating. This provision greatly increases the cost of regulation while simultaneously restricting the regulators' course of action in the future. Once an advance ruling certificate granting approval for a particular act (a merger, for example) has been issued, the agency cannot challenge it at a later stage, however socially destructive or ruinous the consequences turn out to be. From the business point of view, this is a "win–win" situation: uncertainty is lessened, predictability increased, profitability promoted, freedom of action increased, and the elusive "business climate" considerably improved.

Under the Competition Act, investigations begin with a preliminary examination. If there are grounds, the director is obliged to commence an inquiry. Inquiries can also be launched by the application of six Canadian residents, or by directive from the Minister of Consumer and Corporate Affairs. Once begun, records and documents (including computer records) can be searched and seized and oral examinations commenced, but only following a successful application to senior judicial authority. If the investigation is subsequently discontinued, the director must report on the reasons for this. However, these provisions are all somewhat fluid. Because of the strength of the corporate sector, and the passage of the Charter of Rights and Freedoms, powers given to the state under this act (and many others) are subject to regular legal challenges. The powers of search and seizure provided in the 1976 revisions, for example, were substantially weakened following the Southam Corporation's Supreme Court of Canada victory in 1984 (Canada, 1989:30). The rights of regulators as set out here, then, may well be weakened by more court victories for the corporate sector in the near future (Sheehy, 1992).

For reviewable matters (those no longer subject to criminal proceedings), sanctions that can be imposed under the act are strictly limited at the present time. Regulators can make investigative visits and negotiate with offenders to secure orders on consent. Or they can obtain what are called "the delineation of undertakings" from the company (Canada, 1989). This eliminates further investigation because the company "undertakes" to refrain from the behaviour under discussion (without admitting it ever engaged in such behaviour in the first place). One can no longer refer to the behaviour as a "crime"; it is now a "course of action" subject to negotiation. If the matter remains unsettled, the director may apply to the Competition Tribunal, advocating either resolution on consent (yet another consultative process), or on a contested basis. Should a case actually be contested—or, to use the official language, "where alternative case resolutions do not provide an appropriate remedy to the Director's competition concerns" (Canada, 1989:32)—the tribunal may go so far as to issue an order to the offender. The order may officially instruct the individual or company to follow a particular course of action or refrain from a given set of behaviours.

The Competition Tribunal is itself a "court of record," with the same powers and procedures as all superior courts. Its judgments may be appealed to the Federal Court of Appeal in the usual fashion. The decision of this court is final; no appeal to the cabinet is allowed. Four judges and up to eight lay members make up the tribunal. Lay members come largely from the corporate sector, although other constituencies may also be represented. Appointments are for terms up to seven years in length (Canada, 1989).

For those offences where criminalization remains an option, the director may recommend, at any stage of the proceedings, that the case be referred to the attorney general for action. Normally, a recommendation of the level of sanction recommended will accompany such a request. For example, the director may recommend that an order of prohibition on consent be sought. This can be negotiated without the need to register a guilty plea, conviction, sentence, or fine. However, it is up to the attorney general's office to decide whether to accept such a recommendation, or opt for a more punitive course of action (Canada, 1989:32).

RESULTS OF THE 1986 REVISIONS

This section looks at the results of these expensive and extensive revisions. Because of the complexity of the act, mergers and "the abuse of dominant position," the new term for monopolization, will first be examined. Mergers and monopolies have been decriminalized; what kinds of sanctions are now being assessed? Do they represent an improvement?

Mergers and Monopolies

No one would argue that the old provisions of the Combines Investigation Act were effective. Only thirteen charges were ever laid under section 33 from 1935, when monopolies were actually defined, until 1986 (Canada, 1989:61). The few convictions that resulted were all overturned on appeal. A basic problem with securing convictions that would stick was the wording of the law. Its language was interpreted in legal decisions in a way that required the government to prove that each and every merger resulted (or would result) in a monopoly detrimental to the public interest. This was a tall order, in face of the massive resources and expensive legal talent the corporate sector made available to challenge the typically outgunned and underresourced federal prosecutors. A recent government paper puts this differently, attributing the failures of monopoly/merger law to the inadequacies of criminal law. It says: "The rules of evidence, burden of proof and implication of wrongdoing found in criminal provisions are inappropriate to evaluation of a merger's future impact on the competitive environment" (Canada, 1989:18). With the abandonment of criminal law, the Crown does not have to prove public detriment; remedial action can be taken as soon as investigators are convinced that a merger will "likely prevent or lessen competition substantially" (Canada, 1989:35).

The first director appointed under the Competition Act, Calvin S. Goldman, would agree with these sentiments on the ineffectiveness of criminal prosecution. He has been quoted as saying that the revisions, and the philosophical changes they embody, represent a major victory, a giant step forward. At a 1989 conference commemorating the centenary of combines law in Canada, he argued that the new rules make law more effective and efficient. The new Competition Tribunal, he points out, has successfully negotiated deals with industry without resorting to adversarial measures. Here he cites cases such as Nabisco's take-over of Weston, Safeway over Woodward Stores, and Hostess over Frito-Lay, where companies swallowing up their competitors were persuaded to modify their plans in such a way that mono-polization was avoided. The revisions, he says, have created a "modern and realistic framework for addressing antitrust issues," which protect competition without putting "crippling con-straints" on the ability of Canadian industries to compete in international markets (Goldman, 1989:2).

However, when one looks at the record, or asks "in whose interests" the legislation operates, it is hard to adopt so sanguine a view. No one would argue that the opportunity to stop a poten-tially detrimental merger before it occurs (an option not present under the former law) is a bad thing. The issue is whether or not regulators have been put into a position where they lack the bar-gaining power and access to information to determine what is harmful. Assuming they can make this judgment, do they have sufficient tools to act on their evaluations? Although the process has been altered, the result appears to be that the corporate sec-tor can do much as it pleases, with the additional security of knowing its actions cannot be legally challenged because the regulatory agency has approved them in advance. Indeed, the director's implicit definition of the "success" of the revisions is premised on their allowing the regulatory agency to avoid taking adversarial measures. As outlined below, the changes have not even led to a leaner and meaner agency; they require more regu-latory staff, thereby vastly increasing costs to government. Add-ing more resources to regulatory agencies is not necessarily a bad thing. In this case, however, the regulators are prevented by law from using their increased resources to represent more effectively the public interest; the criterion of public interest was specifically excluded from the act.

This outcome may be advantageous for business and indus-try; indeed, the blue ribbon committee of corporate elite who designed the legislation must be proud. The benefits for everyone else, however, are hard to see. As a speaker at the aforemen-tioned conference on the centenary of combines law pointed out, in what has to rank as a massive understatement, the new merger policy is "very timid" (Davidson, 1989:31). By not challenging takeovers or subjecting price-fixers to criminal law, the director sends out a signal that consensual solutions will always be favoured. Any corporation with good legal advice will therefore enter negotiations with "intended changes or give-aways dressed up as major concessions" (Davidson, 1989:32). Regulatory officials now enter a bargaining relationship with business where one side is constrained by a policy that seeks cooperation and consensus at all costs, while the other, with nothing to lose, can "go for broke" each and every time. The utterly predictable result, outlined below, is that regulators are outmanoeuvred. Satisfaction for the director and the Bureau of Competition Policy may be achieved, but at the expense of Canadian consumers, workers, and communities. Moreover, because tests of the statutory law are eschewed in the interests of cooperation, even self-policing becomes impossible because no legal limits have been put on the parameters of the negotiation process. This leads to a limitless expansion of the work of the bureau, as well as limitless expense. On top of this, the public has no way to resist or question because it has no access to information on the bureau's secret deals; the dominance of business interests has made routine a level of secrecy that would never be countenanced in other enforcement arenas. Routine disclosures of information may be "long overdue" (Davidson, 1989:35), but they are unlikely to occur without heavy countervailing pressure, and that is not, so far, on the horizon.

Sanctions Assessed

Turning to sanctions assessed, one finds that few mergers have been contested. Even in the face of clear and unambiguous evidence combined with deliberate intent to flout Canadian law, regulators have been reluctant to act. Weaknesses in merger policy are obvious. The takeover of Wardair by Pacific Western was not challenged despite the fact that the director himself formally recognized that it would lessen service and competition if allowed to go ahead. It went ahead, nevertheless, with token changes. Imperial Oil was permitted to acquire Texaco despite the high levels of concentration and the rampant number of uncompetitive practices that were recognized (by the agency itself) as characteristic of the entire petroleum industry. In one of the very first cases under the new act, the director overruled the recommendations of its own Competition Tribunal to allow the takeover of Palm Dairies by the Fraser Valley Milk Producers in 1986. Similar examples of regulatory "cooperativeness" abound.

For conspiracy, discriminatory and predatory pricing, misleading or deceptive practices, and price maintenance cases, the 1986 legislation was significant only in terms of the philosophical shift in regulatory policy it signalled. These sections of the act were left substantially unaltered, although new defences against these charges were added, and the maximum level of fines increased. These offences remained criminal matters, subject to criminal procedures, with the onus of proof resting firmly on the prosecution or Crown. The sanctioning record before and after the revisions went into effect can be examined to see what effect, if any, the philosophical shift has had on these behaviours.

Table 6.1 shows the number of cases opened, the number referred to the attorney general for further action, and the number of prosecutions or other proceedings commenced, for three different time periods. Two of these periods, 1982–84 and 1984–86, predate the latest revisions while one, 1986–88, shows regulatory activity in the immediate post-revision period.

Notice the sharp decline in the number of cases referred for further action, and in the number of legal proceedings launched, in the post-revision (1986–88) period. These figures cover too short a period of time to be definitive; moreover, they exclude misleading advertising and deceptive marketing provisions (which are examined below). Nonetheless, a decline of 50 percent in the number of cases referred, and a similar drop in the number of proceedings commenced does not bode well from an enforcement perspective.

T A B L E   6 . 1

Sanctions for Criminal Matters (Excluding Trade Practices) Before and After Competition Act

	Number of Cases	Referred to AG	Prosecutions or Other
1982–84	441	44	37
1984–86	506	48	36
1986–88	475	24	23

Source: Bureau of Competition Policy. 1989. *Competition Policy in Canada: The First Hundred Years*. Ottawa: Consumer and Corporate Affairs: 59.

The post-revisions director himself, however, does not share these misgivings. He points with pride to a phenomenon the table does not reveal, an increase in the number of orders of prohibition assessed in price-fixing cases in the 1986–88 period. He sees this as evidence that the new law is providing "immediate protection," in addition to being "less costly than contested litigation" (Goldman, 1989:19). Moreover, he claims that fine levels have increased since the revisions came into effect, citing a $1.6 million fine in one 1988 bid-rigging case.

Once again, data are not available for a more rigorous assessment of the director's claims. Scattered reports of record-high fines are hardly convincing, however, since longitudinal studies have reported wide variations in fine levels from year to year (see, for example, Goff and Reasons, 1978; Stanbury, 1988; or Snider, 1978). One record fine can hardly be taken as evidence of an upward trend. It is also hard to argue that orders of prohibition represent a novel initiative when a full twenty-two of the eighty-nine prosecutions launched between 1952 and 1975 were "settled" in that fashion (Snider, 1978:157).

It is considerably easier to find qualitative evidence that links the decline in prosecutions recorded in Table 6.1 to the cooperative stance of the regulatory agency, the Bureau of Competition Policy. Indeed, examples of the lengths to which the bureau is now willing to go to avoid adversarial action are legion. Consider, for example, the elaborate scheme to fix the price of legal services undertaken by two professional associations of lawyers in Ontario. The rationale most frequently advanced for a failure to lay charges under the new act is that the groups or organizations in question were ignorant of the law—hardly a credible excuse when the offending bodies are composed entirely of lawyers. A second rationale is that the offences were short-lived, or that no party benefited from them to any extent. Yet this price-fixing scheme was blatant, longstanding, and highly profitable. It ensured that no one in Ontario could receive legal services without paying uniformly high fees, and saved lawyers from the embarrassment of competing for customers.

All the same, it was "settled" with a consent order. No sanctions were imposed, and of course, few details about either the original conspiracy or the subsequent consent agreement were released. As far as can be seen, the relevant law associations were merely instructed to cease price fixing from that time forward. There is no mention of their being required to compensate past clients for the thousands of dollars in excess lawyers' fees clients paid. Similar examples of lenience abound in the director's annual reports (Canada, 1989:59).

Financial Effects

The change in philosophy and procedure from the old act was premised on the belief that criminalization was expensive and inefficient, and that cooperation was, in contrast, cheaper and more cost effective. Has this in fact been the case? Ironically, the answer is a resounding no. The new cooperative approach (designed and sanctified by the corporate sector itself, it must be remembered) has turned out to require a large increase in the number of regulatory staff, particularly in the office of the Director of Investigation and Research. While regulatory staff numbers have been steadily increasing in the postwar period, the passage of the Competition Act appears, far from arresting this trend, to have accelerated it.

Average yearly staff numbers went from 156 in 1971–75 to 256 in 1986–88, and average expenditures from $2,758,000 to $15,284,000 (Canada, 1989:58). Lest it be thought that all these officials were idle, 402 merger files were opened in the period from June 1986 to May 1989. Each required at least two person-days for preliminary registration and assessment, and twenty-six required monitoring. Seven cases were abandoned, a total of nine mergers were restructured, five went to the Competition Tribunal, and two will be appealed before it.

This makes for a vastly increased workload, requiring endless consultations and negotiations with few tangible results and even less public benefit. Somehow we have managed to double the size and number of regulators while simultaneously making them less effective (a very Canadian achievement). Indeed, regulators have been turned into free consultants for industry, making the business climate better by assuring corporations in advance that their contemplated takeovers and monopolies will be legally blessed. This situation is a direct result of the government's rejection of adversarial proceedings. As Davidson points out, "one or two substantive judicial pronouncements would ... concentrate the forces of the Bureau's activity and save resources for everyone" (1989:34). However, the director of the Competition Act apparently saw things quite differently. He was still convinced, as quoted in 1989, that the effect of the revisions was entirely positive: "Since 1986 ... it is fair to say, a quiet revolution has taken place" (Goldman, 1989:1). The evidence to date, fragmented and inconclusive as it is, indicates that he is right. A regulatory revolution has indeed occurred, but the prime beneficiaries have certainly not been the Canadian public.

Misleading Advertising and Deceptive Marketing Practices

Finally, let us examine the statutes governing misleading advertising and deceptive marketing practices. These were the sections revised in 1976 in the Stage 1 Amendments to the Combines Investigation Act; they were therefore left substantially unchanged in 1986.[1] These sections have been, since their introduction in 1960, the most vigorously enforced components of the Combines Investigation Act (as it was then). Trade practices are visible in a way that combines and mergers are not, because these messages, through advertisements, are visible to the public; indeed, that is their point. Advertising is big business in Canada, worth $6 billion per annum. Because it is so visible it attracts a lot of attention, from politicians, media critics, pressure groups, churches, and the like, and no public regulatory body can afford to ignore it. Each year thousands of allegedly false, misleading, or deceptive advertisements are reported to the Department of Consumer and Corporate Affairs. There were, for example, 12,382 official allegations in the fiscal year 1986–87, 90 percent of them originating with consumers (*Collins Report*, 1988:5).

As Table 6.2 indicates, enforcement activity has increased consistently and dramatically over the past twenty-five years. The number of files opened went from thirty-three in 1968–69 to 12,374 in 1987–88. Attrition rates, however, have been consistently high as well. A very small number of the total cases opened eventuate in recommendations to the attorney general that charges be laid, and the number of convictions actually registered is lower yet. The statistics may be somewhat misleading, however, because the amount of discretion granted to regulators to decide whether a given complaint should become a file has varied somewhat over the years.

Table 6.2 provides additional evidence that the more lenient attitude toward business signalled in the 1986 revisions has been felt, despite the fact that these sections were basically unaltered. Nevertheless, a substantial drop can be seen in the number of matters referred to the attorney general for further action, and in the number of convictions recorded in the post-revision 1986–88 period. Once again, it is too early to know whether this is a trend or a temporary blip. Similarly, once again Mr. Goldman, the

T A B L E   6 . 2

Percentage of Files Resulting in Charges: Misleading Advertising/Price Misrepresentation

	1968–69	1973–74	1978–79	1983–84	1987–88
Number of files opened	33	4387	8091	10,091	12,374
Matters referred to attorney general	n.a.	123	174	181	113
Convictions	13	70	119	138	84

Source: Bureau of Competition Policy. 1989. *Competition Policy in Canada: The First Hundred Years*. Ottawa: Consumer and Corporate Affairs: 60.

director at that time, explains away the declines as "small," arguing that the figures show that his staff are becoming more selective, weeding out the insignificant offences and prosecuting only the serious ones (Goldman, 1989:24). Although comprehensive data are not available (which is why fines are not included in the table), Goldman again asserts that there has been a "significant increase" in fine levels, with averages topping $13,000 in 1986–87, considerably higher than the $6000 average in 1985–86 or the $3783 per case assessed in the fiscal year 1979–80 (Goldman, 1989:24; Varrette et al., 1985:35–36).

To sum up, then, there is reason to believe that a nonpunitive and accommodating regulatory agency, which is what the earlier data depict, has become even more lenient since the Competition Act came into effect in 1986. As Stanbury has said: "Canada's new competition legislation reflects the lengthy and conflict-ridden process which produced it. Scores of political, professional and analytical compromises have obviously been made" (1986–87:41).

COMPARATIVE SANCTIONS IN OTHER JURISDICTIONS

The study above indicates that the Canadian federal government has embraced the cooperative philosophy with considerable enthusiasm since Brian Mulroney's Conservatives came to power in 1984. However, it is also obvious that enforcement was perfunctory under previous regimes with presumably very different philosophies. Perhaps, then, this reluctance to sanction business is a peculiarly Canadian phenomenon, rooted in our elitist, non-revolutionary past and longstanding traditions of respect for constituted authorities? Perhaps corporate crime has been more effectively sanctioned elsewhere? There is little evidence for such an interpretation, at least in the Anglo-American democracies where data are available.

Looking first at the United States, it is necessary to examine the omnibus study of sanctions and corporate crime done by Clinard and Yeager in the late 1970s (Clinard and Yeager, 1980). Although planned as a replication of Sutherland's study almost fifty years earlier, the authors took advantage of the methodological and epistemological progress social science had made in the ensuing decades to employ a sophisticated and ambitious research design. They looked at all charges laid against 477 of the largest publicly owned corporations in the United States, by a total of twenty-five federal regulatory agencies, over the two-year period 1975 to 1976. Their conclusion was that companies were not subjected to "the full force of the law" (Clinard and Yeager, 1980:122).

Their conclusion was based on findings such as the following: of the total 1529 sanctions assessed, fully 85 percent of the penalties were administrative rather than criminal in nature; a grand total of sixteen executives over the two-year period received jail sentences; and all the sentences together totalled only 594 days of incarceration. In fact, when one atypical case is excluded from the data—two executives in the same case were each sentenced to six months in jail—the average becomes a meagre nine days apiece (Clinard and Yeager, 1980:291). Nor were all defendants treated equally. Antitrust offenders, those who committed offences against the economy or another corporation, were most likely to receive penal sanctions. Offenders who caused physical injury to workers or consumers, through manufacturing unsafe products or dumping toxic wastes, for example, were treated far more leniently than those whose offences hurt the economy. Ninety-nine percent of the former escaped all criminal sanctions, whereas only 28 percent of the latter were handled in a noncriminal fashion (King, 1985:15–16).

Corporate size was a factor in sanctions as well. Giant firms, those with annual sales of $1 billion or more, had an average of 5.1 violations each, compared to the total average of 2.7 offences per company overall. However, the median fine for such firms was only $1000, significantly less than the $1650 average fine given medium-sized firms (although more than the $750 average fine the smallest firms received) (Clinard and Yeager, 1980:124). There was a reluctance to charge executives in addition to companies; regulators preferred to lay charges against the organization only. Thus, only fifty-six executives were singled out for charges over the two-year period.

Eighty percent of all fines assessed were for $5000 or less. Average fines varied widely by type of offence, however, with a clear tendency for offences against the economic system to attract the highest sanctions. Fines for financial cases averaged $148,644 (although this figure is unnaturally high because one $23 million fine was handed out during the period under study), and those for restraint of trade (offences such as price fixing and illegal combines) averaged $47,400. Fines for other offences were much lower, with manufacturing offences averaging $10,000; violations against labour codes $1275; and those against the environment a mere $1424 (Clinard and Yeager, 1980:126). More than half of the sanctions (44.2 percent) consisted of nothing more than a warning; 12.9 percent received consent orders and decrees (roughly analogous to the Canadian order of prohibition); 23.4

percent were assessed monetary penalties; and the remainder received a variety of miscellaneous sanctions: all in all, an impressive picture of lenience and inaction.

A second study documenting sanctions was done by Susan Shapiro, who looked at the operation of the Securities and Exchange Commission (SEC) in the United States. The SEC is the federal agency that regulates stock exchanges and trading. One would expect rigorous enforcement in this area, for many of the financial transactions that influence the health of capitalist economies occur in this sector and (as seen above) financial offences attract the largest fines in the field of corporate crime. Shapiro observed enforcement procedures at the agency for much of 1976 and 1977, then analyzed a random sample of 499 investigations with a total of 2101 suspects in the time period from 1948 to 1972. Her findings largely reinforce the picture presented by Clinard and Yeager.

The typical offence involves three individuals or organizations, victimizes between twenty-six and fifty investors, and nets around $100,000 in profit (Shapiro, 1985:185). The most common offence preferred against corporations was misrepresentation and failure to register. Under SEC rules, all corporations wishing to offer shares for sale and trade on public stock exchanges are required to disclose certain information, including statistics on the company's financial health, prospects, and assets. These have to be registered with the SEC in a prospectus available for stockbrokers and potential investors to evaluate. When companies do not register, the SEC is empowered to take action. Such charges are relatively easy to lay, because the behaviour in question is visible, straightforward, and easily monitored. More significantly, enforcement action would usually be supported by the powerful corporations already registered on exchanges, since it is not in their interests to allow competitors to divert investment away from their own offerings, which are likely to be long-registered, highly respected "blue chip" stocks. This explanation is supported by Shapiro, who observes that investigated offenders tend to be newer, smaller firms rather than companies on the Fortune 500 list.

The sanctioning powers of the SEC provide regulators with four options. They can take no legal action; institute administrative proceedings under SEC administrative law; launch civil actions in federal district courts; or refer the case to the U.S. Department of Justice for criminal action. Criminal options are generally regarded as the most punitive, the no sanction option is clearly the least punitive, and the administrative and civil options range in the middle. The regulators' choices, and the results of these, are illustrated in Table 6.3.

Table 6.3 clearly illustrates the lenience accorded corporate offenders (and the SEC, for reasons to be discussed in the next chapter, ranks as one of the most efficient regulatory agencies). For most of the offences listed, the most common sanction is none at all. Only when funds are "misappropriated" (stolen) as well as misrepresented, and in stock manipulation cases, does the SEC take formal action in more than 50 percent of the cases. Even in these instances, however, criminal charges are laid only 27 and 25 percent of the time respectively. Finally, as Shapiro points out, although ninety-three of every 100 suspects have committed violations that carry criminal penalties, this route is taken for only eleven of every 100 cases (Shapiro, 1985; for Canadian data in similar areas, see Hagan, 1989b:19–70; Hagan and Parker, 1985).

It would be wrong to conclude, however, that the civil or administrative procedures handed out by the SEC are uniformly insignificant and nonpunitive, or are perceived as such by those on the receiving end. Shapiro presents data to show that, for a small minority of offenders, the sanction can be as severe as the suspension or cancellation of trading privileges on the stock exchange. This is guaranteed to get the attention of the most hardened corporate criminal, since it affects the ability of the offender/organization to earn money and amass profits, unlike

T A B L E   6 . 3

Disposition of SEC Cases

Type of Offence	None	Criminal	Civil	Adminis-trative	Total
Nonregistration Alone	71%	1%	23%	9%	(109)
Misrepresentation Alone	58	6	16	25	(79)
Misrepresentation with Nonregistration	56	9	31	12	(187)
Misappropriation Alone	40	17	23	35	(99)
Nonregistration, Misappropriation, & Misrepresentation	41	27	29	19	(121)
Self-Dealing	52	19	23	12	(84)
Stock Manipulation	46	25	35	20	(91)

Source: Shapiro, 1985:195–97.

the majority of regulatory options up to and including criminal charges. Once again, however, the offenders most likely to have trading privileges suspended are small companies or isolated entrepreneurs, not major traders. The majority of sanctions handed out under civil and administrative proceedings are actually negotiated consent agreements where the corporation admits no wrongdoing, but pledges not to do it again all the same!

Agencies may have good reasons for avoiding criminal sanctions. Rules of evidence frequently require allowing the offending behaviour to continue long after its discovery, in order to amass sufficient evidence for prosecution. Or they may introduce a new level of uncertainty into the procedures by taking enforcement out of the hands of the agency that specializes in that offence and handing it over to one with no such expertise. This is almost always the case with federal offences in the United States, for these are typically channelled through the Department of Justice, an organization with very different priorities and procedures than the typical regulatory agency. Furthermore, criminal procedures may take away the possibility of forcing offenders to make restitution to those they have defrauded.

Whatever the rationale, the minimum measures commonly employed do little to deter corporate offenders, particularly when the average profit realized from the typical financial crime far surpasses the average sanction. The weakness of deterrence is exacerbated by the fact that companies quickly realize that their chances of receiving no sanction at all are excellent. Under such circumstances, the stigma of criminal charges may be the only regulatory action with any force, symbolically if not instrumentally. Moreover, when these kinds of sanctions are put beside those meted out to average blue-collar thieves, whose thefts are minuscule by comparison, the perception of systemic bias is hard to avoid.

Nor is lenience restricted to the United States. Clarke reports that, in the United Kingdom, fines under the Health and Safety at Work Act *never* exceeded 16 percent of the maximums specified by law during the 1976 to 1979 period examined (Clarke, 1990:205–6). The average fine imposed for safety and health offences under the Factories Act was £40 (roughly $100 Canadian) in 1970; the average increased to £474 (less than $1000 Canadian) in 1985. Controlled for inflation, this represents a real increase, but a mid-size industry assessed the average 1985 fine would still be paying a minuscule amount of its operating budget (Pearce and Tombs, 1990:415). As Ermann and Lundman have pointed out in their overview of American data: "We have calculated the equivalent fine for a person earning $15,000 per year. A 'small' corporation with annual sales of $300 million paying a $5000 fine is paying the equivalent of 2.4 cents. If the same corporation pays a $100,000 regulatory fine, a rare occurrence, it would be paying the equivalent of less than a half dollar" (Ermann and Lundman, 1982:234). Less than 50 cents, in other words, for jeopardizing the lives and health of workers.

THE EFFECT OF SANCTIONS

Thus far it has been documented that the average sanctions assessed against corporate criminals are small in absolute terms, and positively microscopic in relative ones, that is, when compared with sanctions against those who steal or endanger the lives of others in more traditional criminal contexts. One school of thought, particularly common among the judiciary, maintains that this discrepancy is more apparent than real because corporate criminals suffer disproportionately from the publicity surrounding the sanctioning process. Respectable citizens and corporations, the argument goes, lose a great deal before their particular case even comes to trial, because of the damage done to their reputations and good names.

This argument makes several dubious assumptions, the most obvious being that the good name and reputation of lower-class people is not affected by criminal charges (or, worse yet, that their good name does not matter). It also overlooks the fact that the vast majority of actions against corporate criminals are taken in virtually complete secrecy, with the identity of suspected offenders known only to regulators in one agency. If identities are released at all, it is likely to be in an obscure annual report to Parliament or Congress. Nevertheless, the question of how formal and informal sanctions actually affect corporate criminality is an important one that warrants further examination.

The evidence to date indicates that, far from suffering more, corporations and their executives experience only a fraction of the shame, stigma, and loss of job opportunities endured by lower-class people found guilty of criminal offences. Quite the reverse, in fact; in some cases identification as corporate criminals seems to make them more desirable, both to their own employer and to competitors. The Ford Motor Company was fined a total of $7 million in 1972, and in 1973 the salaries of all the chief executives were increased (Coleman, 1989). Clinard and Yeager point out that the few executives who resign or get fired following sanctioning tend to reappear on the corporate payroll as "consultants" a little while later, sometimes in a matter of days (1980:297). In a famous electrical industry conspiracy, several of the convicted conspirators received promotions or were elected to prestigious honorary positions in industry associations shortly after their convictions (Geis, 1967).

A series of studies on celebrated corporate crimes in the United States, Europe, Australia, New Zealand, and Japan uncovered virtually no evidence that either the publicity or the ensuing convictions caused any long-term negative consequences for the organization or its executives (Fisse and Braithwaite, 1983). The price of the company's stock, its reputation, sales, or most significantly, its profitability—none of these suffered more than a temporary decline. Most of the executives involved resumed their normal jobs after the furor died down, and virtually none suffered financially from the experience since legal costs and fines were typically handled by the corporation. Contrast this with the experience of their victims, who often lost their lives, their health, or their way of life.

These are tangible losses. What about the intangible effects, the loss of reputation, the social stigma? There is little evidence that the peers or communities of corporate criminals exert negative pressure or shun the offenders. The president of A.H. Robbins, the company responsible for marketing the Dalkon Shield, was publicly lauded while the media and courts were full of horror stories on the suffering endured by victims of the Shield and the company's complicity in marketing a device it knew to be risky. The president of the University of Virginia praised the president of A.H. Robbins for his contributions to the community and described him as a man whose "example will cast its shadow into eternity, as the sands of time carry away the indelible footprint of your good works" (Sherrill, 1987:56).

The legal system is also incredibly forgiving when it comes to corporate crime. Not only does it provide dozens of ways for corporations to avoid admissions of guilt, it happily erases the few convictions that have been registered, demanding very little evidence that the company has mended its ways. For example, Revco, a large drug discount chain in the American Midwest, defrauded the Ohio Department of Public Welfare of more than half a million dollars by creating false invoices for prescriptions it filled for welfare recipients. When the fraud was discovered, two senior executives pleaded no contest to two counts of fraud and paid $2000 each to the state. In addition, the company pleaded no contest to ten counts of falsification, paid a $50,000 fine, and made $521,521.12 in restitution. (This was one of the very few offences that did not produce windfall profits for its perpetrators.) Note, however, that neither the executives nor the company were ever found guilty of any wrongdoing. All parties escaped official culpability with negotiated "no contest" pleas (Vaughan, 1979). Even this seems to have been viewed as unusually harsh. A mere four years after the original trial, Revco applied for, and received, permission to have its record officially expunged (Vaughan, 1982).

SUMMARY

Regulatory agencies have an enormous and difficult task to perform. Adequately controlling and sanctioning corporate criminality, given all the legal, political, and ideological barriers, is challenging to say the least. As demonstrated earlier, complex bureaucracies shield individuals and mask their behaviours, and the larger the corporation the more effective the shield. Corporate structures and associated levels of responsibility can be incredibly complex. Businesses *do* provide an important source of employment in this society; they also produce objects that are central to our affluent way of life. One does not interfere lightly with them.

Criminal guilt may be costly and difficult to establish in a court of law, in face of a judiciary that identifies with the accused more often than the prosecution (Coleman, 1989; Simon and Eitzen, 1990). There are undoubtedly certain circumstances where accepting a negotiated plea or settling for administrative remedies is more practical than advocating criminal sanctions. It is also true that regulators need to develop and maintain a minimal level of cordiality with those they are regulating, to get access to the information they need to be effective (Thomas, 1982). Regulatory agencies do have limited resources, which severely restricts the number of cases that can be investigated and/or prosecuted at any one time. Most important of all, regulators are daily confronted by powerful, wealthy, and politically astute offenders who know precisely how to extract concessions from regulatory agencies or their political bosses, resist control efforts, or delay cases for years, if not decades. It is not surprising, then, that regulators typically adopt the strategies and attitudes they do.

Given all of these factors, however, to the outside analyst it is evident that regulatory agencies have been, in the main, ineffective, and that sanctions have been minuscule. This is, of course, a relative judgment, meaning that the vast majority of the offences uncovered (which may be only a tiny percentage of the actual offences occurring) are not sanctioned. It is assumed, therefore, that offenders are not deterred from repeating the offensive behaviour. This analysis cannot be confirmed in an absolute manner, obviously, because there is no way of telling how many corporate crimes would occur in a particular sector if there were no regulatory agencies, or conversely, how many would occur if speedy detection and punishment were the norm. All the same, it is hard to imagine any organization, however small, being deterred under present circumstances, for in almost all cases the offence is highly profitable, the chances of being caught are small, and the probable sanction if apprehended (receiving friendly advice from an official of a toothless regulatory agency, for example) is anything but intimidating. Those who would argue that this lax and compassionate form of social control is the most effective type fail to explain why such an approach is not regularly employed with those who steal bicycles or break into houses, offenders who cause much less damage to the social fabric and steal negligible amounts by comparison.

This chapter, then, has examined the sanctions actually handed out to corporate offenders. Choosing a wide variety of acts from several countries, it has been shown that the sanctions are tiny, especially when compared with the harm done and the profit made in the typical corporate crime. The next chapter looks at the reasons for this ineffectiveness and examines possible remedies to overcome it.

NOTES

1. The federal government is studying proposals to decriminalize false advertising, replacing the present laws with statutes that would allow offenders merely to "make an undertaking ... not to repeat" the offences when caught (*The Globe and Mail*, Tuesday, March 19, 1991:B1). Since many companies would qualify as habitual criminals, having been found guilty on several occasions, and since the offence is very profitable, such an approach seems excessively kind. Whatever else it does, it should ensure continued excellent relations between the present Conservative government, the regulatory agencies, and the corporate sector—at the expense, one would suspect, of the interests of the public.

Understanding Ineffectiveness

INTRODUCTION

This chapter examines the reasons why corporate crime has been ineffectively regulated, and looks at some ways of changing this. There has been no shortage of remedies suggested, at both the level of prevention and the level of deterrence. Preventive remedies focus upon psychological, organizational, and structural conditions that shape the motivation to engage in occupational and corporate crime; deterrence strategies examine the mechanisms and institutions that control such offences.

Straightforward occupational offences can be conceived as primarily crimes of greed, committed wherever susceptible individuals have opportunities they see as worth the risk. To deter these, strategies would be required that either make the individual less susceptible by removing such opportunities, or increase the risk and concomitant consequences of being caught. Changing individual inclinations is difficult, however, since a major impact would require altering structural conditions that reinforce these inclinations. In theory it might be possible to reduce peoples' perceived need to consume by eliminating advertising, promoting systems of self-worth that are not related to the ownership of commodities, strengthening community and family life, discouraging mobility, and building up religious and other nonmaterial value systems.

However, ignoring for a moment the social engineering and wholesale invasions of privacy that would be necessary to shift cultural priorities in this way (and the fact that the effort would likely fail), moves in this direction would be tremendously disruptive for the economy. Since such policies would hurt profits far more than all the annual occupational crimes combined, it is highly unlikely that this course of action would ever be officially endorsed. The remedies vouchsafed by mainstream institutions have therefore seldom gone beyond rhetorical exhortations about improving moral education and ethics, which in no way threaten the dominant consumer ethos. Policy initiatives have concentrated on deterrence rather than prevention, through reducing opportunities and increasing risks for prospective offenders. Recommended courses of action include increasing surveillance, overt and covert, at all levels of the corporation; changing its structure and chain of command; hiring more security forces; and increasing penalties. These suggestions will only be seriously considered if the amount of damage the organization suffers from occupational crime is greater than the cost (in financial and morale terms) of the remedies. Occupational criminality is decried in ethical and moral terms; but the issues that appear to determine actual policy initiatives are essentially economic ones (Hollinger and Clarke, 1983; Coleman, 1989).

Some of these same factors apply to the control of corporate crime. However, the fact that the organization itself benefits from the crime is a key factor shaping both official rhetoric on the morality of corporate crime and the corporate behaviour that follows from it. Securing effective enforcement of corporate crime, then, requires strategies that weaken the power of the corporate sector (economic as well as ideological), while simultaneously strengthening that of oppositional forces (also economic and ideological). Given present-day economic exigencies, the dominance of marketplace ideologies following the downfall of communism, and the antiregulatory climate still dominating major Western democracies, this will be a major challenge.

Moreover, the degree to which macro-level structures influence behaviour and personality is far from settled (Giddens, 1981), which means that it cannot be assumed that changing structures will necessarily have any easy, direct, or predictable impact on behaviour. Conversely, oppositional behaviours from those nearer the bottom of the social structure have also given rise to societal change; witness, most recently, the overthrow of dominant Communist states in Eastern Europe and the dissolution of the former Soviet Union (albeit the disintegration of structures at the state level was essential to the success of these revolutions). We must be wary, therefore, of becoming structural determinists, assuming that change must come from the top down, or that structural changes are a necessary or sufficient condition for change elsewhere in the social order.

Nevertheless, key questions remain. At the deterrence level, why is corporate crime so little understood and ineffectively controlled? Why has sixty years of research by some of the best scholarly minds, in Australia, Britain, the United States, and Canada, been either ignored or implemented in a totally ineffective manner? This chapter focuses on regulatory ineffectiveness, and argues that the answers lie in the political economy of enforcement; the solutions in an unending series of struggles. Without an understanding of the forces that shape regulation, we are doomed to continue repeating the alternating cycles of boom and bust that have marked regulation, and regulatory theory, up to the present time.

This chapter presents, first, an overview of the dynamics of the enforcement process, the political and economic factors that shape overall regulatory patterns for corporate crime. This requires an examination of the role of the state, pressure groups, and academic research, and the sketching of a model that explains the factors that make regulation effective or ineffective. The focus then shifts to specific initiatives and remedies, beginning with the blind alleys of criminalization and cooperation. Finally, the model is applied to four distinct areas of corporate crime—occupational health and safety, antitrust and monopoly offences, insider trading and stock market fraud, and environmental crimes—and the conditions that apply to successful and unsuccessful regulation are discussed. In this section, strategies that have the potential to succeed are highlighted.

THE POLITICAL ECONOMY OF ENFORCEMENT

The regulation of corporate crime by the polity or state is an ever-changing dialectical process. It is, in other words, a struggle between opposing forces at several different levels of analysis. At the micro level, the balance of power between one particular firm and a relevant regulatory agency depends on very specific mechanisms. A decision to ignore, advise, counsel, or prosecute will depend on some combination of the following factors. First and foremost is the nature of the legislation governing agency behaviour, or specifically, what the law says. This is the bottom line because both regulators and regulated bargain within legislative parameters (or their concepts thereof), and neither side wishes its position to be weakened or overturned by a court challenge. Both usually prefer to avoid the time, expense, and publicity of court cases (although there are situations when they will be promoted by one side or the other, to make a political point close to an election or a key legislative decision, for example).

The power of the business or industry involved, its size and the nature of its capital (whether it is local, national, or international), is a second variable. The portability or mobility of the capital at question is crucial. Can the industry move with impunity or is it, like resource-based industries, constrained to remain in one place? If the latter, its ability to play a key card, the threat to pull out and remove jobs if faced with what it sees as regulatory "unreasonableness," is limited, although it can still threaten to downsize or close facilities.

Third, the relationships that have developed between the regulated firm and the regulatory agency, and between both of these and broader political supervisory bodies, are important. Such relationships and the trust (or lack of it) that has been established with regulators can determine the regulatory decisions taken in a specific case. When, for example, does one give an organization the benefit of the doubt? The nature of the specific offence, particularly its visibility and the perceived harm it has caused, is a fourth factor. Pressure groups and opposition MPs play a role here, by publicizing offences and attracting media attention to their consequences for the environment, workers, or consumers. Finally, the local political environment shapes particular regulatory actions. Upcoming elections can prompt more or less enforcement, depending on the visibility of the offence and the importance of the firm in question to the employment picture and prosperity of the region or nation.

At the macro level of analysis, the overall shape of regulation and control, in Western industrial democracies, depends on two broad factors. The first is the level and nature of the consent that exists between the state (usually at the federal level) and capital. There are big differences between nation-states in this regard. For example, the amount the state is "entitled" to intervene in the affairs of business varies considerably between Canada and the United States, the United Kingdom and Sweden, or Australia and Germany.

The second macro-level factor is the relationship between the state and the broad electorate, as represented by relevant pressure groups. Pro-regulatory pressure groups (for example, environmental activists, "green" politicians trying to eliminate chemicals from farmers' fields, unionists working to secure stronger health and safety laws in the workplace, and feminists trying to control the pharmaceutical industry) are absolutely central to the regulatory process. It is the pressure they exert, by maintaining a high level of struggle and dissent, that provides much of the leverage to force the state to maintain a particular level of enforcement activity.

It is in this context that intellectual work enters into the regulatory equation. The work of "experts," university-based social or natural scientists, is important in this struggle for hearts, minds, and legitimacy because such research carries the aura of "objective knowledge." It therefore becomes part of the debate, used by pro- and antiregulatory forces (as the case may be) to buttress particular arguments and strengthen particular positions. Over several generations, this process of struggle and resistance leads to ideological change, a shift in the commonly accepted ideas of what constitutes "reasonable" working conditions and levels of risk. When such redefinitions favour increased safety levels for employees, as has been the case in the Anglo-American democracies over the last century, considerable improvements in lifestyle and life chances can be secured.

These general arguments rest on a set of assumptions about modern states and about regulation itself. The first is that the typical regional, provincial, or federal state, left to its own devices, will not "automatically" provide enforcement for most corporate crimes at the level required by legislation, despite the fact that this same state body created, passed, and officially endorsed the law in the first place. If permitted to do so (by being left alone), it will settle, through its regulatory agencies, into an accommodation with the regulatory target(s), which will provide a level of enforcement that the target can live with. This will not be rigorous; "capture" is the term used in earlier chapters to describe such relationships.

This is the "natural" outcome, because corporate crime occupies a particular niche in the political economy of the modern state. Laws banning false advertising or unfair labour practices are not at all like standard criminal laws. The latter, sanctioning those who rob banks or assault their mates in taverns, are offences where the state and its officials (police) willingly maintain a high level of enforcement even in the absence of direct pressure from victims' groups or banking executives. It is in the interests of dominant forces, structurally, to enforce these laws. To secure even minimal enforcement of laws against corporate crime, on the other hand, constant pressure is required. Modern states are peculiarly dependent on the business sector and the capital it generates to provide jobs and investment and to create wealth, because there is no comparable alternative mechanism to achieve these ends in capitalist societies. Regulation, because it may scare capital away, must therefore be eschewed wherever possible. The creation of a global marketplace adds ideological clout to anti-regulatory arguments, strengthening them much more than the merits of "need-to-compete" arguments dictate. Regulation will only be thorough and rigorous when the state is forced by external pressure to respond, and when a visible response is necessary to maintain the legitimacy of the state and thus the stability of the hegemonic order overall.

Pressure groups have the potential to force the state's agenda, threaten legitimacy, and arouse and channel dissent, particularly in a democratic society with universal suffrage and active mass media. In such societies, this occurs in the classic style of pressure group politics; that is, pressure is exerted through demonstrations, agitation, the dissemination of supportive information, and sometimes strikes, and more is demanded at any particular time than the state, typically under the strong influence of antiregulatory corporate forces, is able to give. If the pressure is strong and continuous, a mild form of regulation will be passed into law. Enforcement may be weak or nonexistent at this stage. However, with continuing pressure and intermittent crises (Bhopal, Love Canal, Missouri Beach, and the U.S. savings and loan debacle, to name a few recent examples), stronger laws and enforcement may be secured.

Academic research provides studies that can be used by pressure groups to strengthen their calls for reform, and by antiregulatory forces to legitimate their resistance. Research documenting the extent and cost of corporate criminality, as well as ideas to control it more effectively—through changing company law to make boards of directors responsible, eliminating limited liability, creating citizens' rights to a clean and safe environment, providing treble damages to encourage civil suits, etc.—all yield ammunition that can be cited by one side (and denigrated or ignored by the other). The purpose and role of academic research is not straightforward, because it is typically sponsored by the richest and most powerful groups in the regulatory struggle, namely the corporate sector. Thus, it is in no sense "objective" data. However, this does not mean it is totally compromised or resolutely ideological in nature, because a scientific consensus on a particular issue, partially independent of sponsorship, will eventually emerge in most cases.

This kind of overview must necessarily oversimplify the relationships and tendencies involved; they are all, in reality, extremely complex. Regulation does not always proceed in a linear fashion from a weak initial position to a stronger one. As demonstrated by events in the United States, Canada, and the United Kingdom in the 1980s, regulatory reversals can occur; resistance never goes away, and backlash generated by the forces of capital is a continuing threat. Hence the need for a never-ending struggle. Reverses such as these are significant because they set back the clock of expectations and redefine "rigorous enforcement" in a more lenient direction. Thus, they affect the parameters within which "reasonable" enforcement levels are negotiated, and can therefore cause dangerous business activities that would previously have been sanctioned to be overlooked.

"Better regulation" and "rigorous enforcement" are relative concepts whose meaning depends on the nature and level of consensus negotiated for that particular act at that particular time in that particular state; events that change the content of these terms may therefore have significant effects. There are also large differences in regulatory policy and potential between different types of corporate crime, because some are much easier than others to discover and sanction. Similarly, there are differences introduced by the nature of the capital involved; capital originating in Canada, for example, may require a different control strategy than that used for transnational corporations. Nor is the corporate sector always diametrically opposed to regulation. Each of these issues will be looked at in turn.

The key body to understand in the regulatory process is the modern state and the role it plays in capitalist democratic systems. Although the increasing globalization of trade and the creation of ever-larger international trading blocks threaten the autonomy and power of the nation-state, it remains a dominant player at the present time, if only by default, for no international regulatory bodies with significant strength have yet emerged. As outlined in earlier chapters, the state, government, or polity encompasses the major institutions and top officials of governing bodies at federal, provincial/state, and sometimes local or county levels as well (depending on the degree of centralization of government power). Although initial formulations in the Marxist literature conceptualized the state as the handmaiden of the bourgeoisie, these instrumentalist and deterministic modes of thought were justifiably criticized, and have been extensively rethought. Nonetheless, it is obvious that modern states take a considerable interest in facilitating the development, growth, and accumulation of capital by the private sector, and in promoting the extraction by capital of surplus value. Whether this is an eternal verity dictated by the structural requirements of capitalism is less obvious and, for the purpose of understanding regulatory ineffectiveness, less important. The empirical reality is that, as Gough (1979), Offe (1982), and others have pointed out, the survival of the nation-state, its revenues, its social welfare, educational, and military programs (as well as the fate of the political party in power) are all dependent, directly and indirectly, on the profitability of the private sector.

Attracting capital and avoiding its flight are therefore central criteria by which all policy initiatives are judged, although these concerns may be articulated up front or remain unrecognized in the background. Indeed, business power may play its most significant role in the background by ensuring that certain policy options, those perceived as most damaging to business, never make it onto state agendas. This initial "cut," which shapes the kind of policy alternatives seen as possible, operates far below the level of formal politics, that final stage where political actors in different parties openly compete for scarce resources. It even underlies agenda setting, the crucial intermediary layer where certain options get defined in or out of the political process. At this level as well, "radical" policy options, those that might cause capital to take flight, are likely to be weeded out. The real and perceived interests of business, then, shape everyday government discourse at every policy level; they are therefore an intrinsic part of government decision-making operating outside the public consultative process (Offe, 1982; Schrecker, 1989:182–83).

More directly, the centrality of capital in the modern state means that those who own and control the means of production must receive official encouragement. Thus, states typically provide billions of dollars in grants, income tax loopholes, facilities for training, infrastructure, transportation, and "forgivable loans" to the corporate sector to get them to invest, create jobs, and produce wealth (Hurtig, 1991; Simon and Eitzen, 1990). They are wary of offending capital because they have little direct control over it, and it is typically fluid while they and their constituencies are not. Governments are even reluctant to force industries to live up to the terms of the bargains they have made. For example, they are loath to prevent companies from leaving the north of England or abandoning plants in Cape Breton despite the millions of taxpayer dollars that were originally put up to attract industry to these locations, and the promises of long-term employment and investment the companies made to secure the grants. Such "severity" with the corporate sector, it is felt, frightens off the much sought investment, and engenders the equally dreaded loss of (business) confidence (Gough, 1979).

However, because the political party in charge of the state apparatus must get elected, some leverage is possible, and some level of control over the corporate sector has emerged. Despite the extensive manipulation of public opinion that is now commonplace, this may require the passage (and even occasionally the enforcement) of laws in the "public" interest that promote the "public" good, laws that go against the wishes of particular factions of the corporate elite. As specified above, the definition of policy alternatives will be limited to those the state considers "feasible"; alternatives outside this consensus are generally not amenable to public discussion and debate. This consensus changes over time. In general, however, state actions that capital opposes are taken only when necessary to protect the long-range stability of the state, its systemic hegemony, or the survival of the existing relations of production.

Thus, where a strong, organized working-class movement is exerting pressure, the interests of manufacturers as a class in minimizing production costs may have to be sacrificed to satisfy demands for safety equipment and laws that raise costs. The rhetoric of the democratic system is that lives are more important than profits: where this belief is revealed as false (when, for example, a major accident caused by faulty mine construction occurs), and where this contradiction has become public (when groups defending worker safety are strident, organized, and persistent), states can be forced to pass laws specifying minimum safety standards for manufacturers (O'Connor, 1973; Miliband, 1969; Panitch, 1977).

This general thesis explains both state timidity to pass and state reluctance to enforce laws penalizing corporations, since both potentially endanger accumulation. It also provides us with a way of understanding differences in regulatory laws and enforcement among the major democracies. It must be remembered, however, that democratic states are not monolithic entities with universally defined or identical interests and strategies. There are real differences between nation-states, and between the various levels within them (federal versus provincial versus local). There are also real differences in the levels of struggle and resistance, and the impact such struggles exert. The significance of agents, rights struggles, and organized pressure groups cannot be overlooked, as they have the potential to make real gains in face of heavy corporate and political resistance (and their absence in many communist countries helps explain the frequently abysmal levels of corporate crime that have existed there).

States, then, do not have a direct and unproblematic interest in wiping out corporate crime. There is ample evidence that the modern state, despite the documented damage corporate crime causes, has frequently acted to vitiate laws against it. It has drawn up ineffective laws (Calavita, 1986; Carson, 1980a, 1980b, 1982), impeded enforcement (Coleman, 1985; Levi, 1981, 1984; Gunningham, 1974, 1987), savagely cut the budgets of regulatory agencies, and interfered in their decision-making processes if they were upsetting important business interests. Time and again a major crisis or lawsuit has been necessary to force political authorities to take action of any sort.

It would also be incorrect to assume that states have the resources necessary to control the predatory activities of the private sector. There are instances where even the richest countries have been forced to back down because they could not afford to mount successful challenges against major multinationals. Consider, for example, the failed attempt to lay charges against the oil companies after the 1973 oil crisis (Sampson, 1975), or to force chemical companies to clean up their toxic dumps and oil companies their disastrous spills (Molotch, 1973). Many multinational companies have assets and profits larger than the gross domestic product of the majority of countries. The way in which countries in the Third World have been held hostage is well known, as are some of the ensuing disasters (Clarke, 1990; Pearce and Tombs, 1989; Pearce, 1991).

On the other hand, there have been some success stories over the short and long term, which prevent us from conceptualizing a conspiratorial model of total capitalist control. As documented earlier, states have, on occasion, strengthened the hand of regulators. Improvements have resulted, in various economic and industrial spheres (Paulus, 1974; Whiting, 1980; Lewis-Beck and Alford, 1980; Hopkins, 1979; Pearce and Tombs, 1988:3–4). In fact, some evidence of long-term improvement is visible: many rivers are cleaner, the air above some cities is less polluted than it was twenty years ago, lead has been removed from gasoline in many countries, and automobiles are safer. Understanding the political economy of enforcement, then, requires taking into account many often contradictory factors.

SPECIFIC INITIATIVES AND EXAMPLES

Drawing from the traditions of criminalization and compliance and utilizing a perspective that takes account of the dialectical nature of the regulatory process, how, then, can more effective control of corporate crime be attained? There is certainly no shortage of academic research prescribing solutions. The literature is replete with ideas; many of them unfortunately conflicting with each other. As discussed in Chapter 5, those advocating criminalization point to enforcement deficiencies, specifically the reluctance of regulatory agencies to "get tough," as the basic problem. These scholars, therefore, advocate more use of prisons, and higher, more punitive fines. As they see it, if criminal sanctions were to be deployed regularly, if corporations knew that their chances of escaping criminal conviction were slight, if fines commensurate with the size of the firm and the profitability of the crime were imposed, if jail sentences were given, and if all this was backed up with more enforcement personnel and more punitive laws, then corporate crime would be more effectively controlled (Glasbeek, 1984, 1989; Reasons et al., 1981; Nader and Green, 1973; Watkins, 1977; Stone, 1980; Coffee, 1984).

Unfortunately, these proposals fail to specify how such a reality can be brought to pass. Since the main obstacle to efficient enforcement is the power of the corporate sector, those advocating criminalization must specify how this power can be neutralized or overcome. Since most countries already have laws on the books that call for more stringent and punitive sanctions than judges ever employ, one wonders how passing still more laws to be ignored will solve the problem.

Theorists advocating cooperative models, on the other hand, basing their arguments on the undeniable failures of criminalization policies, argue that the dependence of modern states on criminal law, and the adversarial relationship this necessitates, is a major cause of regulatory ineffectiveness (Bardach and Kagan, 1982; Ackerman et al., 1974; Kagan and Scholz, 1984; Kneese and Schultze, 1975). Criminalization strategies are rigid techniques, they say, that alienate potentially cooperative individuals and corporations. Moreover, criminal laws are inflexible, resistant to technological change and economic development. Furthermore, because they are based in the nation-state (or even smaller governmental units), they are not equipped to deal with transnational conglomerates (Braithwaite, 1980, 1982).

Over the last two decades this academic approach has been overtaken by the renaissance of the New Right, a powerful social movement that has launched a major attack on all government regulation. Its proponents argue that regulation is a socialist idea, promoted by antibusiness forces and weak-willed politicians. Unwise government decisions have imposed hundreds of unnecessary regulations on business and added millions to the cost of running a corporation. The New Right favours a major behavioural and philosophical shift in regulatory practice, from one promoting criminalization and coercive control to one that removes regulation and abolishes regulatory agencies. Where this is not practical, cooperation between regulatory agencies and their clienteles must become the modus operandi. Given the high costs of regulation and the record deficits incurred by many governments during the 1980s, plus the need to attract and retain investment in face of global competition, these critiques have been very appealing to policy-makers, and often to taxpayers as well.

Outright deregulation models represent fairly transparent attempts to reverse whatever gains workers and consumers have made; they are overtly ideological and must be judged as such. The cooperative movement, on the other hand, presents ideas that must be assessed on their merits. However, close examination makes it clear that cooperative solutions do not provide workable alternatives in the struggle to control corporate crime. Indeed, they can only weaken proregulatory forces, and savage the already underwhelming efforts of regulatory agencies.

To understand why this is so, one must remember earlier discussions on the nature of the state, and examine the role of pressure groups and publicity in securing enforcement. In this context, one of the most crucial reasons for retaining criminal law in the struggle against corporate crime is a symbolic one. Criminal law in Western societies is universalistic and absolute. Those who offend against it are criminals, a term that connotes the evil, villainous, and antisocial. This discourse carries no shades of grey, no sense that there can be a debate about "criminal" behaviour, or that there is another side that should be presented and known. The language covers up all traces of the underlying political process that transformed the behaviour in question from a disputed act to a legal category. This is highly significant, because "interests can be both constrained and enabled by the discourses through which they operate" (Condon, 1992:26). Having to operate through a discourse of criminalization puts those who would defend "criminal" behaviours very much on the defensive, for who can be in favour of criminality?

When arguing for more equitable law enforcement procedures or improved civil rights for traditional criminals, these characteristics of criminal law become a distinct disadvantage. However, in the struggle to prod a reluctant bureaucracy not to ignore corporate offences, they are advantageous. As we have seen, publicity is an important tool in forcing regulators to take action against corporate crime, and ignoring *criminal* offences is linguistically and societally defined as serious. With the switch to cooperative systems, corporate criminals turn into "regulatory evaders," and crimes into value-free "acts whose meaning is under negotiation." The connotations for making a case in public are strikingly different. Pressing a case against an "uncooperative executive" is a nonevent; a judgment that will be reflected in the journalistic play such a story receives. Corporate criminality ignored, on the other hand, might just make it into the newspaper, or into parliamentary question period.

Pressure groups need both the symbolism and the universalism of criminal law. They also need the public access to information about charges laid and dropped, and decisions of innocence or guilt that have traditionally accompanied the criminal process. Because there is no comparable public right to know in regulatory procedures (access varies widely, but is seldom complete), the ability to monitor performance will be virtually destroyed by a wholesale switch away from criminalization. Moreover, the key lever pressure groups use to embarrass regulatory personnel, the failure of the agency to live up to its official mandate to enforce the law, would be irretrievably weakened. Advocacy derives its ideological power from the gap between what the law demands and what the agency actually does. The stronger and more universalistic the agency mandate, then, the greater the potential bargaining strength of pro-regulatory forces. The potential to embarrass the regulatory agency and to shame the offending corporation increases in a similar fashion. As Winter has recognized:

> Without the clear power and duties to interfere with private interests, the administrative agency would not have a position from which to barter effectively. If legal doctrine allowed clear cut rules to be discarded whenever an agency preferred non-enforcement ... the value of the legal rule as a bargaining chip would be diminished, for the regulatory process would begin with the assumption that full enforcement was not even a benchmark. (Winter, 1985:240–41)

An official shift to cooperation also affects the expectations of corporations, providing them with additional excuses to delay compliance. It must be remembered that corporate crime is profitable, so the motivations for prevarication are strong. Moreover, corporations will be better positioned to protest all regulatory actions on the grounds that they are precipitate and premature: "We were going to cooperate," they would say, "but we were not allowed sufficient time to negotiate the terms." Adopting the cooperative model has the potential both to undermine the power of the regulatory agency and simultaneously to legitimate this loss of power.

Like criminalization models, then, cooperative approaches also fail to deal with the meaning and implications of corporate power. However, unlike criminalization models, cooperative approaches are likely to be adopted and translated into policy. And enshrining cooperative approaches into law—the movement is well advanced already—would weaken or remove the potential of pro-regulatory forces to contribute to the struggle by undermining their central legitimating rationales as well as their most important weapons.

Thus far the shortcomings of criminalization and cooperation for improving the enforcement of corporate crime have been examined. But what about reforming the regulatory agency? Is there potential for making a difference there? Cranston (1982), for example, suggests the following changes. First, states should introduce more controls against the "revolving door" syndrome, to prevent job moves from the regulated industry into the regulatory agency and back again. There should also be an increase in the number of public representatives on regulatory and industry boards, despite the danger that the representatives will be co-opted by business. He further suggests that both regulators and regulated bodies should be compelled to hold bargaining sessions in public and to publish the results of all investigations.

These are all good suggestions. Advocated in isolation, however, they are inadequate, for they and similar ideas (and there are many of them) also overlook the root cause of regulatory inadequacy, that crucial power of the corporate sector to vitiate policies that challenge its profitability or dominance. It must always be remembered that, although corporate crime has many causes, one fact ultimately makes it worthwhile: its profitability. Corporate crimes pay. In one sense, every reform proposal recognizes this, in that they all attempt to subvert profitability, attacking it at the social-psychological, organizational, or macro levels. However, when it comes to considering the implications of this fact on the chances of getting a particular reform scheme passed into law (let alone enforced), reformers too frequently ignore it.

APPLYING THESE PRINCIPLES

The focus will now switch to see how the principles discussed above affect the control of specific kinds of corporate crime. Factors shaping regulatory effectiveness will be examined for four types of corporate crime: occupational health and safety, antitrust and monopoly, insider trading/stock market frauds, and crimes against the environment. These four have all been extensively studied, and each exemplifies a somewhat different constellation of political and economic factors.

This examination begins with the overall expectation, outlined earlier, that the state's willingness to enforce regulatory law will vary with the strength of the forces promoting and opposing regulation; the type of corporate crime, especially its visibility; the perceived regulatory alternatives; the relation of the corporate crime to key structural factors such as the needs of capital; its relation to dominant societal values; and the past and present relationship of the particular state and its bureaucracies to the major classes. The nature of the language, the discourse employed to enunciate and conceptualize and understand these factors, underlies all the above forces. As a result, the chances of successful state action vary widely for different instances of corporate misbehaviour. Because the variables at play are complex and abstract, they must be applied to specific forms of corporate crime in order to understand how they are transformed, in a concrete instance, into regulatory behaviour.

OCCUPATIONAL HEALTH AND SAFETY LAWS

Occupational health and safety laws have been classified as "social" or "new" regulations, as opposed to economic or industry-specific rules such as antitrust laws (Cranston, 1982:2; Fels,

1982:31). "Social" regulation laws are not seen as directly related to the survival of capitalism, unlike antitrust or monopoly laws. The distinction is in some senses an ideological one underlaid by corporate-inspired value judgments about the relative validity of occupational health and safety when compared to economic ones. But it is important for any analysis to recognize that a key segment of the academic, political, and business communities differentiates between types of legislation in precisely this way. This helps one understand why, under typical occupational health and safety laws, regulators are instructed to balance the need to safeguard workers against the need to keep down the costs of production. The importance of not jeopardizing the regulated industry's competitiveness, then, shapes the very wording of the law. In this instance, the enabling legislation builds compromise and bargaining, the necessity to trade off one set of benefits and dangers against another, directly into law. The obligation to enforce the law in a uniform and universalistic manner, an expectation that dominates other areas of Anglo-American law, is thereby negated from the beginning.

A second crucial factor is the potential impact that rigorous regulatory action may have on the viability (meaning essentially the profitability) of the target industry. This is significant in determining how vigorously the industry will resist regulation. Unfortunately for workers and employees, health and safety laws directly affect the profits and ultimately the survival of virtually every business with a human workforce. The laws are especially significant to primary and secondary industries, firms that extract resources or manufacture products, where the job frequently requires interaction with heavy machinery or chemical processes. Because there are typically fewer hazardous substances or procedures in the service or tertiary sector (although research on the perils of ennui and the emerging health hazards of daily contact with video display terminals may change this), health and safety laws have been considered less critical for this sector.

However, the direct link between health and safety laws and corporate survival for major manufacturing industries has given employers a significant interest in working to ensure that these laws remain weak and ineffectual. Employer resistance has also been fuelled by the empowering potential of legislation; typically, health and safety laws allow workers the right to refuse to work in unsafe conditions, thus directly challenging one of the traditional prerogatives of management. Resistance, therefore, is fierce and only weakly counterbalanced by the necessity to attract and maintain a productive labour supply, or corporate desire to avoid developing a reputation as a careless employer with a dangerous workplace. In most jurisdictions employers also have economic reasons to minimize workplace dangers, because the workers' compensation rates they are obliged to pay are based on the company's rates of accidental injury and death. Nevertheless, as illustrated by the Texas petrochemical industry discussed in Chapter 5, there are ways of avoiding such strictures. Most of the time, in most countries, mitigating factors such as these are too weak to win the day against corporate opposition.

States, on the other hand, are caught in a dilemma. They cannot appear to be enthusiastic backers of the rights of the private sector to expose workers to risks in the name of higher profits without sacrificing their own institutional legitimacy. The protection of life, limb, and health is an absolute value in Western democracies. However, state officials will not wish to jeopardize the generation of surplus value, upon which the entire economic system rests, by being too fussy about providing safe conditions for workers, who are, after all, a low-status, low-power group. As Walters states: "Immediate expenditures would be high [to improve occupational health and safety] and returns could not be expected for decades" (1985:59). Moreover, workers themselves (and their unions) have been known to demand unsafe jobs over unemployment, if these are perceived as their only choices. Thus, one can predict that states will do as little as possible to enforce health and safety laws.

However, there are a few factors that promote regulatory action. These are rooted in resisters' ability to organize, attract publicity, and put pressure on political and regulatory authorities. Occupational health and safety issues primarily affect employees and their immediate families, which means they lack the potential to imperil (and therefore alarm) the general public that other corporate crimes, such as those that lead to environmental disasters, possess in abundance. This apparent disadvantage can be a political advantage. Prospective victims, often small, geographically contiguous groups, are relatively easy to identify and organize. Moreover, the moral equation is so stark— trading lives and health for profits—that generating pressure through publicity is easy, especially after an accident provides an immediate news "handle" (a hook to hang the story on). In addition, many unions, over the last two decades, have increased their vigilance as well as their knowledge of workplace hazards, although their overall clout has been weakened by the economic retrenchments and accompanying job losses that have savaged unionized staff in particular in the 1980s and 1990s.

Academic research has played a quixotic role in this struggle. On the one hand, it has been extensively used by the corporate sector to substantiate its arguments, by highlighting the difficulties of pinpointing the origin of illnesses that can appear decades after the original exposure to a particular toxic substance or workplace contaminant. As one might expect, then, many industry-sponsored studies argue that employee lifestyles, specifically obesity or tobacco use, are plausible alternative causes of medical conditions that develop in later life. On the other hand, academic studies have sometimes been crucial in documenting the nature and extent of the harm particular substances have caused; they have been cited in landmark court cases, and have been instrumental in securing redress for victims.

When combining all of these factors, then, one can predict that states will pass laws regulating occupational health and safety only when pressured by outside forces to do so, strengthen them reluctantly, weaken them whenever possible, and enforce them in a manner calculated not to impede profitability seriously. In examining case studies of regulation in occupational health and safety, these predictions appear to be borne out. Calavita (1986), Gunningham (1987), Yeager (1991), Walters (1985), Carson (1982), Reasons et al. (1981), and Tucker (1987), in studies done in Britain, Canada, the United States, Australia, and Italy, find that regulators are reluctant to get tough, although the definition of toughness, as expected, varies over different nation-states. States have typically been willing to back off on enforcement whenever and wherever possible. Public crises have been required to create the pressure to secure both passage and enforcement of occupational health and safety laws.

National variations are found, with right-wing regimes admitting and even bragging about their laxity, while left-leaning ones downplay or deny it. Such variations between nation-states do matter. They make real differences in the lifestyle and life chances of the workers involved, and they illustrate the importance of battles that were undertaken and won (or overlooked and lost) in the near or distant past. They also reflect cultural and historic differences between peoples. The relatively lax health and safety laws found in the province of Alberta in comparison with relatively strict laws in the state of Victoria (Australia) were traced to specific differences such as lower levels of unionization in Alberta, a free enterprise–oriented conservative government with total domination of the legislature, a provincial economy heavily reliant on one volatile staple (oil), and a high level of integration between the province and capital (Reasons, 1986). The state of Victoria, on the other hand, had a less volatile economic base, high unionization, a labour government, and a historic affinity between government and labour.

These arguments imply, then, that it will be easier for pro-regulatory forces to secure real improvements in legislation and working conditions when the connection between workplace and victim is an obvious one. The asbestos industry provides an excellent example of this, in that the cancers caused by asbestos exposure are practically never seen in populations lacking contact with asbestos. Similarly, corporate liability is straightforward and beyond debate in many on-the-job accidents.

To maximize regulatory effectiveness, social action should peak immediately following such incidents. A series of struggles for new rights in the workplace—and the discourse of "rights" as opposed to "privileges" is an important one—by unions or left-wing political parties, at this time, has the potential to produce changes at the ideological level that will, in turn, push up the lower limits of "reasonable" business behaviour. As part of this ideological struggle, several specific organizational reforms have some potential. Forcing companies to draw up and register realistic self-regulation schemes and pay at least some of the costs of regulation is one example (Braithwaite, 1982).

As argued earlier, criminalization strategies must not be abandoned, because of the crucial leverage and moral legitimacy criminal law lends to regulatory watchdogs, opposition politicians, and other pro-regulatory forces. For example, a criminal statute prohibiting "reckless employing," one that would require employers to prove they have taken every reasonable measure to prevent injuries (reversing the onus of proof now employed), would be useful (Pearce and Tombs, 1988).

Thus, while it might be impossible under the present socio-economic system to secure full and total enforcement of health and safety laws, or to punish adequately those responsible for thousands of annual deaths and injuries, this must paradoxically remain the official goal of regulatory legislation if even greater laxity is to be avoided. Getting more effective laws passed is a necessary part of this struggle, but as a goal in itself, if it does not strengthen the power base that will make the laws effective, it is useless. For health and safety violations, then, ideological struggle, a redefinition of the levels of risk deemed acceptable for workers in a particular nation-state at a particular time, combined with pro-regulatory moral pressure, will be the primary mechanisms to secure significant improvements.

ANTITRUST

Antitrust legislation embodies a very different set of constraints. One principle of a free market economy is that maximum efficiency is derived by forcing all businesses to compete against each other, the premise being that efficient enterprises will survive and prosper, while inefficient ones will disappear. Neither prediction has turned out to be accurate. As discussed earlier, the economies of all industrialized democracies have increasingly come to be dominated by transnational corporations and giant oligopolies, in private hands or occasionally under public ownership, with the result that meaningful competition (as envisaged by the original proponents of a laissez-faire economy) has virtually disappeared. Typically there is one dominant sector where one or a handful of megaglomerates exercise near-monopoly control. This situation is repeated in virtually every part of the economy, typically including oil refining, insurance, car manufacturing, retail food production, and others. Meanwhile, on the periphery of each sector hundreds of small concerns fight for the spoils, the roughly 10 percent market share that remains.

As outlined in Chapter 1, economic concentration is increasing rather than decreasing, and the number of dominant corporations has continually declined over the postwar period (Clement, 1975, 1977; Carroll, 1984). In the United States, the largest 500 corporations control three-quarters of all manufacturing assets; fifty out of 67,000 companies in transportation and utilities control two-thirds of the airline, railway, communications, electricity, and gas industries; three firms control most of the revenues in television and four control the movie industry; and two insurance companies alone have 25 percent of the business (Simon and Eitzen, 1986:10) Similar concentrations of power mark Western European and Australian economies as well (Hopkins, 1978).

Because of their market domination and size, monopoly sector producers can realize higher profits at less cost, so they have a natural and significant structural bias against increasing competition. Thus, the largest and most powerful parts of the corporate sector do not want monopoly laws passed or enforced. However, such laws are in the interests of businesses in the peripheral sector, struggling to get a toehold in the market against tremendous odds. Indeed, Canada's first laws against combines were passed at the behest of competitors left out of a conspiracy (Bliss, 1974). But even small businesses provide less than total support for antitrust laws, because they frequently identify with large business (which they hope to one day be), and display the mandatory ideological distaste for government regulation or "interference" in the marketplace. Once again, there are national and regional variations in these sentiments. They vary with the strength of free market ideologies in each sector and country. In addition, because real competition may exist between small and middle-size businesses in the peripheral economy, they tend not to speak on this or any other issue with one unified voice. All of these factors limit the amount of pressure favouring antitrust put on the state.

The situation of the typical state vis-à-vis competition/antitrust is quite unlike that encountered in laws on occupational health and safety. For one thing, these laws tend to be passed and enforced at a federal or national level, unlike health and safety statutes, which are usually the responsibility of lower-level governments. This gives the state an advantage, making it harder for companies to play one level of government against another within a single nation-state. Second, federal states have a direct interest in promoting a certain level of competition in the economic system, because they need to maintain an efficient economy to maximize the surplus value upon which their political fortunes, and prosperity, ultimately depend; and, beyond a certain level, monopolies are not efficient. Third, governments are major customers of private industry, and want reliable, high-quality goods and services for the public sector at minimum cost. Too high levels of monopolization carry the risk that governments will be held to ransom by their suppliers. States also have an abstract interest in preventing too much economic power from being concentrated in too few hands, as it can be a threat to the nation-state. One final point that favours antitrust enforcement is the fact that, in most countries, enforcement can be initiated by the private sector, typically through a petition from competitors requesting an investigation of specific complaints. The initiative for making the first move in such instances is thereby taken off the regulatory agency.

However, these advantages for pro-regulatory forces generally go for naught. They are countered by strong opposition, because the forces resisting regulation—corporations in the monopoly sector—are among the largest and most powerful economic groupings in the nation-state, and in the developed world (Barnett, 1982). Moreover, the relationship between competition and efficiency is not straightforward. A laissez-faire economy with many small economic units is functional for internal markets, according to most economists, up to a certain level. However, too much competition, too many small, unstable, undercapitalized firms, may work against the interests of the nation-state at the international level. Such a pattern may make a profitable export market, a key money-maker these days, particularly difficult. Academic researchers, particularly economists, have been employed by both sides to examine the relationship between size and efficiency; neither side appears to be satisfied that the one "right" size of an organization has been identified.

In addition, most countries have an extensive set of monopolistic operations that states themselves initiated, in sectors such as uranium mining, airlines, or telephone service. Government spokespeople promoting antitrust, then, usually have to speak with forked tongues on the virtues of competition. And on the public side, there are no significant forces promoting competition and opposing monopolies. Weak consumer groups make representations and testify to government committees opposing rate increases or mergers, but the lack of consensus on the overall benefits of competition frequently render their pronouncements equivocal. Moreover, their popular base is weak, with membership levels that seldom rise to significant levels. One might expect, then, that antitrust enforcement will be ambivalent and uncertain, varying with the dominant interests of the state at any particular time and with the power of the central versus peripheral corporate sectors.

This does not appear to be true. The literature shows, overall, that regulations promoting competition or banning monopolies have been almost totally ineffective. Barnett argues from American data that monopoly sector firms are virtually ignored by regulators (1979:171–72). Coleman describes enforcement of antitrust laws in the United States as an "unbroken record of failure" (1985:174). In Australia, the Trade Practices Act (roughly comparable to the U.S. Sherman Act for our purposes) has been studied by Hopkins, who shows that business lobbyists from the monopoly sector virtually dictated the content of the legislation that was to control them. The corporate sector as a whole met with almost complete success in shaping regulation and promoting the long-term interests of capital, where no countervailing pressure from the electorate was exerted. They were less successful in those few instances where pro-regulatory forces were present and pressing (Hopkins, 1979:79). In Canada, in the transition from the Combines Investigation Act to the new Competition Act, the federal government enthusiastically embraced the business position to such a degree that no semblance of a battle between the two sides remains (see Chapter 6). The victory of monopolistic corporate voices is complete.

Whether this situation reflects the naked power of the monopoly sector or the weakness of pro-regulatory forces is not clear. The impact of pressure groups on the state, in an area as complex and morally amorphous as antimonopoly law, has been minimal. The policy issues at stake are academic and complicated, and it is not always clear that breaking up monopolies is in the interests of the general public. Even if such a benefit could be unequivocally demonstrated, there is no automatic or clear beneficiary when tackling monopolistic enterprises. While consumers may gain in their role as consumers, they may lose as citizens or employees. From a moral perspective it is not obvious that the "right" to buy a product at a cheap price should automatically take precedence over the right of workers to jobs, or the right of the public to a clean environment. These may indeed be the tradeoffs insofar as breaking up a monopoly results in the creation of a bevy of competing companies, each desperate to cut corners, keep costs down, and stave off bankruptcy.

To sum up, then, this area of regulation occupies a particular niche such that the strongest forces of capital oppose enforcement; the academic community is divided (and does not exert independent influence at any rate); pro-regulatory pressures are weak; and the state is ambivalent at best and "captured" at worst. It is not surprising, therefore, that enforcement has been weak.

SECURITIES AND REGULATION OF THE STOCK MARKET

The third area to be examined, insider trading and stock market fraud, has frequently been very efficiently regulated relative to the standards prevailing for corporate criminality elsewhere. This is true despite the frequency of ruinously expensive scandals, most recently the savings and loan crisis in the United States outlined in the introductory chapter. Indeed, it is partly because regulatory failures in this area have the potential to create such debacles that enforcement has reached present standards. As will be recalled, the massive failure of hundreds of savings and loan companies came directly out of the Reagan administration's desire to cut back on government regulation of business. All forms of regulation and regulatory bodies were weakened, politically, economically, and ideologically, with disastrous results. Not surprisingly, then, a certain level of regulation appears to be very much in the interests of the corporate sector overall, as well as being compatible with key objectives of the modern state.

Securities law is a North American phenomenon, originating in a few American states between 1900 and 1910. (In Europe, corporate disclosure by public companies is handled as one component of general corporate law.) Federal laws in the United States were passed in response to a major domestic and international disaster, the collapse of stock markets in 1929, which led to the Great Depression. The Securities and Exchange Commission (SEC) was set up to enforce disclosure and monitor self-regulatory organizations such as stock exchanges as part of Franklin Roosevelt's collection of "New Deal" reforms (Condon, 1992:6; Seligman, 1982). In Canada, the day-to-day regulation of stock exchanges remains a provincial responsibility, backed by federal laws.

Such regulations, when efficiently enforced, protect the sanctity of the investment market, which is itself central to the ability of corporations to raise money through the issuing of shares. Investors must have some degree of confidence that stock markets are operated in an honest and efficient manner, or the supply of capital, the engine of expansion and prosperity, will dry up. States, on the other hand, view healthy stock markets as necessary to ensure high standards of living and overall prosperity. Moreover, as players in the market themselves (investing the pension funds of government employees, for example), state officials have a direct interest in clean dealing. They will also experience pressure from high-income people and negative publicity if investors are cheated or banks fail. Under such circumstances it may even be necessary for governments to step in and rescue defrauded investors, a very expensive proposition indeed.

This does not mean that forces opposed to regulation are absent. Pressures against enforcement are omnipresent because of the potential for powerful corporate actors and stockbrokers to make incredibly large sums of money. As inside traders, for example, they can realize huge profits from their knowledge of the "real" financial circumstances of a firm, or their access to sources who know about takeovers in the early stages of negotiation. Entrepreneurs will also insist that their ability to raise capital for speculative ventures is hampered by "excessive" regulation. However, such arguments are weakened by the fact that the primary benefits of lawbreaking in this sector accrue to individuals, while the costs are shared collectively by business as a whole and, to a smaller degree, government; that is, frauds such as insider trading bring large gains to individual actors or companies, but their costs and consequences are borne by capital (and capitalism) as a whole (through loss of investor confidence), and by provincial and federal bodies of the state. This would weaken the chances of effective enforcement less if the benefit was being realized at the expense of the weak and unimportant—consumers or workers, for example. Instead, it comes at the expense of corporate peers, fellow businesses competing to raise capital on international exchanges.

Thus, we should expect enforcement of securities laws to be relatively efficient, and that is indeed how it appears, in North America at any rate. The U.S. Securities and Exchange Commission has been extensively studied; on the whole it ranks as one of the most efficient regulatory agencies (Coleman, 1985; Shapiro, 1985). This is not to argue that the SEC catches every offender or prosecutes every offence. As Shapiro's 1985 study (described in Chapter 6) demonstrates, it does not. It is caught by dilemmas rooted in the power of the sector it regulates, and the primary role capital plays in the functioning of the modern state. However, given the standards set by regulatory agencies overall, it is clearly more effective than most. Indeed, the need to safeguard the legitimacy of stock markets forced even the Reagan administration, notorious for ignoring crimes against the environment, consumers, and workers, to take action against insider trading and fraud, albeit too late to avoid the collapse of the savings and loan sector (Yeager, 1986:4).

In Canada, the record is complicated by the fact that the primary responsibility for enforcement lies with the provinces. Hence there are a number of different enforcement systems. Several studies of regulation in Ontario, however, have produced mixed results. Hagan and Parker (1985), using interviews with investigators involved in prosecuting securities violators over a seventeen-year period, found prosecutions and convictions went up over the period studied, but the severity of sentences went down. They also found evidence that social class, and the kinds of criminal behaviour it makes possible, influences punishment in a fairly direct fashion. Condon, on the other hand, concluded that some protection for minority shareholders was obtained through a series of reforms orchestrated by the Ontario Securities Commission and the Toronto Stock Exchange (1992:26).

ENVIRONMENTAL PROTECTION

The fourth and final area to be examined, environmental protection, has only recently become a major regulatory issue. This is certainly not because corporate behaviours that damage the environment are new in any sense; they are woven into the very history of the Industrial Revolution. Corporations are frequently responsible for environmental damage, directly through their manufacturing and discharge processes, and indirectly by their promotion of, and dependence upon, throwaway, high-consumption philosophies and lifestyles. Control over corporate pollution, however, has been weak to nonexistent. Most of the laws transforming these behaviours into administrative or criminal offences have been passed only in the last two decades.

Historically, environmental law provides an interesting illustration of the naked role power plays in shaping law. Under feudalism, when aristocrats owned huge tracts of agricultural land, agricultural needs received precedence over every other use in English common law. With the arrival of the Industrial Revolution, a clash between agricultural and industrial interests began, with the old land-based aristocracy pitted against the new industrialists. Conflicts over rights to use watercourses, air, and land were loud and long, largely because the two groups were relatively equal in power. (Where they were not, as in clashes between peasants and lords, or workers and bosses, naked power politics quickly decided the issue with minimal accommodation made to the interests of the weaker party.) The first stage of legal accommodation was an "ad hoc" solution that allowed judges to decide, in each specific dispute, which usage "best advanced societal interests" (Caputo et al., 1989:169).

As industrial power gained ascendancy, and as many land-based aristocratic families gained a stake in industry, legal decisions came to privilege the interests of industry over those of agriculture. The result was that, in most countries, industries gained the *right* to deposit their wastes in oceans and rivers, incinerate them into the air, or dump them onto "their" property (Caputo et al., 1989:164–71). The general public, landowners, fishers, and all the other groups whose livelihood and enjoyment was threatened by such acts lost even the limited legal protections they once had. The rights to use freely the resources of land, water, and air and to dispose of the waste-products of production in the cheapest possible way have been important ones for corporations. They reduce the costs of production in the same way that cheap child labour once did. Taking such rights away from capital, by making such acts illegal or criminal, will directly increase costs and threaten profits.

In Canada, there were only two major pieces of federal legislation aimed at controlling pollutants before 1975. These were the Fisheries Act and the Clean Air Act, and neither was effectively or enthusiastically enforced. The first omnibus federal law, the Environmental Contaminants Act, came into being in 1975 and was extended in 1988. The earlier acts were repealed and became part of the Canadian Environmental Protection Act. However, the act was passed only after industry representatives approved each draft, and the standards specified in the act were directly negotiated with the corporations that made up the major offenders!

Not surprisingly, from 1975 to 1988, "the federal government never once used its power ... to require toxicological testing of chemicals new to industry and commerce" (Schrecker, 1989:174). Indeed, whenever political pressure seemed to be making some gesture of enforcement inevitable, the federal government rushed to provide subsidies to the offenders. In 1985, for example, it offered $150 million to the notorious nonferrous smelter companies, despite the fact that the industry was highly profitable at the time and a special parliamentary committee had reported just one year earlier that no such help was necessary, or appropriate (Schrecker, 1989:183; see also Gordon and Coneybeer, 1991). Similarly, in the United States, Molotch (1973) and Coleman (1989) assert that environmental protection varies from poor to nonexistent, basically, once again, because of the power of business.

States—federal, provincial, or local—are typically paralyzed. As with occupational health and protection laws, provinces and countries fear they will be at a competitive disadvantage if they strengthen environmental regulations unilaterally. Industries have always tried to minimize the costs of operation by moving to the cheapest locations they can find. Free trade between Canada and the United States has often resulted in industries from Canada and northern U.S. states relocating to the less regulated south (North Carolina has been particularly successful in this regard). With an extension of the free trade agreement to Mexico, many can be expected to join the already extensive migration across the Rio Grande to Mexico, taking advantage of cheap labour and lax environmental regulations there. Companies with the required degree of mobility have increasingly moved to the Third World, to countries too desperate for investment to impose any conditions on it, as evidenced by the disaster in Bhopal, India.

Thus, even federal nation-states in developed societies are reluctant to act, fearing that they will frighten business away. Yet states are increasingly facing public pressure to do something; there are a number of strong lobbies promoting environmental protection on both national and international levels. This has forced most developed countries to set up numerous regulatory agencies, both specialized and general, whose mandates often overlap. It has not, thus far, forced many to risk annoying industry by introducing measures to guarantee serious and effective enforcement, despite the considerable research (academic and otherwise) documenting the short- and long-term hazards of every kind of pollutant, up to and including holes in the ozone layer that make it unsafe merely to go out in the sun. Public opinion, moreover, supports stricter enforcement, and there have even been numerous environmental crises that should have forced politicians and regulators to pass stricter laws and enforce them more effectively.

Public support for regulatory action has been particularly visible when the issue is one that pits corporate profits against citizens' health and safety. In one celebrated instance, a U.S. federal court judge took the dramatic step of siding with a private environmental group to strike down a weak and ineffective statute on pesticides, a statute that was supported by the state legislature, the chemical corporations, *and* the regulatory agency responsible for enforcement (Macintyre, 1985). In this case, the pressure group itself, the Environmental Defense Fund, had to take the regulatory agency to court to force it to do its job.

The laws allowing similar legal actions exist in very few countries to date, however. What is required is legislation granting legally actionable environmental rights to private citizens and groups. Moreover, as argued earlier, legal victories are likely to be hollow if the underlying power base remains unchanged. The victory cited above, therefore, may well prove to have been a hollow and symbolic one, for it is the reluctant regulatory agency that has to rewrite the old laws and enforce the new ones, and there is no reason to suppose a legal decision will cause an agency to shift its basic priorities. Once the spotlight of publicity has been turned off and the public has taken up other issues, the pressures from industry are likely to prove as irresistible as they were before, at least until another crisis occurs or another legal challenge is launched.

Nor can one hope that the federal state will suddenly see the error of its ways and take up the cudgels of environmentalism. Some even argue that empowering citizens through law can backfire in a more direct fashion. Vogel (1983, 1986) maintains that the reversals of the 1980s in the American environmental movement happened precisely because victories such as the one described above (along with other reforms of the 1970s) caused an intense backlash in the corporate sector. This produced heavy business lobbying that, as part of Reaganism, led to the deregulation craze, and turned back the clock on environmental reform (Vogel, 1986).

In view of this history, the latest fashionable business initiatives on the environment, particularly the concept of "sustainable development," should give pause to those interested in effective regulation. Such ideas assume a great deal about both the capacity and the desire of nation-states and international capital to put social and environmental concerns ahead of profitability. History does not allow us to take an optimistic view of this possibility, despite the fact that the survival of our species is ultimately at stake. Getting capital to put the long-term interests of humans first (let alone plants or animals) has required decades of struggle in the past, and further delays may allow irretrievable damage to be done. (Indeed, in the case of the ozone layer, it may already be too late.) The fact that the struggle is likely to increase the impoverishment of the already impoverished, the Third World countries presently being exploited to allow First World peoples to continue using many times their allotted share of resources and wealth, further complicates the issue.

Given the gravity of the situation, the paucity of action taken thus far must reflect the power of the corporate sector and the strength of its resistance. Nor is the problem limited to the capitalist world. At one level government inaction may also reflect genuine uncertainty, in that many politicians, academics, regulators, corporate executives, and general citizens simply do not know what course of action to follow to turn things around. Ceasing to damage the environment (or even damaging it less) demands reforms that challenge the lifestyles and philosophies underlying all industrialized societies. The idea that humans have a right, if not an obligation, to use the resources of the planet and all the life forms therein to ensure their domination over the beasts of the air and the fishes of the sea is one of the basic tenets of Judeo-Christian thought. It is premised on the deep-seated belief that animals, birds, plants, trees, and mountains are all there to serve human needs (more precisely, the needs of man), and that humankind has no long-term obligations either to future generations or to the natural world.

On a less philosophical plane, real environmental protection demands numerous changes in the mode of production that raise costs and challenge the rights of stockholders and managers. Descending from the abstract to the specific, there are many concrete steps that could be taken, right now, to curb environmental offences. It is neither philosophically nor intellectually controversial to recognize that companies that hire rogue truckers to dump hazardous wastes secretly into the ocean are causing environmental damage in addition to creating massive public health problems (Szasz, 1986). Putting an end to many corporate crimes against the environment is a relatively straightforward matter of monitoring and sanctioning offenders in a way that makes it preferable (cheaper in all senses) for the company to obey environmental laws than to flout them.

This is the theory; the reality, as has been documented throughout this book, is considerably more complex because of the power relationships involved. Public concern is mounting, however, and pressures on state bodies are thereby increasing. Academic research, as well as documenting the extent and costs of environmental destruction, has come up with many plausible suggestions. Economists, for example, suggest that fines to offending corporations be levied in proportion to the emissions or effluent volume produced; or based on the number of days that polluters fail to comply with regulatory orders. Requiring companies to post surety bonds in advance, to be refunded only when compliance has been demonstrated, is another interesting idea (Schrecker, 1989:185). Providing a role for citizen initiatives in legislation through the creation of actionable environmental rights, as the United States has done, has potential despite the ever-present possibility of backlash. Improving corporate law by challenging the privilege of limited liability, and making individual members of corporate boards of directors responsible to the community, not just to shareholders, is another intriguing initiative (McQueen, 1990).

None of these suggestions is a panacea, and none will come about in the absence of protracted public struggle. Corporate power must be constantly challenged, and resistance and backlash are almost guaranteed if any of the measures outlined above threaten actually to work. In order to generate the momentum to take a step forward, however, such risks must be taken.

SUMMARY

This chapter has explored the causes of regulatory ineffectiveness, and sketched some of the social mechanisms and ideological changes that will be necessary to improve the situation. Four areas of corporate crime—occupational health and safety violations, antitrust and monopoly, insider trading and stock market frauds, and environmental offences—were examined, and sources of resistance and compliance were suggested for each. In a political democracy, governments have to make some response to intense pressure, and protest and pressure have been major catalysts for current legislation, and for long-term progress. As Walters (1985) and Carson (1980a, 1980b) have observed, it is not in the best interests of business, in capitalist democracies, for corporate crime to be seen as rampant. Too many workers who are not paid enough to maintain their health, too many toxic dumps that poison the water and air, and too many combines that fix prices at very high levels all cause problems for a corporate sector that ultimately depends upon a minimally healthy workforce able to buy the products produced and on the elusive "good will and confidence" of at least some of the population. Advertising and corporate public relations cannot undo all corporate wrongs.

As an added complication, government regulation is often necessary to save business from itself. It may, for example, compel industries to take actions in their own interests that they could not take unilaterally. If only one firm pays a minimum wage of $10 an hour, or provides pensions, or installs scrubbers in its smokestacks, the added costs may make its products uncompetitive and put it out of business. If all industries are required by law to take these actions, and as long as the option of moving their operations to areas lacking such controls is not available, everyone benefits—the labour force is healthier and happier and better able to buy the products it is producing, the environment is cleaner, and the elusive "image" of the industry is improved. Under such conditions, regulation can be a "win–win" situation.

Conclusion

This book has examined the harm done by corporate crime, its causes and incidence, sanctioning mechanisms and the regulatory agency, and finally, the reasons corporate crime is so ineffectively controlled. It should by now be clear that understanding and controlling corporate criminality is not an easy task. Many factors that produce high levels of corporate crime also produce a thriving economy, healthy profit levels, and high standards of living, for those who are not directly victimized, at any rate. Encouraging individuals and companies to invest time and money to create a better product, beat out their competitors, or produce higher profit levels cannot be done without also encouraging a certain amount of risk-taking behaviour, a willingness to innovate and experiment, and a commitment to the "bottom line." It is easy to see how these "healthy" behaviours may also produce people and companies willing to take short cuts and sacrifice their employees, customers, consumers, and the environment to attain these goals.

This does not mean that corporate crimes are necessarily or universally functional in free enterprise economies; as we have seen, above certain levels of incidence they are dysfunctional, because people lose faith in the economic system, become too poor to buy the goods they are producing, or turn to disruptive behaviours such as political organizing or terrorism. Where corporate crime is harmful to free enterprise or capital, and is *seen* as being such, it should be relatively easy to control. Yet even this is not necessarily so, as the examination of securities fraud in Chapter 7 illustrated. How much more difficult, then, will it be to control the many types of corporate crime that are perceived as an essential risk of providing the freedom of action necessary to create dynamic, profit-driven market systems?

At the highest level of analysis, as Clarke (1990:31) has said, there is a basic dichotomy between an economic system that promotes private enterprise and self-interest (with the ever-present risk that it will degenerate into the oppression of vulnerable groups), and the "service ethic" of the welfare state (which tends to stifle initiative with bureaucratic rules and high taxes). The tension is between the creation versus the distribution of wealth. The private enterprise model generates surplus (wealth) well, but distributes it inequitably; the welfare state distributes it in a more equitable fashion, but does not generate it efficiently or in large quantities. (The latter model, especially in its logical extension of state socialism, also nourishes its own, quite specific kinds of corporate crime.) At the moment, with the first model definitely in the ascendancy, the corporate crimes most compatible with it are the most worrisome. These are the subset of corporate offences driven by profit maximization, with little attendant concern for who or what gets hurt along the way. While exact figures on the proportion such crimes constitute are impossible to generate, they clearly make up a large percentage of the corporate crimes discussed in this book.

Factors such as these only make it more crucial for those interested in effective regulation to tip the balance in the other direction, and redouble efforts to secure measures that minimize risks to the environment, employees, and other vulnerable groups. Corporate crime kills and maims, impoverishes and endangers hundreds of thousands of women, men, and children, and other species as well. It may be true that this tension between incompatible aims—profit maximization and risk-taking versus safety nets and care for vulnerable populations—will never be successfully resolved (Clarke, 1990:31). However, the importance of continuing to struggle, and of refining and developing strategies to make the struggles more effective, cannot be overemphasized. This means coming to a clearer understanding of the centrality, potential, and contradictions inherent in capitalist states, law, and capital itself.

The political state is not neutral; as this book has illustrated, it will not immediately or easily respond to initiatives to tighten control over corporate crime. It is more amenable to the goals and strategies of more powerful groups, but the state in democratic countries cannot be "totally closed to the aspirations of less favoured groups" (Pearce, 1991:6). Similarly, law can be a repressive force, but it can also facilitate social action and safeguard specific policies of amelioration. Capital, too, has the potential to be used against itself. As Pearce reminds us, capital is a force that must not be discounted; it will "block progressive change wherever it can" (1991:6), and reverse previously won gains under certain conditions as well. However, the corporation, too, is a site of struggle where gains can be made if intelligent and timely tactics are employed. With this in mind, some specific strategies will be looked at in conclusion.

ITEM

Gerber (1990), in a case study of the effectiveness of Braithwaite's self-regulation scheme (described in Chapter 5), analyzed the response of the Nestle Corporation to the infant formula crisis. Nestle came under severe international pressure because its marketing practices were causing thousands of unnecessary infant deaths in Third World countries. The company distributed free samples of baby formula to new mothers; when the formula was used to supplement or replace nursing, the mothers' breast milk dried up. However, because few women could afford to buy formula in the recommended amounts when it was no longer free, they watered it down, with the result that many babies died of malnutrition. Moreover, clean, safe water was frequently not available, so babies would pick up dysentery and other diseases as well.

In response to an international media campaign and subsequent boycott, Nestle set up and financed an internal monitoring agency, the Nestle Infant Formula Audit Commission or NIFAC by acronym. However, the efficacy of NIFAC was compromised because there was no multinational government agency capable of supervising and monitoring it effectively (Gerber, 1990:107). Thus, the strongest force influencing agency behaviour became the corporation the agency itself was set up to monitor—a recipe for disaster, as we have seen. It was therefore predictable that efficiency would wane shortly after the international spotlight and attendant pressure shifted to other crises. Gerber argues, however, that such an international regulatory agency, if monitored in its turn by activist groups, has the potential to be effective. "Consumer activism," he says, "combined with negative publicity, may be the best hope for effective control of a variety of corporate behaviours" (Gerber, 1990:108).

ITEM

In October 1981, a district court in Los Angeles authorized the United States Probation Office to form a nonprofit benefit corporation called "Foundation for People Incorporated." Judge Manuel Real subsequently ordered a company convicted of bid-rigging to either pay $300,000 to the court, or make a $100,000 "donation" to the foundation. Not surprisingly, the company chose the cheaper option. Subsequently, fund monies were used for social service programs, counselling, and job training. The rationale was that fines do not deter corporate offenders, and prison is never employed—so why not use the money to service some of the vulnerable populations victimized by corporate crime (Yeager, 1984:225)?

Programs such as those above deliver important benefits. First, they forge an important ideological link between corporate crime and traditional offences in the minds of the judiciary and the public at large. Second, because alternative sanctions such as these are innovative and unusual, they are newsworthy and get extensive media coverage. Third, they are cost-effective, in that they deliver worthwhile programs to dispossessed groups (such as those in central Los Angeles in the example above) without requiring politicians to increase taxes.

Other strategies centering around law have been developed and employed in recent years. The language and sanctions used in criminal law against traditional crime provide the best beginning models, for ideological as well as tactical reasons. The mode of reasoning regularly used in criminal law is applicable here because corporate crime has severe negative effects and is preventable; that is, it would not have occurred if certain courses of action had been followed or others eschewed (Pearce, 1991). Although there are few perfect parallels, arguments by analogy can be effective. If imprisoning a corporation is impossible (and prison sanctions for specific executives not likely to be secured), why not fight for equivalent punishments such as temporary or permanent loss of licence, or temporary nationalization of the offending corporation? If probation and rehabilitation are impractical, why not advocate similar organizationally appropriate punishments such as external monitoring and forced restructuring of the administrative system that allowed the crime to occur (Braithwaite, 1982)? Under the U.S. Sentencing Commission Guidelines for organizations, which became law on November 1, 1991, organizational probation has become an officially approved sanction. It will be a mandatory sanction when an organization with more than fifty employees lacks an effective program to prevent and detect law violations; when it has been convicted of a similar offence in the last five years; when high level officials participated in the offence; and when no fine was assessed (Lofquist 1991:4).

Corporate manslaughter has already made its way into American and British law, although no prosecutions to date have been sustained through all levels of court proceedings. Still, progress is being made, as one case has now succeeded at the initial courtroom level. This is the aforementioned Film Recovery Systems case, where the corporation and three executives were convicted of manslaughter for causing the death by cyanide poisoning of a Polish-speaking worker who could not read the English-language warning signs on the vats of chemicals he worked with daily (Coleman, 1989). Although the conviction was overturned on appeal, it must still be considered an important precedent; the only previous American case, the prosecution of the Ford Motor Company for design flaws in the Pinto car (Cullen et al., 1987), was unsuccessful in that no conviction was registered at the initial level. In the United Kingdom, charges of reckless manslaughter against the directors and owners of the *Herald of Free Enterprise*, the ferry that sank in 1987 causing 188 people to drown, were dismissed (Clarke, 1990). No similar parallel cases yet exist in Canadian law, although the Westray mine disaster in Nova Scotia (May, 1992) may lead to criminal charges.

Battles to secure more effective control of corporate crime, therefore, must be ongoing if the progress achieved thus far, fragile and partial as it is, is to continue. If the last 200 years provide any meaningful lessons, successes and failures, reversals and gains will follow each other in an unpredictable manner, as long as total ecological disaster does not intervene. However, since the lives of people in the developed world are considerably longer and healthier than they were even 100 years ago, there is some, small reason to be optimistic—provided the optimism does not impede the struggle.

REFERENCES

Ackerman, B., S. Rose, J. Sawyer Jr., and D. Henderson. 1974. *The Uncertain Search for Environmental Quality*. New York: Free Press.

Anderson, J.E. 1975. *Public Policy-Making*. New York: Praeger.

Balbus, I. 1977. "Commodity Form and Legal Form: An Essay on the 'Relative Autonomy' of the Law." *Law and Society Review* 11:571–88.

———. 1973. *The Dialectics of Legal Repression: Black Rebels Before the American Criminal Courts*. New York: Russell Sage Foundation.

Bardach, E., and R.A. Kagan. 1982. *Going By the Book: The Problem of Regulatory Unreasonableness*. Philadelphia, Penn.: Temple University Press.

Barnett, H. 1982. "The Production of Corporate Crime in Corporate Capitalism." In P. Wickman and T. Dailey, eds., *White Collar and Economic Crime*. Toronto: Lexington Books: 157–70.

———. 1979. "Wealth, Crime, and Capital Accumulation." *Contemporary Crises* 3:171–86.

Bartel, A.P., and L.G. Thomas. 1985. "Direct and Indirect Effects of Regulation: A New Look at OSHA's Impact." *Journal of Law and Economics* 28 (April): 1–25.

Baumhart, R.C. 1961. "How Ethical are Businessmen?" *Harvard Business Review* 39:6–19.

Baxt, B. 1989. "Lessons from the Past: Present Experience from Other Countries." Paper presented to the National Conference on Competition Law and Policy in Canada, Toronto, October 24–25.

Bell, D. 1970. "Is There a Ruling Class in America?" In M. Olsen, ed., *Power in Societies*. New York: Macmillan: 262–69.

Benson, M. 1989. "The Influence of Class Position on the Formal and Informal Sanctioning of White-Collar Offenders." *Sociological Quarterly* 30, no. 3 (September):465–79.

———. 1985. "Denying the Guilty Mind: Accounting for Involvement in White Collar Crime." *Criminology* 23:585–607.

Benson, M., F. Cullen, and W. Maakestad. 1990. "Local Prosecutors and Corporate Crime." Crime and Delinquency 36, no.3: 356–72.

Bequai, A. 1978. *White-Collar: A 20th Century Crisis*. Lexington, Mass.: Lexington Books.

Bernard, T.J. 1984. *"The Historical Development of Corporate Criminal Liability." Criminology* 22:3–17.

Bernstein, B.H. 1955. *Regulating Business by Independent Commission*. Princeton, N.J.: Princeton University Press.

Blau, P. 1955. *The Dynamics of Bureaucracy: A Study of Interpersonal Relations in Two Government Agencies*. Chicago: University of Chicago Press.

Bliss, M. 1974. *A Living Profit: Studies in the Social History of Canadian Business*. Toronto: McClelland and Stewart.

Blum, R.H. 1972. *Deceivers and Deceived.* Springfield, Ill.: C. Thomas.

Bonger, W. 1916. *Criminality and Economic Conditions.* Boston: Little, Brown.

Box, S. 1983. Power, *Crime and Mystification.* London: Tavistock Publications.

Braithwaite, J. 1988. "Toward a Benign Big Gun Theory of Regulatory Power." Canberra: Australian National University, unpublished manuscript.

———. 1985a. "White Collar Crime." *American Review of Sociology* II:1–25.

———. 1985b. *To Punish or Persuade: The Enforcement of Coal Mine Legislation.* Albany, N.Y.: State University of New York Press.

———. 1984. *Corporate Crime in the Pharmaceutical Industry.* London: Routledge and Kegan Paul.

———. 1982. "Enforced Self-Regulation: A New Strategy for Corporate Crime Control." *Michigan Law Review* 80, no. 7:1466–507.

———. 1980. "Inegalitarian Consequences of Egalitarian Reforms to Control Corporate Crime." *Temple Law Quarterly* 53:1127–146.

———. 1979. "Transnational Corporations and Corruption: Towards Some International Solutions." *International Journal of the Sociology of Law* 7: 125–42.

———. 1978. "An Exploratory Study of Used Car Fraud." In P. Wilson and J. Braithwaite, eds.,*Two Faces of Deviance.* St. Lucia, Queensland: University of Queensland Press.

Braithwaite, J., and B. Fisse. 1983. "Asbestos and Health: A Case of Informal Social Control." *Australian and New Zealand Journal of Criminology* 16:67–80.

Braithwaite, J., and G. Geis. 1982. "On Theory and Action for Corporate Crime Control." *Crime and Delinquency* 28:292–314.

Braithwaite, J., and P. Grabosky. 1986. *Of Manners Gentle: Enforcement Strategies of Australian Business Regulatory Agencies.* Melborne: Oxford University Press.

Brannigan, A., and S. Goldenberg, eds. 1985. *Social Responses to Technological Change.* Westport, Conn.: Greenwood Press.

Brenner, S.N., and E.A. Molander. 1977. "Is the Ethics of Business Changing?" *Harvard Business Review* 55:57–71.

Brooks, N., and A. Doob. 1990. "Tax Evasion: Searching for a Theory of Compliant Behaviour." In M.L. Friedland, ed., *Securing Compliance.* Toronto: University of Toronto Press: 120–64.

Brown, M. 1989. "A Toxic Ghost Town." *The Atlantic* (July): 23–28.

Bruck, C. 1988. *The Predator's Ball: The Inside Story of Drexel Burnham and the Rise of the Junk Bond Raiders.* New York: Penguin Books.

Calavita, K. 1986. "Worker Safety, Law and Social Change: The Italian Case." *Law and Society* 20, no. 20:189–229.

———. 1983. "The Demise of the Occupational Safety and Health Administration: A Case Study in Symbolic Action." *Social Problems* 30, no. 4:437–48.

Calavita, K., and H. Pontell. 1991. "'Other People's Money' Revisited: Collective Embezzlement in the Savings and Loan and Insurance Industries." *Social Problems* 38, no.1: 94–112.

———. 1990. "'Heads I Win, Tails You Lose': Deregulation, Crime and Crisis in the Savings and Loan Industry." *Crime and Delinquency* 36, no.3: 309–41.

Cameron, M.O. 1970. "The Five Finger Discount." In E.O. Smigel and H.L. Ross, eds., *Crimes Against Bureaucracy.* New York: Van Nostrand Reinhold.

———. 1964. *The Booster and the Snitch.* New York: Free Press.

Canada. Bureau of Competition Policy. 1989. *Competition Policy in Canada: The First Hundred Years.* Ottawa: Consumer and Corporate Affairs.

Canada. Department of Justice. 1982. *The Criminal Law in Canadian Society.* Ottawa (August).

Caputo, T., M. Kennedy, C. Reasons, and A. Brannigan, eds. 1989. "Overview—Political Economy, Law and Environmental Protection." In Caputo et al., eds., *Law and Society: A Critical Perspective.* Toronto: Harcourt Brace Jovanovich: 164–72.

Carroll, W.K. 1984. "The Individual, Class and Corporate Power in Canada." *Canadian Journal of Sociology* 9, no. 3 (Summer): 245–68.

Carson, W.G. 1982. "Legal Control of Safety on British Offshore Oil Installations." In P. Wickham and T. Dailey, eds., *White Collar and Economic Crime.* Toronto: Lexington Books.

———. 1980a. "The Institutionalisation of Ambiguity: Early British Factory Acts." In G. Geis and E. Stotland, eds., *White Collar Theory And Research.* Beverly Hills, Calif.: Sage.

———. 1980b. "The Other Price of Britain's Oil: Regulating Safety on Offshore Oil Installations in the British Sector of the North Sea." *Contemporary Crises* 4:239–66.

———. 1970 "White Collar Crime and the Enforcement of Factory Legislation." *British Journal of Criminology* 10:383–98.

Casey, J. 1985. "Corporate Crime and the State: Canada in the 1980s." In T. Fleming, ed., *The New Criminologies in Canada.* Toronto: Oxford University Press.

Cavanaugh, J., and F. Clairmonte. 1983. "From Corporations to Conglomerates." *Multinational Monitor* 4 (January):16–20.

Chenier, N.M. 1982. *Reproductive Hazards at Work: Men, Women and the Fertility Gamble.* Ottawa: Canadian Advisory Council on the Status of Women.

Chesney-Lind, M. 1991. "Patriarchy, Prisons and Jails: A Critical Look at Trends in Women's Incarceration." *The Prison Journal* (forthcoming).

Clark, I.D. 1989. "Legislative Reform and the Policy Process: The Case of the Competition Act." Address given to the National Conference on Competition Law and Policy in Canada, Toronto, October 24–25.

Clarke, M. 1990. *Business Crime.* Cambridge: Polity Press.

Clement, W. 1977. "The Corporate Elite, the Capitalist Class, and the Canadian State." In L. Panitch, ed., *The Canadian State.* Toronto: University of Toronto Press: 225–48.

———. 1975. *The Canadian Corporate Elite.* Toronto: McClelland and Stewart.

Clinard, M.B. 1979. *Illegal Corporate Behaviour.* Washington, D.C.: U.S. Government Printing Office.

Clinard, M.B., and P. Yeager. 1980. *Corporate Crime.* New York: Free Press.

Cobb, R.W., and C.D. Elder. 1972. *Participation in American Politics: The Dynamics of Agenda Building.* Boston: Allyn and Bacon.

Cobb, R.W., J. Ross, and M. Ross. 1976. "Agenda Building as a Comparative Political Process." *American Political Science Review* 70:126–38.

Cochran, T. 1977. *200 Years of American Business.* New York: Basic Books.

Coffee, J.C. 1984. "Corporate Criminal Responsibility." In S.H. Kadish, ed., *Encyclopedia of Crime and Justice,* vol. 1. New York: Free Press: 253–64.

Cohen, A., A. Lindesmith, and K. Schuesser, eds. 1956. *The Sutherland Papers.* Bloomington, Ind.: Indiana University Press.

Cohen, S. 1985. *Visions of Social Control.* Cambridge: Polity Press.

———. 1979. "The Punitive City: Notes on the Dispersal of Social Control." *Contemporary Crises* 3:339–63.

Coleman, J.W. 1985. *The Criminal Elite: The Sociology of White Collar Crime.* New York: St. Martin's Press; 2nd ed. 1989.

Collins, M. (Chair). 1988. *Report of the Standing Committee of Consumer and Corporate Affairs on the Subjects of Misleading Advertising.* Report to the House of Commons, Ottawa, June.

Colvin, M. 1986. "Controlling the Surplus Population: The Latent Functions of Imprisonment and Welfare in Late U.S. Capitalism." In B. MacLean, ed., *The Political Economy of Crime.* Scarborough: Prentice-Hall: 154–65.

Comack, E. 1988. "Law and Order Issues in the Canadian Context." Paper presented at the annual meeting of the American Society of Criminology, Chicago.

Condon, M. 1992. "Following up on Interests: The Private Agreement Exemption in Ontario Securities Law." *Journal of Human Justice* (forthcoming).

Cranston, R. 1982. "Regulation and Deregulation: General Issues." *University of New South Wales Law Journal* 5:1–29.

Craven, P. 1980. *An Impartial Umpire: Industrial Relations and the Canadian State, 1900–1911.* Toronto: University of Toronto Press.

Cressey, D. 1953. *Other People's Money: A Study in the Social Psychology of Embezzlement*. Glencoe, Ill.: Free Press.

Cullen, F., B. Link, and C. Polanzi. 1982. "The Seriousness of Crime Revisited." *Criminology* 20, no. 1:83–102.

Cullen, F., W.J. Maakestad, and G. Cavender. 1987. *Corporate Crime Under Attack: The Ford Pinto Case and Beyond*. Cincinnati, Ohio: Anderson Publishing.

Dahl, R.A. 1961. *Who Governs? Democracy and Power in an American City*. New Haven, Conn.: Yale University Press.

Dalton, M. 1959. *Men Who Manage: Fusion of Feeling and Theory in Administration*. New York: Wiley.

Daly, K. 1989. "Gender and Varieties of White Collar Crime." *Criminology* 27:769–94.

Davidson, R. 1989. "Independence Without Accountability Won't Last." Paper presented to the National Conference on Competition Law and Policy in Canada, Toronto, October 24–25.

Dekeseredy, W., and R. Hinch. 1991. *Woman Abuse: Sociological Perspective*. Toronto: Thompson Educational Publishing.

Denzin, N. 1978. "Crime and the American Liquor Industry." *Studies in Symbolic Interaction* 1:87–118.

———. 1977. "Notes on the Criminogenic Hypothesis: A Case Study of the American Liquor Industry." *American Sociological Review* 42 (December):905–20.

Deverell, J. 1975. *Falconbridge: Portrait of a Canadian Mining Multinational*. Toronto: J. Lorimer.

Dewees, D.N., and R.J. Daniels. 1986. "The Cost of Protecting Occupational Health: The Asbestos Case." *Journal of Human Resources* 21:381–89.

Ditton, J. 1977. *Part-Time Crime: An Ethnography of Fiddling and Pilferage*. London: Macmillan.

Diver, C. 1980. "Modesty and Immodesty in Policy-Oriented Empirical Research." *Administrative Law Review* 32:73–78.

Domhoff, G.W. 1970. *The Higher Circles: The Governing Class in America*. New York: Random House.

———. 1967. *Who Rules America*. Englewood Cliffs, N.J.: Prentice-Hall.

Dowie, M. "Pinto Madness." In S. Hills, ed., *Corporate Violence, Injury and Death for Profit*. Tatowa, N.J.: Rowman-Littlefield:4–29.

Downing, P., and K. Hanf. 1983. *International Comparisons in Implementing Pollution Control Laws*. Boston: Kluwer-Nijhoff.

Downs, A. 1967. *Inside Bureaucracy*. Boston: Little, Brown.

Dugger, N. 1988. "An Institutional Analysis of Corporate Power." *Journal of Economic Issues* 22, no.1:79–111.

Edelhertz, H. 1970. *The Nature, Impact and Prosecution of White-Collar Crime*. Washington, D.C.: National Institute for Law Enforcement and Criminal Justice, Department of Justice.

Elkins, J.R. 1976. "Decisionmaking Model and the Control of Corporate Crime." *Hobarth Law Journal* 85:1091–129.

Ericson, R.V. 1982. *Reproducing Order: A Study of Police Patrol Work.* Toronto: University of Toronto Press.

———. 1981. *Making Crime: A Study of Detective Work.* Toronto: Butterworths.

Ericson, R.V., and P. Baranek. 1982. *The Ordering of Justice: A Study of Accused Persons as Dependents in the Criminal Process.* Toronto: University of Toronto Press.

Ermann, D.M., and R.J. Lundman. 1982. *Corporate Deviance.* (2nd ed.) New York: Holt, Rinehart and Winston.

———. 1978. "Deviant Acts by Complex Organizations: Deviance and Social Control at the Organizational Level of Analysis." *Sociological Quarterly* 19, no.1:55–67.

Etzioni, A. 1985. "Will a Few Bad Apples Spoil the Core of Big Business?" *Business and Society Review* 55 (Fall):4–5.

Fellmeth, R. 1973. "The Regulatory-Industrial Complex." In R. Nader, ed., *The Common and Corporate Accountability.* New York: Harcourt Brace Jovanovich.

Fels, A. 1982. "The Political Economy of Regulation." *University of New South Wales Law Journal* 5:29–60.

Finn, D. 1969. *The Corporate Oligarchy.* New York: Simon and Schuster.

Fisse, B., and J. Braithwaite. 1983. *The Impact of Publicity on Corporate Offenders.* Albany, N.Y.: State University of New York Press.

Foucault, M. 1979. *Discipline and Punish: The Birth of the Prison.* New York: Pantheon Books.

Francis, D. 1986. *Controlling Interest: Who Owns Canada.* Toronto: McClelland and Stewart.

Friedman L. 1977. *Law and Society.* Englewood Cliffs, N.J.: Prentice-Hall.

Galanter, M. 1974. "Why the Haves Come Out Ahead: Speculations on the Limits of Legal Change." *Law and Society Review* 9:95–160.

Gavigan, S. 1987. "Women and Abortion in Canada: What's Law Got to Do With It?" In H. Maroney and M. Luxton, eds., *Feminism and Political Economy.* Toronto: Methuen: 263–82.

Geis, G. 1973. "Deterring Corporate Crime." In R. Nader and M.J. Green, eds., *Corporate Power in America.* New York: Viking Press.

———. 1967 "White Collar Crime: The Heavy Electrical Equipment Antitrust Cases of 1961." In M.B. Clinard and R. Quinney, eds., *Criminal Behaviour Systems: A Typology.* New York: Holt, Rinehart and Winston.

Geis, G., and R.F. Meier. 1977. *White-Collar Crime: Offences in Business, Politics and the Professions,* rev ed. New York: Free Press.

Gerber, J. 1990. "Enforced Self-Regulation in the Infant Formula Industry: A Radical Extension of an Impractical Proposal." *Social Justice* 17, no.1:98–112.

Gibbons, D. 1969. "Crime and Punishment: A Study in Social Attitudes." *Social Forces* 47:391–97.

Giddens, A. 1981. *The Class Structure of Advanced Societies,* 2nd ed. London: Hutchinson.

Glaeser, M.G. 1957. *Public Utilities in American Capitalism.* New York: Macmillan.

Glasbeek, H. 1989. "Why Corporate Deviance is not Treated as a Crime." In T. Caputo, et al., eds., *Law and Society: A Critical Perspective.* Toronto: Harcourt Brace Jovanovich: 126–45.

———. 1984. "The Corporation as Criminal." *Our Times* (September): 21–24.

Goff, C., and N. Mason-Clark. 1989. "The Seriousness of Crime in Fredericton, New Brunswick: Perceptions toward White-Collar Crime." *Canadian Journal of Criminology* 31:19–34.

Goff, C., and C. Reasons. 1986. "Organizational Crimes against Employers, Consumers and the Public." In B. MacLean, ed., *The Political Economy of Crime.* Scarborough: Prentice-Hall: 204–32.

———. 1978 *Corporate Crime in Canada.* Toronto: Prentice-Hall.

Gold, M. 1975. "Recent Developments in Marxist Theories of the Capitalist State," *Monthly Review* no. 27:323.

Goldman, C. 1989. "The Impact of the Competition Act of 1986." Address given to the National Conference on Competition Law and Policy in Canada, Toronto, October 24–25.

Gordon, R.M., and I.T. Coneybeer. 1991. "Corporate Crime." In M. Jackson and C.T. Griffiths, eds., *Canadian Criminology.* Toronto: Harcourt Brace Jovanovich.

Gottfredson, M.R., and T. Hirschi. 1990. *A General Theory of Crime.* Stanford, Calif.: Stanford University Press.

Gough, I. 1979. *The Political Economy of the Welfare State.* London: Macmillan.

Grabosky, P., and J. Braithwaite. 1986. *Of Manners Gentle: Enforcement Strategies of Australian Business Regulatory Agencies.* Melbourne: Oxford University Press.

Graham, J.M., and V.H. Kramer. 1976. *Appointments to the Regulatory Agencies: The Federal Commerce Commission and the Federal Trade Commission.* Washington, D.C.: U.S. Government Printing Office, Committee on Commerce, U.S. Senate, 94th Congress, 2nd Session (April).

Gramsci, A. 1971. *Selections from the Prison Notebooks of Antonio Gramsci.* New York: International Publishers.

Grayson, J.P., and L. Grayson. 1980. "Canadian Literary and Other Elites." *Canadian Review of Sociology and Anthropology* 17, no.4:338–56.

Green, M. 1972. *The Closed Enterprise System.* New York: Grossman.

Gross, E. 1980. "Organizations as Criminal Actors." In F. Wilson and J. Braithwaite, eds., *Two Faces of Deviance*. St. Lucia, Queensland: University of Queensland Press.

———. 1978. "Organizational Crime: A Theoretical Perspective." *Studies in Symbolic Interaction* no.1:55–85.

Gunningham, N. 1987. "Negotiated Non-Compliance: A Case Study of Regulatory Failure." *Law and Policy* 9, no.1:69–97.

———. 1984. *Safeguarding the Workers*. Sydney: Law Book Co. Ltd.

———. 1974. *Pollution: Social Interest and the Law*. Oxford Centre for Socio-Legal Studies.

Hagan, J. 1991. "A Power-Control Theory of Gender and Delinquency." In R. Silverman, J. Teevan, and V. Sacco, eds., *Crime in Canadian Society*, 4th ed. Toronto: Butterworths: 130–36.

———. 1989a. "Why is there so Little Criminal Justice Theory? Neglected Macro- and Micro-Level Links Between Organization and Power." *Journal of Research in Crime and Delinquency* 26, no.2:116–35.

———. 1989b. *Structural Criminology*. New Brunswick, N.J.: Rutgers University Press.

Hagan, J., and P. Parker. 1985. "White Collar Crime and Punishment: The Class Structure and Legal Sanctioning of Securities Violations." *American Sociological Review* 50 (June):302–16.

Hall, A. 1988. "Managing Contradictory Interests—Health and Safety in Mining." Paper presented at the annual meeting of the Canadian Sociology and Anthropology Association, Windsor.

Hartung F. 1953. "Common and Discrete Values." *Journal of Social Psychology* 38:3–22.

Hawkins, K. 1984. *Environment and Enforcement: Regulation and the Social Definition of Pollution*. Oxford: Clarendon.

Hay, D., P. Linebaugh, J. Rule, E. Thompson, and C. Winslow. 1975. *Albion's Fatal Tree: Crime and Society in 18th Century England*. Harmondsworth: Penguin Books.

Hazeldine, T. 1989. "Trade Policy as Competition Policy." Paper presented to the National Conference on Competition Law and Policy in Canada, Toronto, October 24–25.

Henry, F. 1986. "Crime: A Profitable Approach." In B. MacLean, ed., *The Political Economy of Crime*. Scarborough: Prentice-Hall: 182–203.

Herring, E.P. 1936. *Federal Commissioners: A Study of their Careers and Qualifications*. Cambridge, Mass.: Harvard University Press.

Hirschi, T. 1969. *Causes of Delinquency*. Berkeley: University of California Press.

Hollinger, R.C. 1990. "Hackers: Computer Heroes or Electronic Highwaymen?" Paper presented at the annual meeting of the American Society of Criminology, Baltimore.

———. 1973. *Employee Deviance: Acts against the Formal Work Organization*. Ann Arbor, Mich.: University of Michigan (microfilm).

Hollinger, R.C., and J.P. Clarke. 1983. *Theft by Employees.* Toronto: Lexington Books.

Holloway, J., and S. Picciotto. 1978. *State and Capital.* London: Edward Arnold.

Hopkins, A. 1979. "The Anatomy of Corporate Crime." In P. Wilson and J. Braithwaite, eds., *Two Faces of Deviance.* St. Lucia: University of Queensland Press.

———. 1978 *Crime, Law and Business: The Sociological Sources of Australian Monopoly Law.* Canberra: Australian Institute of Criminology.

Horton J. 1981."The Rise of the Right: A Global View." *Crime and Social Justice* 15 (Summer):7–17.

Howe, A. 1990. "The Problem of Privatized Injuries: Feminist Strategies for Litigation." In S. Silbey and A. Sarat, eds., *Studies in Law, Politics and Society* 10:119–42.

Howe, M. 1989. "A British Look at Canadian Competition Law and Policy." Paper presented to the National Conference on Competition Law and Policy in Canada, Toronto, October 24–25.

Hundloe, T. 1978. "Heads They Win, Tails We Lose: Environment and the Law." In P. Wilson, and J. Braithwaite, eds., *Two Faces of Deviance.* St. Lucia, Queensland: Queensland University Press.

Hunt, A. 1985. "The Ideology of Law: Advances and Problems in Recent Applications of the Concept of Ideology to the Analyses of Law." *Law and Society Review* 19:11–37.

Hurtig, M. 1991. *The Betrayal of Canada.* Toronto: McClelland and Stewart.

Hutchins, B.L., and A. Harrison. 1962. *A History of Factory Legislation*, 3rd ed. London: King and Son.

Inglehart, R. 1981. "Post-Materialism in an Environment of Insecurity." *American Political Science Review* 75, no.4:880–900.

Jamieson, M. 1985. *Persuasion or Punishment—The Enforcement of Health and Safety at Work Legislation by The British Factory Inspectorate.* Oxford: Oxford University, unpublished M.Phil. thesis.

Jaspan, N. 1960. *Thief in the White Collar.* Philadelphia, Penn.: J.B. Lippincott.

———. 1974. *Mind Your Own Business.* Englewood Cliffs, N.J.: Prentice-Hall.

Johnson, K.A. 1986. "Federal Court Processing of Corporate White Collar and Common Crime Economic Offenders over the Past Three Decades." *Mid-American Review of Sociology* 11, no. 1:25–44.

Kagan, R. 1978. *Regulatory Justice.* New York: Russell Sage.

Kagan, R., and J.T. Scholz. 1984. "The Criminology of the Corporation and Regulatory Enforcement Strategies." In K. Hawkins and J. Thomas, eds., *Enforcing Regulation.* Boston: Kluwer-Nijhoff.

Kanungo, R.N. 1982. *Work Alienation: An Integrated Approach.* New York: Praeger.

Katz, J. 1979. "Legality and Equality: Plea-Bargaining in the Prosecution of White Collar and Common Crimes." *Law and Society Review* 13:431–59.

Keane, C. 1991. "Corporate Crime." In R.A. Silverman, J.J. Teevan, and V.F. Sacco, eds., *Crime in Canadian Society*, 4th ed. Toronto: Butterworths.

Keller, S.I. 1963. *Beyond the Ruling Class: Strategic Elites in Modern Society*. New York: Random House.

Kelman, S. 1981. *Regulating America, Regulating Sweden*. Cambridge: Cambridge University Press.

Kernaghan, W. 1990. "Between Rocks and Hard Places: Bureaucrats, Law and Pollution Control." In R. Paehlike and D. Torgerson, eds., *Managing Leviathan: Environmental Politics and the Administrative State*. Peterborough: Broadview Press: 201–27.

Kettler, D. 1987. "Legal Reconstitution of the Welfare State: A Latent Social Democratic Legacy." *Law and Society Review* 21, no.1:9–47.

King, D.K. 1985. "The Regulatory Use of the Criminal Sanction in Controlling Corporate Crime." Paper presented at the annual meeting of the American Society of Criminology, San Diego.

Kneese, A.V., and C.L. Schultze. 1975. *Pollution, Prices, and Public Policy*. Washington, D.C.: Brookings Institute.

Kolko, G. 1988. *Restructuring the World Economy*. New York: Pantheon Books.

———. 1969. *The Roots of American Foreign Policy: An Analysis of Power and Purpose*. Boston: Beacon Press.

———. 1962. *Wealth and Power in America: An Analysis of Social Class and Income Distribution*. New York: Praeger.

Kramer, R. 1982. "Corporate Crime: An Organizational Perspective." In P. Wickman and T. Dailey, eds., *White Collar and Economic Crime*. Toronto: D.C. Heath.

Lahey, K. 1988. "Civil Remedies for Women: Catching the Critical Edge." In S. Findlay and M. Randall, eds., *Feminist Perspectives on the Canadian State* 17, no.3 (September): 92–95.

Lambert, R. 1963. *Sir John Simon, 1816–1904, and English Social Administration*. London: MacGibbon and Kee.

Lane, R.E. 1977. "Why Businessmen Violate the Law." In G. Geis and R.F. Meier, eds., *White Collar Crime*. New York: Free Press.

———. 1954. *The Regulation of Businessmen: Social Condition of Government Economic Control*. New Haven, Conn.: Yale University Press.

Laxer, R. 1973. *(Canada) Ltd: The Political Economy of Dependency*. Toronto: McClelland and Stewart.

Leigh, P. 1989. "Compensating Wages for Job-Related Death: The Opposing Argument." *Journal of Economic Issues* 23, no.3:823–42.

Leonard, D., and L. Weber. 1970."Automakers and Dealers: A Study of Criminogenic Market Forces." *Law and Society* 4:407–24.

Levi, M. 1987. "Crisis: What Crisis? Reactions to Commercial Fraud in the United Kingdom." *Contemporary Crises* 11, no.3:207–21.

_____. 1984. "Giving Creditors the Business: The Criminal Law in Inaction." *International Journal of the Sociology of Law.* 12:321–33.

_____. 1981. *The Phantom Capitalists: The Organization and Control of Long Term Fraud.* London: Heinemann.

Lewis-Beck, M.S., and J.R. Alford. 1980. "Can Government Regulate Safety? The Coal Mine Example." *American Political Science Review* 74:745–81.

Leys, C. 1989. *Politics in Britain.* Toronto: University of Toronto Press.

Lipman, M. 1973. *Stealing: How America's Employees are Stealing their Companies Blind.* New York: Harper's Magazine Press.

Lofquist, W.S. 1991. "The Development of Organizational Probation: Assessing Its Significance in Criminology." Paper presented at the annual meeting of the American Society of Criminology. San Francisco. November 20–23.

Long, S. 1979. "The Internal Revenue Service: Examining the Exercise of Discretion in Tax Enforcement." Paper presented at the annual meeting of the Canadian Law and Society Association, May.

Luchansky, W., and J. Gerber. 1990. "Antitrust Legislation and State Theory: The Celler-Kefauver Act of 1950." Paper presented at the annual meeting of the American Society of Criminology, Baltimore.

Lynxwiler, J., N. Shover, and D. Clelland. 1983. "Corporate Size and International Contexts: Determinants of Sanctioning Severity in a Regulatory Bureaucracy.". Paper presented at the annual meeting of the American Criminal Justice Society, San Antonio, Texas.

McBarnett, D. 1992. "Legitimate Rackets: Tax Evasion, Tax Avoidance and the Boundaries of Legality." *Journal of Human Justice* 5: (forthcoming).

McCormick, A.E. 1977. "Rule Enforcement and Moral Indignation: Some Observations of the Effects of Criminal Anti-trust Convictions upon Societal Reaction Processes." *Social Problems* 25:30–39.

Macdonagh, O. 1961. *A Pattern of Government Growth, 1800–1860: The Passenger Acts and their Enforcement.* London: MacGibbon and Kee.

McDonald, L. 1976. *The Sociology of Law and Order.* Montreal: Book Centre.

Macintyre, A. 1985. "A Court Quietly Rewrote the Federal Pesticide Statute: How Prevalent is Judicial Statutory Revision?" *Law and Policy* 7, no.2:250–79.

MacLean, B., ed. 1986a. *The Political Economy of Crime.* Scarborough: Prentice-Hall.

_____. 1986b. "State Expenditure on Canadian Criminal Justice." In B. MacLean, ed., *The Political Economy of Crime.* Scarborough: Prentice-Hall: 106–34.

McNully, P.J. 1978. "The Public Side of Private Enterprise: A Historical Perspective on American Business and Government." *Columbia Journal of World Business* 13 (Winter):122–30.

McQueen, R. 1990. "Why Company Law is Important to Left Realists." Paper presented to Left Realist Conference, Vancouver, B.C.

———. 1989. "The New Companies and Securities Schemes: A Fundamental Departure?" *The Australian Quarterly* (Summer):481–97.

Marchak, P. 1975. *Ideological Perspectives on Canada*. Toronto: McGraw-Hill Ryerson; 2nd ed. 1988.

Marcus, S. 1974. *Engels, Manchester and the Working Class*. New York: Random House.

Maroney, H.J., and M. Luxton, eds. 1987. *Feminism and Political Economy: Women's Work, Women's Struggle*. Toronto: Methuen.

Martinson, R. 1974. "What Works? Questions and Answers About Prison Reform." *The Public Interest* 35 (Spring):22–54.

Marx, K. 1973. *Capital*, vol. 1. New York: International Publishers.

Marx, K., and F. Engels. 1959. *Basic Writings on Politics and Philosophy*. Garden City, N.Y: Doubleday.

Meier, R., and J.P. Plumlee. 1978. "Regulatory Administration and Organizational Rigidity." *Western Political Quarterly* 31:80–95.

Meier, R., and J.F. Short. 1982. "The Consequences of White-Collar Crime." In H. Edelhertz, and T. Overcast, eds., *White-Collar Crime: An Agenda For Research*. Toronto: D.C. Heath, Lexington Books.

Melossi, D. 1980. "Strategies of Social Control in Capitalism: A Comment on Recent Work." *Contemporary Crises* 4:381–402.

Merton, R.K. 1957. *Social Theory and Social Structure*. Glencoe, Ill.: Free Press.

———. 1938. "Social Structure and Anomie." *American Sociological Review* 3, no.5:672–82..

Messerschmidt, J. 1986. *Capitalism, Patriarchy and Crime: Toward a Socialist-Feminist Criminology*. Tolowa, N.J.: Rowan and Littlefield.

Michalowski, R. 1985. *Order, Law and Crime: An Introduction to Criminology*. New York: Random House.

Michalowski, R., and R. Kramer. 1987. "The Space Between Laws: The Problem of Corporate Crime in Transnational Context." *Social Problems* 34:34–53.

Miliband, R. 1969. *The State in Capitalist Society*. London: Quartet Books.

Mills, C. Wright. 1959. *The Sociological Imagination*. New York: Oxford.

Mintz, M. 1985. *At Any Cost: Corporate Greed, Women and the Dalkon Shield*. New York: Pantheon.

Mitnick, B.M. 1980. *The Political Economy of Regulation*. New York: Columbia University Press.

Molotch, H. 1973. "Oil in Santa Barbara and Power in America." In W.J. Chambliss, ed., *Sociological Readings in the Conflict Perspective*. Reading, Mass.: Addison-Wesley.

Moore, E., and M. Mills. 1990. "The Neglected Victims and Unexamined Costs of White-Collar Crime." *Crime and Delinquency* 36, no.3:408–18.

Morgenstern, F. 1982. *Deterrence and Compensation: Legal Liability in Occupational Health and Safety*. Geneva: International Labour Organization.

Nader, R., and M.J. Green, eds., 1973. *Corporate Power in America*. New York: Viking Press.

Needleman, M.L., and C. Needleman. 1979. "Organizational Crime: Two Models of Criminogenesis." *Sociological Quarterly* 20, no.4:517–528.

Newman D.J. 1977. "White-Collar Crime: An Overview and Analysis." In G. Geis and R. Meier, eds., *White-Collar Crime*. New York: Free Press.

Noll, R. 1978. *Reforming Regulation: An Evaluation of the Ash Council Proposals*. Washington, D.C.: Brookings Institute.

O'Connor, J. 1973. *The Fiscal Crisis of the State*. New York: St. Martin's Press.

Odagiri, H. 1981. *The Theory of Growth in a Corporate Economy*. Cambridge: Cambridge University Press.

Offe, C. 1982. "Some Contradictions of the Modern Welfare State." *Critical Social Policy* 2, no.2:7–16.

Oliver, O., and M. MacDonagh. 1961. *A Pattern of Government Growth, 1800–60: The Passenger Acts and their Enforcement*. London: MacGibbon and Kee.

Olson, S. 1985. "Comparing Justice and Labour Department Lawyers: Ten Years of Occupational Safety and Health Litigation." *Law and Policy* 7, no.3:286–313.

O'Malley, P. 1988. "Law-Making in Canada: Capitalism and Legislation in a Democratic State." *Canadian Journal of Law and Society* 3:53–87.

———. 1987. "In Place of Criminology: A Marxist Reformulation." Paper presented to the annual meeting of the Canadian Sociology and Anthropology Association, Hamilton, Ontario.

Otake, H. 1982. "Corporate Power in Social Conflict: Vehicle Safety and Japanese Motor Manufacturers." *International Journal of the Sociology of Law* 10, no.1:75–103.

Palmer, B. 1983. *Working Class Experience: The Rise and Reconstitution of Canadian Labour 1800–1980*. Toronto: Butterworths.

Panitch, L., ed. 1977. *The Canadian State: Political Economy and Political Power*. Toronto: University of Toronto Press.

Parenti, M. 1983. *Democracy for the Few*. New York: St. Martin's Press.

Parsons, T. 1970. "The Monopoly of Force and the 'Power Bank.'" In M. Olsen, ed., *Power in Societies*. New York: Macmillan.

Pashukanis, E.B. 1978. *Law and Marxism*. London: Ink Links.

Passas, N. 1990. "Anomie and Corporate Deviance." *Contemporary Crises* 14:157–78.

Passas, N., and D. Nelken. 1990a. "Frauds against the European Community and Criminological Theorizing." Paper presented at the annual meeting of the American Society of Criminology, Baltimore.

———. 1990b. "The Fight Against Economic Criminality in the European Community." Paper presented at the annual meeting of the American Society of Criminology, Baltimore.

Paulus, I. 1978. "Strict Liability: Its Place in Public Welfare Offences." *Criminal Law Quarterly* 20:445–67.

———. 1974 The Search for Pure Food: A Sociology of Legislation in Britain. London: Martin Robertson.

Pearce, F. 1991. "Corporate Structure and Corporate Crime." Paper presented at the annual meeting of the American Society of Criminology, San Francisco.

———. 1990a. "Commercial and Conventional Crime in Islington." *Second Islington Crime Survey*. Funded by the Economic and Social Research Council, United Kingdom.

———. 1990b. "The Contribution of 'Left-Realism' to the Empirical Study of Commercial Crime." Paper presented at Realist Criminology Conference, Vancouver.

———. 1990c. " 'Responsible Corporations' and Regulatory Agencies." *The Political Quarterly* 61, no.4: 415–30.

———. 1976. *Crimes of the Powerful, Marxism, Crime and Deviance*. London: Pluto Press.

Pearce, F., and S. Tombs. 1990. "Ideology, Hegemony and Empiricism: Compliance Theories of Regulation." *British Journal of Criminology* 30, no. 4:409–29.

———. 1989. "Union Carbide, Bhopal, and the Hubris of a Capitalist Technocracy." *Social Justice* (June):116–45.

———. 1988. "Regulating Corporate Crime: The Case of Health and Safety." Paper presented at the annual meeting of the American Society of Criminology, Chicago.

Peltzman, J. 1976. "Toward a More General Theory of Regulation." *Journal of Law and Economics* 19:211–40.

Pepinsky, H. 1974. "From White Collar Crime to Exploitation: Redefinition of a Field." *Journal of Criminal Law and Criminology* 65:225–33.

Perry S., and J. Dawson 1985. *Nightmare: Women and the Dalkon Shield*. New York: Macmillan.

Phillips, D. 1977. *Crime and Authority in Victorian England: The Black Country, 1835–60*. London: Croon Helm.

Phillips, W. 1964. "Canadian Combines Policy: The Matter of Mergers." *Canadian Bar Review* 42, no. 1 (March):78–99.

Porter, J. 1965. *The Vertical Mosaic*. Toronto: University of Toronto Press.

Poulantzas, N. 1978. *State Power and Socialism*. London: New Left Books.

————. 1973. *Political Power and Social Classes.* London: Sheed and Ward.

Presthus, R. 1978. *The Original Society,* rev. ed. New York: St. Martin's Press.

————. 1973. *Elite Accommodation in Canadian Politics.* Cambridge: Cambridge University Press.

Randall, D. 1987. "The Portrayal of Business Malfeasance in the Elite and General Public Media." *Social Science Quarterly* 68, no.2:281–93.

Randall, P.M., L. Lee-Sammons, and P. Hagner. 1988. "Common Versus Elite Coverage in Network News." *Social Science Quarterly* 69, no.4 (December):910–29.

Rankin, M., and R. Brown. 1988. "The Treatment of Repeat Offenders under B.C.'s Occupational Health and Safety and Pollution Control Legislation." Paper presented at the annual meeting of the Canadian Law and Society Association, Windsor.

Ratner, R. 1986. "Specious Extensions of Social Control in the Canadian Penal System." In B. MacLean, ed., *The Political Economy of Crime.* Scarborough: Prentice-Hall: 142–54.

Reasons, C. 1986. "Occupational Health and Safety in Two Jurisdictions: Canada and Australia." In R. Tomacs and K. Lucas, eds., *Power, Regulation and Resistance: Studies in the Sociology of Law.* Canberra: School of Administrative Studies: 33–51.

Reasons, C., W. Ross, and L. Patterson. 1981. *Assault on the Worker: Occupational Health and Safety in Canada.* Toronto: Butterworths.

Reed, J., and R. Reed. 1975. "Doctor, Lawyer, Indian Chief: Old Rhymes and New on White-Collar Crime." *International Journal of Criminology and Penology* 3:279–93.

Regush, N. 1991. "Health and Welfare's National Disgrace." *Saturday Night* (April):9.

Reiman, J. 1990. *The Rich Get Richer and the Poor Get Prison,* 3rd ed. New York: Macmillan.

————. 1984. *The Rich Get Richer and the Poor Get Prison,* 2nd ed. Toronto: J. Wiley and Sons.

————. 1982. *The Rich Get Richer and the Poor Get Prison.* Toronto: J. Wiley and Sons.

Reisman, W.M. 1979. *Folded Lies: Bribery Crusades and Reforms.* New York: Free Press.

Reiss, A.J., and A.D. Biderman. 1980. *Data Sources on White Collar Law-Breaking.* Washington, D.C.: Bureau of Social Science Research.

Robin, G. 1967. "The Corporate and Judicial Disposition of Employee Thieves." *Wisconsin Law Review* (Summer):685–702.

Rose, A. 1967. *The Power Structure: Political Process in America.* New York: Oxford University Press.

Rossi, P.H., C.E. Bose, and R.A. Berk. 1974. "The Seriousness of Crimes: Normative Structure and Individual Differences." *American Sociological Review* 39 (April):224–37.

Rothman, D. 1980. *Conscience and Convenience: The Asylum and its Alternatives in Progressive America*. Boston: Little, Brown.

———. 1971. *The Discovery of the Asylum: Social Order and Disorder in the New Republic*. Boston: Little, Brown.

Sabatier, P. 1977. "Regulatory Policy-Making: Toward a Framework of Analysis." *Natural Resources Journal* 17:415–60.

———. 1975. "Social Movements and Regulatory Agencies: Toward a more Adequate—and less Pessimistic—Theory of 'Clientele Capture.'" *Policy Sciences* 6:301–41.

Sampson, A. 1975. *The Seven Sisters: The Great Oil Companies and the World They Shaped*. New York: Viking.

Sands, P. 1968. "How Effective is Safety Legislation?" *Journal of Law and Economics* 11:165–79.

Sargent, N. 1990. "Law, Ideology and Social Change: An Analysis of the Role of Law in the Construction of Corporate Crime." *Journal of Human Justice* 1, no.2:97–116.

Sass, R., and R. Butler. 1982. "The Poisoning of Canada." *Canadian Dimension* 16, no.3:2–7.

Schmidt, R.R. 1975. "Executive Dishonesty: Misuse of Authority for Personal Gain." In S. Leininger, ed., *Internal Theft: Investigation and Control*. Los Angeles: Security World Publishing: 69–81.

Scholz, J. 1984a. "Deterrence, Cooperation and the Ecology of Regulatory Enforcement." *Law and Society Review* 18:179–224.

———. 1984b. "Voluntary Compliance and Regulatory Enforcement." *Law and Policy* 6:385–404.

Schrecker, T. 1989. "The Political Context and Content of Environmental Law." In T. Caputo et al., eds., *Law and Society: A Critical Perspective*. Toronto: Harcourt Brace Jovanovich: 173–204.

Science Council of Canada. 1977. *Policies and Poisons: The Containment of Long-term Hazards to Human Health in the Environment and Workplace*. Ottawa: Science Council of Canada.

Seavoy, R. 1978. "The Public Service Origins of the American Business Corporation." *Business History Review* 52 (Spring):30–60.

Selcraig, B. 1992. "Bad Chemistry." *Harper's* (April):62–73.

Seligman, J. 1982. *The Transformation of Wall Street: A History of the Securities and Exchange Commission and Modern Corporate Finance*. Boston: Houghton Mifflin.

Selling, L.S. 1944. "Specific War Crimes." *Journal of Law, Criminology and Police Science* 34 (January-February).

Shapiro, S. 1990. "Collaring the Crime, Not the Criminal: Considering the Concept of White-Collar Crime." *American Sociological Review* 55 (June):346–65.

————. 1985. "The Road Not Taken: The Elusive Path to Criminal Prosecution for White Collar Offenders." *Law and Society Review* 19, no.2:179–217.

————. 1984 *Wayward Capitalists*. New Haven, Conn.: Yale University Press.

Shearing, C.D., and P.C. Stenning. 1983. *Private Security and Private Justice: The Challenge of the 1980s: A Review of Policy Issues*. Toronto: Institute of Research on Public Policy.

Sheehy, G. 1992 "Strict Liability for Regulatory Offences: 'Too Monstrous to be Accepted as Law?'" *Journal of Human Justice* (forthcoming).

Sheleff, L.S. 1982. "International White Collar Crime." In P. Wickman and T. Dailey, eds., *White Collar and Economic Crime*. Toronto: D.C. Heath: 39–58.

Sherrill, R. 1987. "Murder Inc.—What Happens to Corporate Criminals?" *Utne Reader* (March–April).

Shover, N., D.A. Clelland, and J. Lynxwiler. 1983. *Developing a Regulatory Bureaucracy: The Office of Surface Mining Reclamation and Enforcement*. Washington, D.C.: National Institute of Justice.

Shover, N., and M. Mills. 1990. "Victim Impacts of Economic Crime." Paper presented at the annual meeting of the American Society of Criminology, Baltimore.

Silberman, C.E. 1980. *Criminal Violence, Criminal Justice*. New York: Vintage Books.

Simon, D.R., and D.S. Eitzen. 1990. *Elite Deviance,* 3rd ed. Boston: Allyn and Bacon.

————. 1986 *Elite Deviance,* 2nd ed. Toronto: Allyn and Bacon.

Simpson, S. 1986. "The Decomposition of Antitrust: Testing a Multi-Level Longitudinal Model of Profit Squeeze." *American Sociological Review* 51:850–75.

Smandych, R. 1991. "The Origins of Canadian Anti-Combines Legislation, 1890–1910." In E. Comack and S. Brickey, eds., *The Social Basis of Law,* 2nd ed. Halifax, N.S.: Garamond Press: 35–48.

Smart, C. 1989. *Feminism and the Power of Law*. London: Routledge.

Smigel, E.O., and H.L. Ross. 1970. *Crimes against Bureaucracy*. New York: Van Nostrand Reinhold.

Smith, R. 1979. "The Impact of OSHA Inspections on Manufacturing Injury Rates." *Journal of Human Resources* 14:145.

————. 1976. *The Occupational Health and Safety Act*. Washington, D.C.: American Enterprise Institute.

Snider, L. 1990. "Cooperative Models and Corporate Crime: Panacea or Cop-Out?" *Crime and Delinquency* 36, no.3:373–91.

————. 1987. "Towards a Political Economy of Reform, Regulation and Corporate Crime." *Law and Policy* 9, no.1:37–68.

————. 1985. "Legal Reform and Social Control: The Dangers of Abolishing Rape." *International Journal of the Sociology of Law* 13:337–56.

———. 1982. "Traditional and Corporate Theft: A Comparison of Sanctions." In P. Wickman and T. Dailey, eds., *White-Collar and Economic Crime.* Toronto: Lexington Books: 235–58.

———. 1978. "Corporate Crime in Canada: A Preliminary Report." *Canadian Journal of Criminology* 20:142–68.

———. 1977. *Does the Legal Order Reflect the Power Structure: A Test of Conflict Theory.* Toronto: University of Toronto, unpublished Ph.D. thesis.

Snider, L., and W.G. West. 1980. "Social Control, Crime and Conflict in Canada." In R.J. Ossenberg, ed., *Power and Change in Canada.* Toronto: McClelland and Stewart.

Spencer, J.C. 1965. "White Collar Crime." In E. Glover, H. Mannheim, and E. Miller, eds., *Criminology in Transition.* London: Tavistock.

Stanbury, W. 1988. "A Review of Conspiracy Cases in Canada, 1965/66 to 1987/88." *Canadian Competition Policy Record* 10, no.1:33–49.

———. 1986–87. "The New Competition Act and Competition Tribunal Act: Not with a Bang, but a Whimper?" *Canadian Business Law Journal* 12:2–42.

———. 1977. *Business Interests and the Reform of Canadian Competition Policy 1971–75.* Toronto: Carswell/Methuen.

Stanley, D.T., D.E. Mann, and J.W. Doig. 1967. *Men Who Govern: A Biographical Profile of Federal Political Executives.* Washington, D.C.: Brookings Institute.

Statistics Canada. Canadian Centre for Justice Statistics. 1990. *Catalogue # 85–205.* Ottawa: Ministry of Supply and Services.

Stenning, P., C. Shearing, S. Addario, and M. Condon. 1987. "Controlling Interests: Two Conceptions of Order in the Regulation of a Financial Market." Paper presented at the annual meeting of the American Society of Criminology, Montreal.

Stigler, G. 1975. *The Citizen and the State: Essays on Regulation.* Chicago: University of Chicago Press.

Stone, C. 1980. "The Place of Enterprise Liability in the Control of Corporate Conduct." *Yale Law Journal* 90:1–77.

———. 1978. "Social Control of Corporate Behaviour." In D. Ermann and R. Lundman, eds., *Corporate and Government Deviance.* New York: Oxford University Press.

———. 1975. *Where the Law Ends: The Social Control of Corporate Behaviour.* New York: Harper and Row.

Sutherland, E.H. 1978. "White Collar Crime in Organized Crime." In D. Ermann and R. Lundman, eds., *Corporate and Governmental Deviance.* New York: Oxford University Press: 49–58.

———. 1977. "White Collar Criminality." In G. Geis and R.F. Meier, eds., *White Collar Crime.* New York: Free Press.

———. 1973. "Crimes of Corporations." In K. Schuessler, ed., *On Analyzing Crime.* Chicago: University of Chicago Press.

————. 1961. *White Collar Crime.* New York: Holt, Rinehart and Winston.

————. 1940. "White-Collar Criminality." *American Sociological Review* no. 5 (February):1–12.

Swartz, J. 1975. "Silent Killers at Work." *Crime and Social Justice* 3:15–20.

Swigert V.I., and R.A. Farrell. 1980. "Corporate Homicide: Definitional Processes in the Creation of Deviance." *Law and Society Review* 15, no.1:161–82.

Sykes, G., and D. Matza. 1957. "Techniques of Neutralization: A Theory of Delinquency." *American Sociological Review* 22 (December):667–80.

Sypnowich, C. 1987. "The 'Withering Away of Law.'" *Studies in Soviet Thought* 33:305–332.

Szasz, A. 1986. "Corporations, Organized Crime and the Disposal of Hazardous Waste: An Examination of the Making of a Criminogenic Regulatory Structure." *Criminology* 24, no.1:1–27.

Tabb. N. 1980. "Government Regulations: Two Sides of the Story." *Challenge* 23:40–48.

Tappan, P.W. 1947. "Who is the Criminal?" *American Sociological Review* 12:96–102.

Tatham, R.J. 1974. "Employee Views on Theft in Retailing." *Journal of Retailing* (Fall):49–55.

Tepperman, L. 1977. *Crime Control.* Toronto: McGraw-Hill Ryerson.

————. 1975. *Social Mobility in Canada.* Toronto: McGraw-Hill Ryerson.

Thomas, J. 1982. "The Regulatory Role in the Containment of Corporate Illegality." In H. Edelhertz H. and T. Overcast, eds., *White-Collar Crime: An Agenda for Research.* Toronto: D.C. Heath, Lexington Books.

Thompson, E.P. 1975. *Whigs and Hunters: The Origin of the Black Act.* New York: Pantheon Books.

————. 1963. *The Making of the English Working Class.* London: Gollancz.

Tombs, S. 1990. "Industrial Injuries in the British Manufacturing Industry." *Sociological Review* 38, no.2:324–43.

Tucker, E. 1987. "Making the Workplace 'Safe' in Capitalism: The Enforcement of Factory Legislation in Nineteenth Century Ontario." Paper presented at the annual meeting of the Canadian Law and Society Association, Hamilton, Ontario.

Vandivier, K. 1992. "Why Should My Conscience Bother Me?" In M.D. Ermann and R. Lundman, eds., *Corporate and Governmental Deviance,* 4th ed. New York: Oxford University Press: 205–28.

Varrette, S.E., C. Meredith, P. Robinson, and D. Huffman, ABT Association of Canada. 1985. *White Collar Crime: Exploring the Issues.* Ottawa: Ministry of Justice.

Vaughan, D. 1982. "Transaction Systems and Unlawful Organizational Behaviour." *Social Problems* 29, no.4:373–79.

————. 1979. *Crime Between Organizations: A Case Study of Medicaid Procedural Fraud.* Columbus, Ohio: Ohio State University, Ph.D. dissertation.

Veltmeyer, H. 1987. *Canadian Corporate Power.* Toronto: Garamond Press.

Vogel, D. 1986. *National Styles of Regulation: Environmental Policy in Great Britain and the United States.* Ithaca, N.Y.: Cornell University Press.

————. 1983. "The Power of Business in America: A Re-Appraisal." *British Journal of Political Science* 13:4–41.

Walker, S. 1985. S*ense and Nonsense about Crime.* Monterey, Calif.: Brooks/Cole.

Walters, V. 1985. "The Politics of Occupational Health and Safety: Interviews with Workers' Health and Safety Representatives and Company Doctors." *Canadian Review of Sociology and Anthropology* 22, no.1:58–79.

Watkins, J.C. 1977. "White Collar Crimes: Legal Sanctions and Social Control." *Crime and Delinquency* 23:290–303.

Weinberg, A., and L. Weinberg, eds. 1961. *The Muckrakers.* New York: Simon and Schuster.

Weisburd, D., E.F. Chayet, and E.J. Waring. 1990. "White Collar Crime and Criminal Careers: Some Preliminary Findings." *Crime and Delinquency* 36, no.3:342–55.

Weldon, J.C. 1966. "Consolidations in Canadian Industry, 1900–1948." In L. Skeoch, ed., *Restrictive Trade Practices in Canada.* Toronto: McClelland and Stewart: 228–79.

Wheeler, S., and M. Rothman, 1982. "The Organization as Weapon in White Collar Crime." *Michigan Law Review.* 80, no. 7:1403–26.

Wheeler, S., D. Weisburd, and N. Bode. 1988. "White Collar Crime and Criminals." *American Criminal Law Review* 25:331–56.

————. 1982. "Sentencing the White-Collar Offender: Rhetoric and Reality." *American Sociological Review* 47:641–59.

Whiting, B.J. 1980. "OSHA's Enforcement Policy." *Labour Law Journal* 31:259–72.

Wickman, P., and T. Dailey, eds. 1982. *White Collar and Economic Crime.* Toronto: D.C. Heath.

Wilson, J.Q., ed. 1980. *The Politics of Regulation.* New York: Basic Books.

————. 1974. "The Politics of Regulation." In J. McKie, ed., *Social Responsibility and the Business Predicament.* Washington, D.C.: Brookings Institute.

Winter, G. 1985. "Bartering Rationality in Regulation." *Law and Society Review* 19, no.2:219–50.

Wolfgang, M. 1980. "Crime and Punishment." *The New York Times,* March 2.

Yeager, M.G. 1984. "Community Redress against the Corporate Offender." *Crime and Social Justice* 21–22:223–27.

Yeager, P. 1991. *The Limits of Law: The Public Regulation of Private Pollution.* Cambridge, Mass.: Cambridge University Press.

———. 1986. "Managing Obstacles to Studying Corporate Offences: An Optimistic Assessment." Paper presented to the annual meeting of the American Society of Criminology, Atlanta, Georgia.

Zeitlin, I. 1978. "Who Owns America? The Same Old Gang." *The Progressive* 6:14–19.

Zietz, D. 1981. *Women Who Embezzle or Defraud: A Study of Convicted Felons.* New York: Praeger.

INDEX